The Irish

SEX AETATES MUNDI

THE IRISH
SEX AETATES MUNDI

EDITED BY
DÁIBHÍ Ó CRÓINÍN

DUBLIN INSTITUTE FOR ADVANCED STUDIES
1983

ISBN 0 901282 75 8

Dom' athair –

Mé an t-ésga, eision an ghrian

CONTENTS

FOREWORD

'My times are in your hands', said the psalmist, in a trusting mood. This edition of the Irish *Sex Aetates Mundi* has been through two stages of preparation: the first took the form of a thesis submitted in July, 1977, for the degree of M.Phil. (Medieval Studies) at University College, Dublin. After two years' subsequent study in Germany, researching different materials, the work was taken up anew when I was granted a research scholarship in the Dublin Institute for Advanced Studies and was invited by Professors David Greene and James Carney to revise the text with a view to publication. The final result was a complete revision of the earlier edition, with a corresponding change of views on many aspects of my earlier work. The revision, then, was a salutary experience and the edition now presented is offered with something of the psalmist's trepidation.

The reader is cautioned against more than a tentative acceptance of the views expressed in this book; they are based on as wide a reading of the manuscript evidence as possible, but with the realisation that new, and perhaps important, witnesses may always turn up. One such manuscript, a sixteenth-century collection now housed in the Public Library in Mullingar, was recently brought to my attention by Mrs. Nessa Doran, and though its evidence did not materially affect my previous conclusions its very appearance was warning enough of the danger, ever-present in Irish studies, of overlooking an important manuscript.

It is not for an editor to say what attracted him to his chosen text. It may be because James F. Kenney, in his great *Sources for the early history of Ireland 1: Ecclesiastical,* p. 737, remarked that 'in Rawl. B 502 the *Saltair na Rann* is followed by some chronological matter with the heading "According to the Seventy",' for the 'chronological matter' concerned is the *Sex Aetates,* here edited in its entirety for the first time. It comprises more than mere chronological material: the *Sex Aetates* has something to offer to scholars of varying disciplines. Historians may find much to interest them in the way that biblical history was taught in the Irish schools of the 11th and 12th centuries; linguists will find much to occupy them in the forms of a text for which we can supply a known and dated author, an almost complete index of his sources, and a near perfectly established text; metrists too will find here many poems to work on. Students of the apocrypha will find in the SAM text many interesting details, some unique and not previously noted in the standard discussions of the topic. Finally, though not perhaps least, cultural historians will find here much that is relevant to the study of the transmission of ideas.

A work of this kind incurs, of course, many debts. Of my teachers and fellow students at UCD I received particular inspiration and help from Professors Francis John Byrne, Proinsias Mac Cana, and Tomás Ó Concheanainn, Dr. Proinséas Ní Chatháin and Mr. Tomás Ó Cathasaigh, from all of whom I have learned a great deal. Dr. Hans Oskamp gave me access to the unpublished materials of his book on medieval Irish manuscripts, from which I also learned much. Fr. Martin McNamara, MSC, was characteristically generous with his knowledge and time, and I have found his book, *The apocrypha in the Irish Church,* an invaluable guide throughout my work.

I owe a particular debt of gratitude to Professor Carney, who compared my text with a transcript of the Rawlinson B 502 recension that he had made many years ago, and who made many very helpful corrections and suggestions for the improvement of text and translation. Dr. Thomas Charles-Edwards, in his capacity as external examiner for the M.Phil., also made many helpful corrections and comments on the first edition. Dr. Hildegard Tristram, of Freiburg, compared my text with a transcript of *R* which she had made, and offered other suggestions for improvement. Professor Brian Ó Cuív also made some helpful corrections and improvements. Ms. Peggy Walsh, of the School of Celtic Studies library in the Dublin Institute, helped considerably by procuring photographs of manuscripts at short notice.

Finally, to my parents and especially to my wife, Maura, I am indebted for providing inspiration and for bearing patiently with me while I was preparing this work.

DÁIBHÍ Ó CRÓINÍN

ABBREVIATIONS

AFM	Annals of the Four Masters.
AT	Annals of Tigernach.
AU	Annals of Ulster.
CCSL	*Corpus Christianorum Series Latina* (Turnhout 1954–).
CCSL, Cont. med.	*Corpus Christianorum Series Latina, Continuatio medievalis.*
Collectanea	(Ps.Bede) *Excerptiones patrum collectanea, MPL* 94, cols. 539–60.
CSEL	*Corpus Scriptorum Ecclesiasticorum Latinorum* (Vienna 1866–).
DIL	Royal Irish Academy *Dictionary of the Irish Language.*
Etym	Wallace M. Lindsay (ed) *Isidori Hispalensis episcopi Etymologiarum sive Originum libri XX.* 2 vols (Oxford 1911[1]/1971).
Eusebius-Jerome	Rudolf Helm (ed) *Die Chronik des Hieronymus (Hieronymi Chronicon)*, Eusebius Werke 7 = *Die griechischen christlichen Schriftsteller der ersten drei Jahrhunderte* (Leipzig 1913[1]/ Berlin 1956[2]).
Hier	Marc Adriaen (ed) *S. Hieronymi presbyteri Hebraicae questiones in libro Geneseos, CCSL* 72.
MPL	Jacques-P. Migne (ed) *Patrologia Latina cursus completus* (Paris 1844–55).
NLI	National Library of Ireland.
OIG	Rudolf Thurneysen, *A grammar of Old Irish* (Dublin 1975).
OIP	John Strachan, *Old-Irish paradigms and selections from the Old-Irish glosses.* RIA (Dublin 1970).
PRIA	*Proceedings of the Royal Irish Academy.*
RIA	Royal Irish Academy, Dublin.
SAM	The Irish Sex Aetates Mundi.
SR	Whitley Stokes (ed) *Saltair na Rann.* Anecdota Oxoniensia, Medieval & Modern Series I iii (Oxford 1883).
TCD	Trinity College, Dublin.
ZCP	*Zeitschrift für celtische Philologie.*

The biblical citations in the Notes and Commentary, pp. 138–80, are from Robert Weber, OSB, and others (ed) *Biblia sacra iuxta vulgatam versionem.* 2 vols (Stuttgart 1975); individual books of the bible are referred to in the abbreviated forms of this version also. The names in the translation have been standardised according to the text in Ronald Knox, *The Holy Bible* (London 1961).

THE SIX AGES OF THE WORLD

> Nec historicos nec commentatores varia dicentes imperite condemnare debemus, quia antiquitas ipsa creavit errorem.
>
> Isidore, *Etymologiae* XV 1. 2

'We are forever talking about time and times', Saint Augustine remarked. 'We use these words and we hear them used, we are understood and we understand. They are the veriest deep-down things and yet, again, they conceal so much and new meanings are always being found for them.'[1] The 'rational' mind has always tried to find order in chaos, to discern a pattern where no such pattern actually exists. Thus countries are often arbitrarily divided according to the direction of a river or the interposition of a mountain-range. The epochs of history, in like manner, are only creatures of the moment, the response to man's insistent desire to find logic in the course of history. But as a geographer's divisions do not alter the flow of a river nor the direction of a mountain-range, so man's exposition of history in terms of eras or epochs does not alter the fact that history itself – *antiquitas ipsa* – is an indivisible unit.[2] For while God was believed to have performed the act of his Creation in six consecutive days, *post namque historiae narrator divisit in sermone, quod Deus non divisit in operis perfectione.*[3]

These words of the seventh-century Irish Augustine, by stressing the human element in the narrative of history, emphasised in particular that the notion of epochs could exist only *in sermone* – only in words could man hope to imitate God and redefine that which God had immutably defined at the Creation. In the beginning was the Word, but the Word was with God, not with men; hence the Irish Augustine saw in all the seemingly miraculous things of the world not the evidence for God's continuous act of Creation (for that had ended on the sixth

[1] Confessions XI 22, 28: 'Et dicimus tempus et tempus, tempora et tempora . . . Dicimus haec et audivimus haec et intellegimur et intellegimus. Manifestissima et usitatissima sunt, et eadem rursus nimis latent et nova est inventio eorum.' *Bibliothèque augustinienne*, Oeuvres de Saint Augustin 14 (Paris 1962).

[2] See Charles W. Jones, *Saints' lives and chronicles in early England* (Ithaca, New York 1947) p. 51 ff.

[3] Augustinus Hibernicus, *De mirabilibus sacrae scripturae* I 1 (*MPL* 35, col. 2152).

day) but the witness to his continued working and governance in nature. Man could not himself presume ever to create, only to understand more deeply the things that already existed in the world.

Nevertheless, the concept of epochs in history was useful for some purposes. When the great James Ussher gave his estimate of 4004 as the number of years that had elapsed from the Creation to the Advent he was not simply displaying 'the pedantry of an archbishop who had constituted himself the self-appointed clerk of God's Court',[4] he was following in the well-worn path of nearly two millenia of ecclesiastical scholarship. The distinction of periods of time had a precise function – to provide a definitive context for the events of Christ's earthly mission. Within that context any event, great or small, could be seen to have some individual significance for the interpretation of the whole; hence the distinction might apply equally to years or to other groupings of time. There was therefore no self-contradiction in the words of Bede, for example, when he said *sex aetatibus mundi tempora distinguuntur,*[5] no dichotomy between Bede the historian and Bede the biblical scholar. For to him anything more than the bare annalistic form was a *descriptio temporum,* as he himself characterised the Chronicle of Eusebius-Jerome.[6] The annalistic form, on the other hand, was to characterise the receding series of years, each by a mark or sign of its own, so that the years might not be confused in the retrospect of those who had lived and acted in them. Historians tend to forget that annal entries were originally intended to distinguish remarkable years, not remarkable people or events.

According to this historical concept, therefore, each epoch not only develops and manifests its own view of the world but, very gradually, refashions or discards entirely the inherited view of the preceding epoch. True, it often discards that inherited image so slowly that we think it is still in focus long after it has begun to dim; but as often as not, the 'backward look' which we associate with the medieval mind (and particularly the Irish mind) is in reality the creation of our own prejudices. But the concept of epochs in history was not exclusive to Christian thought; the dominant characteristic of Christian historiography that set it apart from the historical writing of Antiquity was its new-found theory of *universal* history and chronology. Christian

[4]The verdict of Toynbee, cited by R. Buick Knox, *James Ussher Archbishop of Armagh* (Cardiff 1967) p. 106.

[5]*De temporibus* XVI; see Charles W. Jones (ed) *Bedae opera de temporibus.* Medieval Academy of America Publications No. 41 (Cambridge, Mass. 1943) p. 303 and idem., *Saints' Lives*, p. 36 ff.

[6]Cf. Irish Ps. Bede's *Collectaneum*, *De luminaribus ecclesiae (MPL* 94, col. 552D), who enumerates the three great works of Eusebius thus: 'Canones quatuor evangeliorum . . decem historiae ecclesiasticae . . et chronicon, id est temporum breviarium.'

history was a chronology of man, not of Greece or Rome alone.[7] This history of the world, the mundane microcosm, fell into six parts, to be viewed as typical of man as an individual, but as the reflection too of an abstract or eternal similitude that forms all God's creations. The comparison came quite naturally to literate men, hence the Irish Ps. Bede's *Collectaneum* remarks: *Sic tradunt seniores, quod sex millia annis mundus a Deo omnipotenti censitus fuisset. Sex aetates hominis sunt.*[8]

The six, seven, and eight days of Creation served as a model or prefiguration of the Six, Seven, and Eight historical and chronological Ages of the world. Whether viewed as typological or allegorical (in the strict sense of that word), history was literal and the historical could be prefigured in history, the happenings in the world could be given a significance: *Per historiam namque historia figuratur, cum factura primorum sex sive septem dierum totidem saeculi huius comparatur aetatibus.*[9] Christian history, in other words, presented a completely new picture of the world and conversion to Christianity meant literally the discovery of a new history from Adam and Eve up to contemporary times. The Christian historians, for their part, were characterised by a new kind of historical exposition introduced by Eusebius, distinguished by the importance they attributed to the remote past, by the central position of doctrinal controversies, and by the lavish use of documents. The impact of this kind of history on a society like that of the Irish must have been tremendous.[10]

But there was more involved than the mere pointing out of parallels and prefigurations in Scripture; Christian history had a point to make and was not always subtle in making it. 'To us it naturally appears that there is something in common between the Jews who died in defending the old Jerusalem and the Christians who died in building up the new Jerusalem against the same Roman Empire. Modern scholars have found it easy to prove that in form and substance the Jewish martyr is the prototype of the Christian martyr. Such scholarly discoveries have little relevance to the realities of the fourth century. The pupils hated the masters, and were hated in their turn. With a cry of joy Eusebius, possibly a man of Jewish descent, retells from Josephus the story of the fall of Jerusalem: thus may perish the enemies of Christ!'[11]

[7]See especially on this theme Moses I. Finley, *The use and abuse of history* (London 1975) p. 24 ff. and pp. 82–4.

[8]*De septem peccatis (MPL* 94, col. 556B).

[9]See Jones, *Saints' Lives*, p. 23 ff.

[10]It has long been known, e.g., that some of the versified genealogies in M. A. O'Brien (ed) *Corpus genealogiarum Hiberniae* I (Dublin 1962[1]/1975[2]) draw on Isidore's *Etymologiae*, and as such these poems bear witness to a use of Isidore in secular Irish learned circles already by the mid-seventh century.

[11]Arnaldo Momigliano (ed) *The conflict of paganism and Christianity in the fourth century* (Oxford 1963) pp. 79–80.

Christian historians made no effort to compete with the pagans, but preferred to adapt and integrate what they could into their own writing. Thus biography became hagiography and the lists of kings and emperors of various races were joined to form the synchronistic history of universal man. Christian history, moreover, combined the two streams of messianic doctrine and an inherited number symbolism into a compact unity which could be interpreted either literally or allegorically as suited the context. On the subject of this number symbolism Charles Jones has this to say: 'Augustine's number symbolism revealed a creative Multiplicity in Unity, equally literal (historical) and spiritual (allegorical). Trinity required of all creatures, inorganic, organic, and intelligential, a beginning, middle, and end. The very universe is a creature, with a body (history) and a soul *(nous)*. Christian historians, therefore, assumed all temporalities to be linear, with movement from beginning, through middle to end. On that historical line rested topics.'[12]

When, therefore, the seventh-century Irish commentator on the Catholic Epistles[13] remarked that *sex milibus annorum aetas mundi describitur,* he was following in a tradition already established by ecclesiastical writers as early as the third century. The germ of the doctrine was to be found in the Epistle of Barnabas 'On the Sabbath', which treated of a created universe lasting Six Days, by uniting hexaemeron, chiliasm, and eschatology in a single, short passage:

> 'Notice, children, what is the meaning of "He made an end in six days". He means this: that the Lord will make an end of everything in six thousand years. And he himself is my witness when he says: "Lo! The day of the Lord shall be as a thousand years" [Ps. 89; *Pet* 3. 8]. So then, children, in six days, that is in six thousand years, everything will be completed.'[14]

It required no great imagination to pass from the belief in Six Ages of six thousand years' duration to the notion that every Age had a duration of a thousand years. Thus the author of *Saltair na Rann,* for example, echoed no doubt a belief that was common in Ireland in his time when he said:

> Adfiadat ind ecnaide,
>   do réir na riagla as moo,
> imriadat co héttlaide
>   míli bliadna 'sind loo.

'The wise men declare, according to the greatest law, that they go

[12]Charles W. Jones 'Some introductory remarks on Bede's commentary on Genesis' *Sacris Erudiri* 19 (1969–70) pp. 115–98, esp. p. 191 ff.

[13]See Robert E. McNally (ed) *Scriptores Hiberniae Minores* 1, *CCSL* 108 B, p. 40.

[14]The translation of Kirsopp Lake, *Nicene and Ante-Nicene Fathers,* cited by Jones, art. cit., p. 192.

wearily about – a thousand years in the day!'[15] Evidently the topic of the Six Ages had been long developing before these words were written. Writers followed in the path of Augustine, the Visigothic Fathers, and Gregory the Great. The requirements of teachers and preachers developed the theory into a millenarianism which could be either prophetic or literal and which has continued sporadically even up to our own day. Since Genesis determined this line of history, and Kings and Chronicles seemed to set the historiographical pattern, every commentator was driven back to the vast corpus of patristic literature on these subjects that lay to hand. It is no coincidence that, in the composition of the Irish *Sex Aetates Mundi,* our author should have drawn on Genesis and Kings for the most part, with additional material from Jerome's commentary on Genesis and from the apocrypha. 'Generations have trod'; the Fathers had exercised every form of ingenuity to establish convincing relationships between the Ages, and the history of medieval exegesis is the history of the dissemination of these ideas.[16]

Throughout the Middle Ages the biblical literature was coursed by two divergent streams of influence, exemplified on the one hand by the mysticism of the school of Alexandrine exegesis, and on the other by the literalism of the Antiochan school, a school which, in reaction against the allegorising tendencies of Alexandria, insisted on the literal and historical sense of Scripture, refusing to see prophecies or types of Christ in almost every detail of the Old Testament.[17] The whole of medieval exegesis, then, is dominated by a manifold (generally a three- or four-fold) sense of Scripture, as expressed in the well-known rhyming hexameters:

Littera gesta docet, quid credas allegoria,
moralis quid agas, quo tendas anagogia.[18]

In almost every patristic work that they studied the medieval exegetes found the text of Scripture interpreted according to more than one

[15]Whitley Stokes (ed) *Saltair na Rann.* Anecdota Oxoniensia, Medieval & Modern Series I iii (Oxford 1883) p. 123; the translation is by William W. Heist, *The fifteen signs before Doomsday* (Michigan 1952) p. 21.

[16]There is a good, brief discussion of medieval biblical exegesis, with particular reference to Hiberno-Latin writings, in Robert E. McNally, *The bible in the early Middle Ages,* Woodstock Papers No. 4 (Westminster, Maryland 1959).

[17]See Martin McNamara 'Psalter text and Psalter study in the early Irish Church' *PRIA* 73 C 7 (1973) pp. 201–98, at pp. 257–8; for a wide-ranging discussion of Hiberno-Latin exegesis see the important paper by Bernhard Bischoff 'Wendepunkte in der Geschichte der lateinischen Exegese im Frühmittelalter' *Sacris Erudiri* 6 (1954) pp. 189–279; rev. ed. in Bischoff, *Mittelalterliche Studien. Ausgewählte Aufsätze zur Schriftkunde und Literaturgeschichte,* 3 vols (Stuttgart 1966–7, 1981), Vol. 1, pp. 205–73. There is an English translation of this paper in McNamara (ed) *Biblical studies: The medieval Irish contribution.* Proceedings of the Irish Biblical Assoc. No. 1 (Dublin 1976) pp. 73–164.

[18]Cited by McNally, *The bible,* p. 53, and McNamara, art. cit., p. 257.

sense. It could be understood spiritually as well as literally. But the patristic work which above all others furnished the Middle Ages with the most useful categorisation of the biblical senses was Augustine's *De Genesi ad Litteram* I. 1,[19] which provides a four-fold division: 'In every sacred book one should note the things of eternity which are communicated, the facts of history which are recounted, future events which are foretold, and moral precepts which are enjoined or counselled.' In the Irish *Sex Aetates Mundi,* which follows the characteristically Irish fashion of mixing christological (allegorical) and literal interpretation, we find the literal approach in the passage on the origin of the monsters (§34), the allegorical in the passages on the mystical interpretation of Noah's Ark (§19) and of the *Beati* (§§60–62), while the historical approach is reflected in the detailed genealogies and biblical history, and the moral aspect in the accounts of Cain and Noah (§§17, 18).

Such a combination of the two streams of exegetical interpretation, however, could sometimes lead to difficulties, not least in regard to the concept of the Six Ages. The Chronicle of Eusebius-Jerome, for example, had placed the date of Advent in the 5199th year from Creation and for three centuries the reputation of Jerome was sufficient to ensure that the Chronicle and its continuations dominated western historical thinking, with the result that its chronology (which was never intended by its authors to be definitive) had hardened into tradition, especially after Isidore had adopted the same reckoning. The millenarian interpretation was not in itself a clearly defined one, despite the lengthy duration of its discussion. Lactantius had talked about Six Ages of the world and how each Age equalled a thousand years,[20] but there seem never to have been any profound philosophies underlying the millenarian belief. Even Augustine, the classic writer for the period, was not predicting the millenium when he constantly used the metaphor of Six Ages of the world and compared them (as others did) with other combinations of six, especially the six days of Creation. Augustine thought of himself naturally as living in the sixth, the last, the 'old' Age of the world – *senectus mundi.* 'He thought of this,' however, 'not as a man living under the shadow of an imminent event, but rather, with the sadness of one for whom nothing new could happen.'[21]

But such metaphors 'struck fire' and his more fundamentalist followers, like Isidore, made it a common point of reference. It combined easily in the millenarian mind with 2 *Pet* 3, 7–8:

> 'But the heavens, O earth, which are now, by the same word are kept in store, reserved into fire against the day of judgement and

[19]*CSEL* 28, 3, p. 3.

[20]'Ergo quoniam sex diebus cuncta opera Dei perfecta sunt, per saecula sex, id est annorum sex milia, munere in hoc statu mundum necesse est,' *Div. Inst.*

[21]Peter Brown, *Augustine of Hippo; a biography* (London 1960) p. 296.

the perdition of ungodly men. But, beloved, be not ignorant of this one thing: that one day is with the Lord as a thousand years and a thousand years as one day.'

Charles Jones has explained how these words served as the key to world chronology: 'Now, so careless was the millenarian that he was fascinated by the fact that Jerome and his continuators placed the Advent in the 5199th year from the Creation. With Olympian disregard, he forgot the 199, and concentrated on the round 5000. If five ages of the world last 5000 years the Sixth Age would last a thousand. He set the Second Coming and the end of the secular world at the year A.D. 1000 and, since the time was as yet far distant, no doubt would have conceded a few years one way or the other.'[22] This doctrine, however, could cut both ways; that combination of the literal and the allegorical in exegesis that we mentioned above sometimes led to a misinterpretation of the facts. Thus, the *De comprobatione sextae aetatis* of Julian of Toledo,[23] for instance, was written specifically to combat the Jews, who (according to Julian) were using the doctrine of Six Ages (five to the Incarnation) together with Psalm 79 to argue that, since the Fifth Age had not yet fulfilled its allotted number of years, the Messiah could not yet have come.

Julian wrote to deny that any chronology other than that of the Seventy Weeks of Daniel could provide a sound basis for a Christian chronology of the world. But the problem was not just one of interpretation, it also lay in the fact that the first eight centuries of Christianity knew not just one canonical text of the bible, but several, each with its own peculiar set of figures for the chronology of biblical events. Hence the two introductory poems prefixed to SAM, which give the duration of each Age according to the figures of the Septuagint and the Vulgate respectively, are not the products of pedantic scholarship but reflect a conflict of evidence which had troubled centuries of Christian thinkers. The conflict is perhaps best exemplified in the personality of Bede, who heralded a new era (in more ways than one) in the field of mundane chronology. Bede's distinction was to have set himself against the millenarianism of his time and before, and his first move to counteract the trend was to publish in A.D. 703, in the short chronicle attached to his tract *De temporibus,* his own chronology of the world based on the Vulgate – a chronology which set the beginning of the Sixth Age at 3952 years from Creation.[24] In so doing he did no more than many computists of the third and fourth centuries had done, and the fact that he had found a different answer was not in

[22] *Saints' Lives*, p. 25.

[23] See Jocelyn N. Hillgarth (ed) *Sancti Iuliani opera* 1, *CCSL* 115, pp. lxv–lxvi.

[24] *De temporibus*, ed. Jones, pp. 295–303; see also Bede's *Epistola ad Pleguinam*, ed. Jones, pp. 307–15, where Bede answers his critics, saying: 'Audiat beatum Hieronimum quod non hebraeos sed graecos codices dicat esse falsatos.'

itself disturbing – seldom did two men make a conscientious attempt with the same results. Bede's novelty was to disagree to such a large extent with his predecessors, and he was accused by some contemporaries of having drunk from the cup of heresy.[25]

Besides the fact that the traditional chronology, combined with various interpretations of Augustine's doctrine of the Six Ages, had become a pseudo-scholarly dogma, it was also objected against Bede that Jerome, whose translation of the bible he professedly followed, had himself in the Eusebio-Hieronimian Chronicle been the translator and adapter of a manifestly different chronology from Bede's. So that while it was true that Bede would have known (as not all of his detractors would) that Jerome's adaptation of the Eusebian chronicle had *preceded* his creation of the Vulgate,[26] by his own time the pattern had been immutably set.

Bede was essentially a chronologist, a master of the computus, or ecclesiastical calendar. The ecclesiastical calendar combined the theoretical discussion of Times with the practical, the manual of mathematical-astronomical theory and the survey of history which was intended to illustrate the technical rules. Here, as in other respects, Bede was following in the path of Isidore's *Etymologiae* which, in the same way, had concluded its chronological summary with a short history of the world. The pattern however, was a common one from the fourth century; the makers of computi passed naturally from consideration of the smaller units of time to the larger: from moments, hours, days, weeks and months up to the seasons and the cycles of years, culminating in the Ages of the world. *Tempora momentis horis diebus mensibus annis saeculis et aetatibus diuiduntur* is the opening statement of Bede's shorter tract *De temporibus*[27] and the computist moved easily from chronological theory to historical research. The theory of the *aetates mundi,* the greatest units, induced him (like Isidore) to add a Chronicle exhibiting the duration of the individual Ages of world history.

The notion that a thousand years are as one day in the eyes of God led, as we saw above, to the comparison of history with the week of Creation and with the periods of the individual human life. The founders of Christian chronography, Sextus Julius Africanus and Hippolytus, were firm believers in the idea of a temporal world lasting 6000 years (5,500 to the Incarnation); the fact that they were disproved by experience in the sixth century did not prevent others from following their line of thinking. Bede himself mentions the work of a heretical

[25]See Jones, *Bedae opera,* p. 133.

[26]In his *Expositio Actuum Apostolorum et Retractatio,* ed. M. L. W. Laistner, Medieval Academy of America Publications No. 35 (Cambridge, Mass. 1939), at p. 93, Bede calls attention to Jerome's stated belief that the Vulgate was the final authority.

[27]Jones, *Bedae opera,* p. 295.

chronologist which he had seen in his youth, who had allotted to the world a duration of 5,500 years before the Incarnation and 500 after it, of which 300 and more were then past.[28] But though disapproving of the notion that men could know such things, Bede and others were fond of the comparison with the six days of Creation and the six phases of human life, and consequently fond of the division of history into *sex aetates mundi*. But even Bede, a practised historian, did not trouble to settle the times of single events accurately; the beginnings and ends of great kingdoms are recorded exactly as Eusebius-Jerome and Isidore had done before him – 'the dependence on earlier Christian chronography is so evident that one might at times call the book a compressed Jerome.'[29] The duration of generations and reigns was given only to piece out the length of the Ages. Bede was 'a theologian even when writing history;'[30] we could use the same words when speaking of Dublittir ua hUathgaile's translation of the *Sex Aetates Mundi*.

As it happened, however, the *Hebraica ueritas* in the form of Jerome's Vulgate was to become the standard biblical version of the Middle Ages, and Bede's revised chronology of the Ages, which was based on the Vulgate text, eventually held the field. But this was not so much due to its own intrinsic merits as to the universal reverence shown to Jerome's scholarship. The centuries subsequent to Bede saw numerous other attempts to establish a mundane chronology, the most famous perhaps being the work of Marianus Scottus of Mainz.[31] Ussher, for his part, had his chronology enshrined in the King James bible, but he was only the latest in a long line of computists and biblical scholars. But though the chronologists and exegetes followed Augustine in the belief that there was no predicting the millenium, the doctrine of the Ages was adopted time and time again by both. They saw the world as being in its Sixth Age, with a Seventh from the time of death up to the Last Judgement, leading into an Eighth and final Age of timeless union with God. This thinking is well exemplified in the collection of homiletic and devotional texts known as the *Catechesis celtica*:[32]

> Item isti VIII dies paschae significant VIII tempora vitae praesentis a principio mundi usque ad iudicium, quia sub forma

[28]See Jones, ibid., p. 313.

[29]See Wilhelm Levison 'Bede as historian' in A. Hamilton-Thompson (ed) *Bede, his life, times and writings* (Oxford 1935) pp. 111–51, at p. 121; repr. in *Aus rheinischer und fränkischer Frühzeit*, ed. Walther Holtzmann (Düsseldorf 1948) pp. 347–82, at p. 356.

[30]Levison, art. cit., p. 123 [357].

[31]There is an excellent account of Marianus by Anna-Dorothee von den Brinken 'Marianus Scottus. Unter besonderer Berücksichtigung der nicht veröffentlichten Teile seiner Chronik.' *Deutsches Archiv für Erforschung des Mittelalters* 17 (1961) pp. 191–238.

[32]André Wilmart (ed) *Studi e Testi* 59, Analecta Reginensia (1933) pp. 29–112, at p. 56.

> ebdomadis constituit Deus hunc mundum. Ipsa est VII aetas dies iudicii, in quo fiunt mille anni, dum iudicentur vivi et mortui secundum merita uniuscuiusque. Ipsa est VIII dies vita aeterna, quam dabit Deus sanctis suis sine fine in summa civitate caeli.

The theme was essentially a devotional one and the fact that it was adapted by the chronologists should not distract our attention from the exegetical origins of the idea. Scholars have remarked that it is impossible to understand Bede the historian without reference to Bede the exegete[33] and the same could be said for much of the Irish material as well. The Irish SAM tract is not so much a work of 'synthetic history' as a historical homily on the story of Salvation. The redemption of the lost souls of the first five Ages mentioned in §64 of SAM is only the most obvious statement of ua hUathgaile's intent in composing the work; the devotional element is predominant throughout the whole text and reaches an obvious climax with the passage on Christ's Advent. That this devotional element was eliminated subsequently by degrees only serves to indicate that the inheritors of the tradition had gradually lost sight of its true aims and saw fit to adapt the work to their own contemporary needs and purposes.

[33]See esp. Levison, art. cit.

THE TEXT TRADITION

I. INTRODUCTION

The *Sex Aetates Mundi* is found, in more or less complete form, in eight manuscripts ranging in date from *Leabhar na hUidhre* – the oldest extant codex in Irish – to the seventeenth-century NLI MS. G 131 (the O'Clery MS.). Epitomes of the text, and fragments of varying lengths, occur sporadically in a good many more manuscripts, sometimes incorporated in later compositions such as *Stair chloinde Israhél,* or occurring individually as mere *disjecta membra.*[1] It has been suggested that SAM may have been a standard opening text in many late eleventh- and twelfth-century Irish codices,[2] and it does seem to have enjoyed a widespread popularity with the scribes and compilers of that period.

The manuscripts which contain more or less complete versions of SAM are *Leabhar na hUidhre,* Rawlinson B 502, Rawlinson B 486, the Book of Lecan, the Book of Ballymote (whose text can be completed by reference to TCD MS. H.2.4 [1295] and its derivative, TCD MS. H.1.15 [1289]), and NLI MS. G 131. The fact that Dublittir ua hUathgaile's poem *Rédig dam, a Dé, do nim* (§70) is found in the Book of Leinster suggests the possibility that a full text of SAM may once have been contained in that codex, but the surviving evidence gives no clue to what its extent or quality may have been. It might be surmised likewise, from the fragments of SAM that survive in Laud 610, that a text of SAM once formed a part of that manuscript as well. There is some evidence to suggest that Laud 610 once contained a version of the *Lebor Bretnach,*[3] and we know that this text and SAM are frequently found together in the manuscripts. But in the case of the Laud MS. also we have too little evidence on which to base an

[1] The reader is referred to the concordance of MSS that follows this chapter, pp. 56–61.

[2] See Hans P. A. Oskamp 'The Yellow Book of Lecan proper' *Ériu* 26 (1975) pp. 102–19, at p. 114: 'Of these tracts [SAM, LG, LB] *Sex Aetates Mundi* undoubtedly came first in all synchronistic compilations of the eleventh and twelfth centuries'; it should be stated, however, that this last paper by Oskamp represents a departure from the views expressed by him in his notes on the history of *Leabhar na hUidhre* (1967), and the revised theories—based as they are mainly on an unfortunate confusion of Dublittir ua hUathgaile's poem *Rédig dam, a Dé, do nim* with the poem by Flann Mainistrech of the same title—mark a departure from the direction of his earlier work.

[3] See David N. Dumville 'The textual history of "Lebor Bretnach": a preliminary study' *Éigse* 16 (1975–6) pp. 255–73, at pp. 263–4, and note 41 below.

estimation of the kind of SAM text (if any) it might have contained. The detailed evidence, for what it is worth, will be listed and discussed below.[4]

2. MANUSCRIPTS AND RECENSIONS

(a) *Rawlinson B 502 and related MSS (Recension I)*

The best and most complete copy of SAM is to be found in the Oxford, Bodleian Library, MS. Rawlinson B 502 *(R)*, written probably in the late 1120's in a south-Leinster scriptorium.[5] It occurs in that manuscript immediately following *Saltair na Rann* and is the second text in the biblico-historical section of the manuscript (fols. 18^{r}–46^{v}), being followed by four poems generally ascribed to Airbertach mac Cosse. The whole section is closed by a curious apocryphon about a monster in the Indian Ocean that causes the tides.[6]

The *R* text is a prose-verse recension, containing all but one of the seventy sections in the present edition. The prose text is interspersed with eight poems bearing on the matter there discussed, and is preceded by two further introductory poems (§§2, 3) and a prose prologue (§1), which ascribes the work to Dublittir ua hUathgaile. The *R* text is glossed throughout and some sections, which were obviously intended for inclusion in the body of the prose, were added in the margins or at the heads of pages. Some of these sections have, unfortunately, been lost in *R* due to the work of the seventeenth-century binder, but all those portions of the text so lost have been recovered by reference to other manuscripts.

Copied directly from *R* (or, less likely, from another manuscript almost identical with it) was the Dublin, NLI, MS. G 131 *(P)*, a seventeenth-century transcript. The scribe of *P* had access to at least one eleventh-century codex, and many of his other texts show consistently good readings. The relationship of the *P* text of SAM to that in *R* will be clear from the following select list of comparative readings (passages within arrow brackets indicate glosses on the text):

	R	**P**
§11.21-22	⟨*Hironimus*⟩ *etc.*	Written beside §11, in space left vacant
§13.6	Laméch ⟨.i. *bigamus*⟩	ditto
§20.3	hi sechtmaid fichet ⟨.i. Maii⟩	,,
§20.6-7	cethri lathi coícat ⟨.i. ar tríb cétaib⟩	,,

[4]See also the description of the MSS, pp. 51–53.

[5]See section 4 (a) below, on the date and authorship of SAM.

[6]See Pádraig Ó Néill 'Airbertach mac Cosse's poem on the Psalter' *Éigse* 17 (1977–8) pp. 19–46; Ó Néill seems to me undoubtedly right when he suggests that the tale was inserted to fill up the remaining few lines of a page, since it has no real bearing on what precedes it.

	R	P
§22.3	⟨*Noe primum altare fecit*⟩ *etc.*	Noé. . is lais dorónad altóir, *etc.*
§23.9	i[n] stuag nime	*n*-stroke *om. P*
§28.4-5	⟨La Mesrom⟩ *etc.*	Mesrom. . laiside dorónad altóir, *etc.*
§29.8-9	Tala ⟨*ciuitas*⟩ ⁊ Resen ⟨*ciuitas*⟩	ditto
§30.2	Sidon ⟨.i. *primogenitus*⟩	,,
§30.7	prímchathir na Foénice ⟨.i. Sidon⟩	Gloss incorporated in text
§31.3	Elam ⟨.i. *primogenitus*⟩	,, ,, ,, ,,
§31.6-7	⟨Assiri *ab* Assúr⟩ *etc.*	,, ,, ,, ,,
§31.11	⟨.i. na Lidetai⟩ *etc.*	,, ,, ,, ,,
§35.3	⟨*qui primus*⟩ *etc.*	Nachor, *qui primus, etc.* misplaced
§35a	Cétmac as marb, *etc. om.*	ditto
§38.5	Laban ⟨.i. *filius*⟩ ⁊ Rabecca	Gloss incorporated in text
§39.9	⟨*Saraceni a Sarra*⟩	*S. hautem a S.* incorporated in text
§39.15	⟨*Ismohelitae ab Ismal*⟩	Gloss incorporated in text
§39.16	⟨*a quo Nabatheni*⟩	,, ,, ,, ,,
§44.18	⟨.i. *patrem Moisi* ⁊ *Aron*⟩	,, ,, ,, ,,
§44.9	⟨.i. Galad⟩	,, ,, ,, ,,
§44.21	⟨*qui ambo mortui sunt*⟩ *etc.*	,, ,, ,, ,,
§49.6-15	⟨Rechab ⁊ Banna⟩ *etc.*[7]	,, ,, ,, ,,
§50.4	secht mbliadna ⁊ [sé] mís	sé *om. P*
§50.17	⟨Dá siar immorro Dauída⟩ *etc.*	Gloss incorporated in text
§50.26	⟨Athalas⟩ *etc.*	Gloss incorporated in text
§53.8	Dair mac Arbei ⟨nó Arsabei⟩	Dair mac Arsabei
§55.5	⁊ [sé] crom tornocht	sé *om. P*
§57.11	Cccclxxx. stadi ⟨nó sesca míli⟩	.lx. míli stadi
§59.12	⟨.i. mac Abda⟩	Gloss incorporated in text

Besides these examples from the body of the SAM text, the glosses that were lost in *R* as a result of the binder's trimming of the manuscript are found in their entirety in *P* and are there incorporated into their respective places in the main text.[8]

The *P* text of SAM contains all but the first four sections that make

[7]*P* here mistakenly inserts the gloss *Otholia, filia Achaib meic Ambrae, mater Ochozias* ⟨*.i. rex Israhél*⟩, which should be in §52.3–5.

[8]Note, however, that the scribe of *P* has not, I think, always placed these glosses in their correct contexts; see the note above and the apparatus criticus to §§28, 31, 39, 50.

up the *R* version, excluding, that is, the introductory poems and the prose prologue (with its ascription to Dublittir ua hUathgaile), and the Latin section (§4a) on the Ages of Man. It is perhaps possible that the omission of §§1–3 in *P* is a result of the fact that the section of *R* which contains the bulk of the SAM text, and whose first recto folio (41^{r}) is marked by the very large ornamented initial of *SEX AETATES SUNT MUNDI* (§4.1), may at one time have been regarded as separate from the preceding section of *R,* on whose last verso folio (40^{v}) occur the prose prologue (§1) and almost all of the two introductory poems (§§2, 3).[9]

We are precluded from assuming that §§1–3 were added by the scribe of *R* solely to fill the vacant space at the end of a column, because the large ornamented initial of §4 does not open the new folio but is preceded by the last nine lines of §3 (the poem *Cétaimmser in bethad bind*). Elsewhere in *R* the scribe on occasion crammed the writing space at the end of a folio in order that he might be able to begin a new recto page with the ornamented initial of a new text (or of a main text, if the preceding matter comprised introductory or prefatory material); that he did not do this in the present instance is clear evidence that he felt the prose prologue and the two introductory poems to be integral parts of the text. This statement, moreover, finds additional support in the version of SAM that is preserved in Rawlinson B 486, which is discussed below in section 2 (b).

Apart from these four sections, then, the text of SAM in these two manuscripts *(R P)* is virtually identical and it will be maintained in what follows that they represent the original and uninterpolated first recension of the text. A structural analysis of this text will be given below, in section 3, and the detailed arguments for this view will be held over till then.

The Dublin MS., NLI G 2–3 *(G)* contains copies of §§2, 9, 11 of SAM, taken by Ádhamh Ó Cianáin (†1373) either from *R* or a derivative manuscript almost identical with it. Some of what Ó Cianáin transcribed into this manuscript he copied from *leabhar a oidi .i. Seoan O Dubagan,* perhaps to be identified with an exemplar of the Book of Uí Maine; it will be seen below, in section 3 (d), that the scribe(s) of that codex had access to a part at least of the SAM text, and Ó Cianáin may have shared this material. The Book of Glendalough is cited as a source for some texts in *G*[10] but the SAM extracts in *G* seem to me to come from *R* and it is difficult to decide if the two codices are in fact identical, or whether the SAM sections are copied at first hand from a twelfth-century exemplar or from a

[9]By 'section' here I do not mean 'gathering'; there is no *codicological* separation between the beginning of SAM and what precedes it in *R*.

[10]See James Carney 'The Ó Cianáin miscellany' *Ériu* 21 (1969) pp. 122–47, at p. 125, and the discussion below, pp. 34–35.

later transcript thereof;[11] either way, the *G* texts are of no value in establishing the critical text of SAM; their chief value is in the study of the text tradition.

The last item in this first recension to be discussed is a copy of §3 (the poem *Cétaimmser in bethad bind*) which is to be found in the London, British Library, MS. Egerton 1782, written at Cluain Plocáin (Ballymulconry, Co. Roscommon) in 1572 (TCD MS. H. 4. 17 [1358], copied by Aodh Ó Dálaigh mainly from TCD MS. H. 1. 15 [1289], also has this poem, but collation shows that it derives directly from Egerton 1782 and is of no independent value). This brief extract contains seven of the nine stanzas in §3, but there is no obvious indication of its provenance. The fact that this manuscript was written at Cluain Plocáin raises the possibility that its version of §3 may derive from the material now preserved in Rawl. B 486 (a part at least of which was also at Cluain Plocáin in the fourteenth century); but there is insufficient evidence on which to base a definite judgement about the origins of its SAM texts. If it is listed here as a representative of Recension I, that is only because the manuscripts of Recension II do not now contain that poem; it is not impossible, however, that the Egerton poem was in fact copied from a manuscript of Recension II, since we will see below that the archetype of that recension contained much of the verse that is now found only in the MSS of Recension I.

(b) *Leabhar na hUidhre and related MSS (Recension II)*

The oldest surviving fragment of SAM occurs on what is now the first folio of *Leabhar na hUidhre (U)*, generally believed to have been written ca 1100 A.D. in the scriptorium of Clonmacnois.[12] This fragment, a single leaf of the text, was penned by scribe *A*, the oldest hand in the manuscript. Codicological analysis has not been able to establish with any certainty how much of the text has been lost from *U*, but what remains is sufficient to show that the *U* version of SAM differs markedly from the manuscripts of the first *(R P)* recension.

The *U* text of SAM opens midway through §5 (on the descendants of Japheth) and continues parallel to the manuscripts of the first recension as far as §39.3, when the loss of one or more folios has cut off the rest of the text. Within the space of these few sections, however, *U* has already clearly departed from the pattern (though not the sequence) of the *R P* recension. The characteristic features of the *U* text are: (i) omission of the poem *Ingena Loith, légtar lib* (§37) and its prose introduction (§36); (ii) the insertion of a single stanza (§35a) on the death of Aran, son of Thara; (iii) a tendency to express in Irish

[11]I am more inclined to think they are a direct copy from *R*.

[12]See Hans P. A. Oskamp 'Notes on the history of Lebor na Huidre' *PRIA* 65 C 6 (1967) pp. 117–37, and the same writer's paper 'On the author of *Sex Aetates Mundi*' *Studia Celtica* 3 (1968) pp. 127–40.

the many words and phrases which in Recension I are preserved in their original Latin form.

The structural analysis of SAM that follows below in section 3 will show that the poems incorporated into SAM in the *R P* recension are integral to the text and cannot be shown to have had an independent existence outside of SAM. It will suffice at this point to anticipate the conclusions reached in section 3, where the detailed arguments will be listed, and for the present it will be maintained that the scribe/compiler of the *U* text purposely omitted §§36, 37 of SAM and substituted in their place the single stanza §35a on Aran, the first few words of which are written in the text proper and the remainder added in the margin.

The occurrence of this stanza in *U* raises the possibility that the recension of SAM in that manuscript was a predominantly prose one, with only occasional stanzas or poems interspersed; this is the implication of Oskamp's essay. But, on the other hand, the evidence of the *U* fragment clearly does not rule out the alternative possibility that the original format of the SAM text in that manuscript (or its exemplar) was a prose-verse one, similar to or identical with that of Recension I. The recent discovery of the Rawl. B 486 version enables us to see that it is the scribe/compiler of *U* who has innovated (by omitting the poem *Ingena Loith, légtar lib* and its prose introduction, §§36, 37); there is no sound basis – on the little evidence available – for the claim that *U,* containing as it does a shorter version of SAM, automatically represents an earlier stage in the development of the text. On the contrary, the evidence to follow shows that in the case of SAM, as in so many other cases, *Leabhar na hUidhre* contains an inferior copy of the text. [13]

The Oxford, Bodleian Library, MS. Rawlinson B 486 *(C)* contains two main Irish sections, one or both of which were written ca 1370. The genealogies of kings and saints in this manuscript were clearly copied from a good exemplar of late eleventh- or twelfth-century date, emanating probably from a south-west Leinster scriptorium.[14] The *C* text of SAM seems also to derive from a good early manuscript, perhaps the same exemplar from which the genealogies were copied – though it is not possible to prove this conclusively. Most significant in the case of *C,* however, is that its text of SAM parallels the format and sequence of sections in Recension I, but *textually* it stands closest to the *U* version. The verbal forms common to *U* and *C*, and which set them apart from the SAM text in *R P,* are here listed briefly in order to establish the relationship:

[13]See below, pp. 18, 20–21.
[14]See p. 52 below.

	U	C
§25.14	*filius* Gomér *om.*	ditto
§25.16	Baath, mac do side	B. m. d. sein
§25.17	athair na Scithecda	ditto
§25.21	Burgandus	,,
§26.8	atát *om.*	,,
§26.12-13	frisin . . Toirrén *om.*	,,
§27.4-5	co huilinn talman *om.*	,,
§28.3	uad side Chusi	uadha sein C.
§28.4	is uad Egiptus	i. u. Egipti
§28.5	is uad	ditto
§28.7-8	meic Israhel iar tain iar dílgend na Cannanna ⁊ iarna n-inarba	,,
§28.10	.i. a senainm sin *om.*	,,
§28.11	cétna *om.*	,,
§28.12	ar tús add. after Babilóin	,,
§28.13	is la Nebroth . . Babilóne *om.*	,,
§29.2	Sessach . . cáduis *om.*	,,
§29.3	*ciuitas om.*	,,
§29.4-5	Doram . . Sennáir *om.*	,,
§29.15	Capturim	,,
§29.15	nitat achinti [⁊ nídat derba *om.*]	,,
§30.5	*qui fuit iunior om.*	,,
§31.5-6	*ut supra diximus om.* [reads: .i. cathir mor fil eter Ninue ⁊ Thala	,, [mor *om.*]
§31.8-10	is leis . . indiu *om.*	ditto
§31.14	na Siria *om.*	,,
§31.14	Damascus	Damocscus
§31.17	.i. fodail .i. add. after *diuisio*	ditto
§32.1	*ut numerantur om.*	,,
§32.2	.iiiixl. cenela	cetri ceneal .xl.
§32.3	gabait	ditto
§32.3-4	⁊ araill . . Assia *om.*	,,
§32.7	Coelensiria	Colensiria
§33.5	a cul	ditto
§33.6	⁊ in ball . . dílsi *om.*	,,
§35.4	cccxxxix	,,
§38.5	mac Nachoir *om.*	,,
§38.11	Iadilafac	,,
§39.1	⁊ dia airechaib *om.*	,,
§39.2	In tres aes in domain ise so lin bl. fil inti .i. .dccccxlv.	,,
§39.3	i tír Caldeorum misplaced	i t. C. *om.*

The list of readings could be added to, but the present selection will suffice. We saw that the third feature listed above among the characteristics of the *U* text was the tendency to translate into Irish those words and phrases that occurred in the original version of SAM in Latin; this feature also marks the *C* text of SAM. But here the similarity ends, for the *C* version has preserved two poems of the original SAM (§§7, 43) and a fragmentary text of the final poem, *Rédig dam, a Dé, do nim* (§70), thus clearly showing that its exemplar, though already close to *U* in its textual readings, stood closer to *R P* (Recension I) in the *pattern* of its SAM text, a prose text with poems occasionally interspersed. The *C* version is particularly significant for the history of the SAM text tradition, for it shows vividly the process whereby items in the exemplar were selectively deleted, and shows too the tendency of later scribes and copyists to remove the poems from their natural context and collect them together either at the end of the work or in entirely separate collections.

The structural relationship of the *C* text to the other manuscript versions can be found set out schematically in the concordance of manuscripts; for the present purpose it will suffice to discuss the main similarities of the *C* recension and the manuscripts *R P* of Recension I. We saw that the main prose text in *R* is preceded by a prose prologue (§1) and two introductory poems (§§2, 3); the prologue ascribes the whole work to Dublittir ua hUathgaile. This prologue is found, in a slightly debased form, in *C* also, but the two poems are lacking in that manuscript. However, between the prose prologue and the main body of the text there is a gap in *C* of 5–6 lines; this gap can have no other explanation, it seems to me, than that the scribe of *C*, faced with a version of SAM in a recension close to or identical with that of *R*, copied the prologue but decided (for reasons of his own) to omit the two poems. The gap thus left between prologue and prose text suggests that the scribe may have intended to fill the lacuna at a later date, but he never did so. But that the prologue and the two introductory poems were an integral part of the *C* exemplar cannot reasonably be doubted; the fact that *U* and *C* are textually identical proves also that the exemplar of that recension is best represented by the later of the two manuscripts. *Leabhar na hUidhre,* despite its relative antiquity, does not represent an older stage of the text tradition.

(c) *The Book of Lecan and Book of Ballymote recension (Recension III)*

The SAM text in the Book of Lecan *(Lc)* and the Book of Ballymote *(B)* represents a further development in the text tradition. The basic underlying text is that of the manuscripts *U* and *C,* but most of the poetry in the original SAM has been jettisoned, sometimes being replaced by other later compositions like the poem *Sé bliadna caécud imalle,* which occurs in both manuscripts and which was composed, according to its final stanza, in A.D. 1126.[15] Another such poem interpolated into the SAM text is autographed by one Mugrón Tuama dá Gualann,[16] who may or may not have been the compiler of the *Lc B* recension.

The characteristic feature of this third recension, however, is its elaboration of many SAM sections by the inclusion of material from Isidore's *Etymologiae* and other Latin texts. These insertions detract somewhat from the continuity of the original text and comprise little more than elaboration of genealogical details and the like; the Ballymote version also includes an elaborate account of the gates of Babylon, which derives from the *Historia contra paganos* of Orosius. The detailed variations of this third recension from the SAM original will be discussed below in section 3 (c) and they need not detain us here. The general format of this recension follows more the prose-verse pattern of Recension I, but the verbal forms are closer to the texts of Recension II. The *B* text is now acephalous, but we are able to recover the missing sections from the transcript of *B* (SAM) in TCD MS. H. 2. 4 [1295] by Richard Tipper, and its derivative, H. 1. 15 [1289], made by Tadhg Ó Neachtain in the early 18th century. These transcripts show that *B* followed *Lc* in deleting the first four sections of the present edition, though it has retained the metrical list of the names of Adam's sons (§11).

It is possible that this recension took on its present form ca 1126 A.D., if the poem of that date attached to the text in both manuscripts can be assumed to provide a terminal date. But we have no way of knowing when that poem was added and we do not know anything, so far as I am aware, about Mugrón Tuama dá Gualann (Tuam, Co. Galway).[17] If the *B Lc* recension did take on its present shape ca 1126 A.D. we would have to presume an early dissemination of SAM west of the Shannon; the evidence of *Leabhar na hUidhre* would tend to support such a proposition.

For the purposes of the structural analysis of SAM that follows, then, it will be assumed that comments on the second *(U C)* recension automatically apply to the third *(Lc B)* recension as well, the latter being regarded as a later development of Recension II. The comparison in the next section will be between the manuscripts of the first recension *(R P)*, on the one hand, and those of the second *(U C)* on the other.

(d) *Recension I (R P) and Recension II (U C) compared*

It has been argued in the foregoing pages that manuscripts *R* and *P*

[15]Edited by Bartholomew MacCarthy, *The codex Palatino-Vaticanus No. 830*. RIA Todd Lecture Series 3 (Dublin 1895) pp. 259–60.

[16]Hé do-gní in críchud nád gann/ Mugrón Tuama dá Gualann/ indisis cen láthair lac/ senchus d'Ádam is dá mac/; *Lc* fol. 22^{v}a.

[17]He may possibly be the Mugrón, a verse of whose is cited in AFM, s. a. 941.

represent the original first recension of SAM and that the MSS *U* and *C* represent a second, altered version of the text. The discussion in section 3 (a) below will, it is hoped, show that the original text of SAM can be recovered in its entirety from the combined testimony of *R* and *P;* for the present we will concentrate on those textual readings that distinguish the first recension from the second; for that purpose I list here below the readings of *R P* on the left and those of *U C* on the right:

	R P	**U C**
§25.14	Togorma, *filius* Gomér	*filius* Gomér *om.*
§25.16	Mac don Baath Foénius F.	Baath, mac do side F. F. (do sein)
§25.17	F. F., *a quo sunt* Scithi ⁊ Gothi	F. F. athair na Scithecda
§26.12	insi in mara Tirritae frisin n-abbarar Muir Toirrén	frisin . . Toirrén *om.*
§27.4	in nEspáin n-uilidi co huilinn talman	co huilinn talman *om.*
§28.3	Chuss, *a quo sunt* Chussi	uad side Chusi (uadha sein)
§28.4	Mesrom, *a quo* Aegyptus	is uad Egiptus (Egipti)
§28.8	iar ndilgenn ⁊ iar n-inarba na Cannána	íar dílgend na Cannanna ⁊ iarna n-inarba
§28.9	Saba, *a quo* Sabei	is uad Sabei
§28.10	Sabatheni, .i. a senainm sin	.i. a senainm sin *om.*
§28.11	is leis-side cétna-ro-chumtacht in Babilóin	is leiside ro cumtaiged in Babiloin ar thús
§28.13	is la Nebroth cétna-roacht múr Babilóne	*om.*
§29.2	Sessach *hautem* a ainm cáduis	,,
§29.4-5	Doram dano ainm aili do Maig Sennáir	,,
§29.15	nídat cínte ⁊ nídat derba	nitat achinti (⁊ nídat derba *om.*)
§30.8	for agid Tripolim	ar agid
§30.9	Aradius, *a quo Aradii*	A., is uad atat Aradai
§30.11	Samarius, *a quo Samarii*	S., is uad atat Samari (otat)
§31.5	is leis ro-chumtacht Ninue ⁊ Tala ⁊ Resin, *ut supra diximus*	.i. l. ro-cumtaiged Ninues ⁊ Tala ⁊ Resen .i. cathir mór fil eter Ninue ⁊ Thala
§31.8	is leis ro-chumtacht ind rígcathir . . indiu	*om.*
§31.17	Fallec .i. *diuisio*	Falec .i. *diuisio* .i. fodail
§32.2	Ataat .lxiiii [cenéla]	Atat .iiii.xl. cenela (cetri ceneal .xl.)
§32.3	is iat ro-gabsat	is iat gabait
§32.3	⁊ araill mór dind Assia	*om.*

	R P	**U C**
§32.4	óthá sruth nEofrait aniar	othá in sruth aníar
§32.7	Coél na Siria	Coelensiria (Colen-)
§33.5	a ndrommann rempaib	a cúl rempo
§33.6	in ball diaro-thusmit a colla saindílsi	*om.*
§35.4	Arafaxat ccccxxxix	.s. Arfaxat cccxxxix
§38.4	ruc Melcha .uii. maccu	uiii. maccu
§39.2	Dá bliadain cethrachat ar noí cét isin tres aés in domuin	In tres aes in domain ise so lin bliadan fil inti .i. dccccxlu.
§39.3	ó gein Abráim i tír *Caldeorum* co gabáil rígi do Dauíd	co gabáil ríge do Dauíd i tír *Caldeorum* (i t. C. *om*)

The following points emerge clearly from this comparison: (i) the *R P* recension consistently preserves the original Latin wording in many sections, where the *U C* version consistently translates into Irish; (ii) the *R P* recension preserves more of the text than does the *U C* version (a point which is borne out by reference to the Notes and Commentary, pp. 138–80, where the established sources are cited *in extenso*); (iii) The *R P* recension offers a near flawless text, where the *U C* version already shows signs of corruption.

It is clear then that in those sections of the SAM text where Recension I and Recension II exist in parallel, the substance of the text is to all intents and purposes identical. There are no clear linguistic examples from *U C* that would prove a later date of origin for this recension and we must conclude that both recensions are virtually contemporary. It should be emphasised, however, that though the *U C* version could have derived from the text of Recension I, there is no possibility of the *R P* text having evolved from the version now preserved in *U* and *C*. The linguistic forms of Recension III *(Lc B)* suggest that these manuscripts derived their text from a version of SAM similar to Recension II; whether that version showed the format now characteristic of *U*, or whether it followed the pattern of the *R P* and *C* texts will be discussed in the next section, 3 (c).

Before passing on to a discussion of the third recension, however, we may summarise the main findings of our discussion up to now: (i) The best and most complete text of SAM is now preserved in MSS Rawl. B 502 *(R)* and NLI G 131 *(P)*; (ii) A second, less complete recension is found in the MSS *Leabhar na hUidhre (U)* and Rawl. B 486 *(C)*; (iii) The MSS Book of Ballymote *(B)* and Book of Lecan *(Lc)* represent a third recension of SAM, whose textual readings accord more closely with those of Recension II than of Recension I, but whose format follows the prose-verse pattern of the first recension.

A detailed structural analysis of SAM now follows below, and the points made above will be discussed again in greater detail there.

3. THE ARCHETYPE OF SAM AND ITS DERIVATIVE RECENSIONS

(a) *Structure and content of Recension I (R P)*

The basic structure of SAM, as it stands in the MSS *R* and *P*, is a prose text with eight poems interspersed, to which is attached a prose prologue (§1) and two introductory poems (§§2, 3), and a verse epilogue (the poem *Rédig dam, a Dé, do nim,* §70), which provides a summary of most of the preceding text. The prose prologue is a brief summary of the contents of the text and identifies Dublittir ua hUathgaile as its author; the verse epilogue provides a mnemonic epitome of the prose, and is autographed in its final stanza by ua hUathgaile.[18]

The prose text begins with §4a, a Latin passage on the Ages of Man which provides a microcosmic contrast to the larger discussion of the Ages of the World that follows (§4). The next section (§5) recounts the basic themes to be discussed in the subsequent account, which are the respective Ages and their duration, the principal personalities of each Age and the lengths of their lives and reigns, and an account of the dispersal of the races throughout the world and the manner in which they colonised the continents, and how the continents in turn received their names. The account proceeds therefore from the particular to the general, from the Creation and the nature of the primal language to the story of the continents. Within these parameters the author of SAM recounts the history of Adam and Eve and their offspring, and of all the prominent biblical characters thereafter.

The story of the first language is related in §6 and then rendered into verse in the section following (the poem *Gairthigern ainm in bérlai,* §7); these two sections provide a natural pretext for the account of the dispersal of the races and their languages which follows immediately (§§8–16). In this part also of the prose text there occur verse sections alongside the prose: the list of Adam and Eve's sons (§10) is rendered into mnemonic verse in §11; the discussion of Adam and his contemporary, Methuselah (§15), is also rendered subsequently in verse in §16. This is a pattern which we find repeated throughout Recension I, a pattern in which items of the prose text are repeated in verse for mnemonic purposes.

The narrative in §§17–20 relates the story of the transgression by the races of Seth and Cain and the creation of the monsters that resulted therefrom. The story provides the cause for the Deluge and sets the scene for the end of the first Age and the opening of the second, with the account of its principal character, Noah. Within this section is a remarkable exegetical passage in Latin and Irish on the subject of the Ark and its mystical significance as a symbol of the

[18] Dublittir ua hUathgaile's claims to authorship of SAM will be discussed in detail below, in section 4 (a), pp. 41–48.

Church in its unity and universality.[19] After this mystical exposition there occurs a technical passage on the chronology of Noah's voyage in the Ark, in relation to the calculations of the lunar and solar cycles. To close the account of the first Age then there occurs a synchronistic poem *(Mathusálem, Noé cen lén,* §21), relating the relative ages of the four oldest characters in the Old Testament: Adam and Jareth, Methuselah and Noah; the poem is basically a mnemonic rendering of §14, which lists in tabular form the ages of the chief leaders of the first Age.

Thus far then we have seen a prose-verse pattern of text in which the details of the prose narrative are occasionally repeated in verse, doubtless with a view to their easy memorisation.

The narrative in §§22–25 relates the story of Noah and his three sons, Sem, Japheth, and Ham, and the details of their respective offspring. This section opens with God's covenant with Noah, signified by the image of the rainbow; the doctrine of the seventy-two languages follows, based on the number of peoples descended from Noah's three sons. In this passage (§24) the questions posed earlier in §§6–8 concerning the origins of the languages are now taken up, and the fact that the number of races far exceeds the number of the languages is explained as being due to there being many races in Africa with the same language (§24.10–15). How the divergence came about is then the subject of §§25–31, wherein are described the offspring of Japheth, Ham, and Sem in turn; the closing passage in §31 states that it was in the time of Heber (a great-grandson of Sem) that the languages were dispersed (§31.17).

Within this section of the narrative also is answered the question posed in §5 concerning the Age in which the continents were divided, for it was in this second Age that it came about. But in order not to interrupt the flow of the narrative the account of how the continents received their names is held over until a more suitable opportunity is offered by §69, when the account of the dispersal of the Apostles and Disciples throughout the world provides a suitable pretext for telling how these various parts of the world got their names. The present section concentrates on the detailed discussion of Noah's descendants and the precise geographical disposition of their various settlements.

As with the origins of the continents, so too the foundation of Babylon is mentioned incidentally in this section, and its construction by Nimrod and subsequent reconstruction by Ninus are both related in passing. The detailed description of Babylon is postponed till the narrative about the Jewish captivity there (§§53–62) provides a more appropriate setting for it; in the present section only passing reference

[19]Compare the mystical interpretation of the *Beati* [Ps. 118] in §§60–62, where too the basis of the discussion is a dual Latin-Irish text.

is made to its mystical significance, a subject which is taken up again and elaborated in §§59–62. The basic purpose of the mention of Nimrod in §29 is to show that some traced the origins of the Assyrian peoples back to him; in this case also we see the emphasis on continuity and homogeneity in the SAM narrative.

The next section, on the origins of the various monstrous creatures in the world, has caused some commentators unnecessary difficulty.[20] It was already related in §17, in the period of the first Age, how the transgression by the families of Seth and Cain of God's express command not to intermarry brought about the divine retribution of the Deluge and its consequent destruction of all but the family of Noah. It followed, then, that the monstrous creatures brought about by the initial transgression were drowned in the Deluge along with the rest of humanity. Faced therefore with the attested existence of the monstrous creatures after the Flood, as related, for instance, in the account of them in Isidore's *Etymologiae,* the author of SAM (or perhaps a predecessor) naturally concluded that the post-diluvian cursing of Ham, after his mocking of Noah, was the origin of those monsters that still existed in the world. Hence it is in this second Age, in the time of Noah, that the detailed story of the monsters is given.[21] The fact that Dublittir ua hUathgaile, in his verse epitome *Rédig dam, a Dé, do nim* (§70), follows this scheme bears out the contention that the poem was intended simply as a mnemonic version of the preceding SAM text.

With §35, which lists the chief figures of the second Age, and the lengths of their lives, we begin the account of Abraham and his family. This section opens with the statement that Abraham, Nachor, and Aaron were the three sons of Thara. Aaron had two daughters, sisters of Lot, who in turn married Abraham and Nachor. Aaron then died in Ur of the Chaldees, the first biblical figure to die before his father.

The next two sections in *R* and *P* relate the story of Lot's incest with his two daughters, the first section (§36) relating the details in prose and that following providing a verse rendering of those details. These two sections follow the pattern of previous items in the SAM text by narrating the story in the favoured Irish *tres linguae sacrae* manner.[22] In this case, however, the poem *Ingena Loith, légtar lib* (§37) is not just a verse paraphrase of the preceding prose, but includes

[20] See Charles Donahue 'Grendel and the *Clanna Cain*' *Jnl of Celtic Studies* 1 (1950–1) pp. 167–75, and James Carney, *Studies in Irish literature and history* (Dublin 1955[1]/1979[2]) pp. 103–10.

[21] The linguistic arguments advanced by Donahue, p. 172, in alleged support for his theory of an earlier and later version of this episode in SAM, hardly merit mention.

[22] Cf. §19, on the mystical significance of the Ark, and §61, on the mystical interpretation of the *Beati;* see the notes and commentary also, where literature on the subject is cited.

details which are wanting in the prose; these two sections will interest us again in the discussion of Recension II below, section 3 (b).

The account of the second Age then closes with §38, which relates how Abraham and Nachor both married, and who their offspring were. As with the narrative of events in the first Age then, we find in the account of the second Age the same pattern of prose-verse composition that we can say is a distinctive feature of this first recension of SAM; we will find this pattern repeated in what follows.

The third Age comprises §§39–49 of the text and spans the period from the birth of Abraham to the death of Hisposeth, grandson of Saul. This is much the longest section in SAM and is devoted chiefly to listing the names of the main leaders in this period and the names of their offspring; to this is added much incidental topographical information, a feature characteristic of this recension. The material in §§40–45 gives the names of the leaders of the Twelve Tribes of Israel and related peoples and §43 is a poem on the twelve sons of Jacob attributed to one Oéngus mac Suibni; this is no more than a versification of the details in the preceding section but it will occupy our attention again in the discussion of Recension II below in section 3 (b).

The remainder of the narrative in this Age is occupied with the listing of elders and judges of the tribes of Israel and their ages or reigns, all in tabular form. The Age closes with the accession of David to the kingship of the Two Tribes and of Hisposeth to the kingship of the Twelve Tribes; the final items – an account of the murder of Hisposeth, and an exegetical interpretation of Joseph's name – are added in *R* at the top of a page (43^r) and referred to their proper places in the body of the text by a reference mark (the items occur in *P* also, incorporated into the SAM text).

The fourth Age occupies §§50–55 of the text and opens with an account of David's reign in the kingship of Israel. There then follow synchronistic details about the beginnings of the Macedonian empire and the first Olympic games, and the siege of Troy (§50). The next section tells the story of the foundation of Rome and the epic of Romulus and Remus, which is followed in turn by an elaborate table of the kings of Israel in this Age and the lengths of their respective reigns. Following this is the account (§53) of the destruction of Jerusalem and the carrying away of the Jewish people into the Babylonian captivity.

Within this whole section there falls naturally the account in §54 of the three youths, Sedrac, Misac, and Abdenago, who were cast into the furnace by Nabuchodonosor, and the story of Daniel in the lions' den. But the section that follows, maintaining as it does that Sedechias, last king of Israel, was not in fact led into the captivity in Babylon but was left behind in Reblatha, strikes a curious note, for no such inference can be drawn from any of the biblical sources for this period in Jewish history. That the author of the first recension himself felt this section to be somewhat anomalous is suggested by his description of it as a digression *(etaraisnéis,* §55.15).

After this there follows (§§56–58) a very detailed account of the destruction of Babylon with the subsequent release of the Jewish people and their return to Jerusalem. The narrative here takes up the thread of §29, where Babylon was first mentioned, and fills out the story with detailed genealogies of the chief characters in the period, Balthazar, Cyrus, and Ninus son of Bel, together with an elaborate description (§57) of the city of Babylon itself. Following then on the account of Cyrus's capture of the city is a poem in twenty-two stanzas *(Babilóin ro-clos hi céin,* §58) summarising all the foregoing details.[23] Here, then, as before, the prose-verse pattern of the narrative is maintained.

The remaining sections of this account of the fifth Age are devoted to the deaths of the four chief Prophets of the Exilic period, Isaiah, Jeremiah, Ezekiel, and Daniel, and a poem in six stanzas *(Secht coícait huide co mbríg,* §61) with prose introduction (§60) and prose epilogue (§63) on the mystical interpretation of the *Beati* and of the journey from Babylon to Jerusalem.

The whole narrative of the fifth Age then progresses naturally from the account of Babylon and its grandeur to the closing days of the Jewish captivity and the mystical significance of that and of the Jewish return from captivity to the new Jerusalem. The destruction of Babylon and the return of the Jews to their homeland thus serve as a fitting prelude to the sixth Age, the Age of salvation.

The account of the sixth Age (§§63–68), for which there is reckoned to be no set number of years, is much briefer than that which preceded it. The natural focus of attention is on the Advent and on the events of Christ's life. The manuscripts of the first recension are distinguished by the fact of their containing an elaborate list of the Apostles and Disciples, and a brief summary (in Latin) of the persecutions that they suffered. The inspiration of the Apostles and Disciples then with the gift of tongues leads up to the account of their dispersal throughout the world in order to preach the Gospel. It is at this point that the cue given in §5 (where it was asked how the continents had got their names) is taken up and answered.

As an epilogue to the whole SAM text there follows the poem *Rédig dam, a Dé, do nim,* by Dublittir ua hUathgaile (§70), which summarises in verse much of what has preceded in the body of the SAM text.[24]

[23]MacCarthy, op. cit., pp. 310–17, has edited a synchronistic poem dealing with related material, from the Book of Ballymote.

[24]The precise parallels between prose and verse are noted in the commentary to §70.

We see, therefore, that the SAM text in Recension I is an elaborate work, balanced and measured in the sequence of its sections. The narrative progresses logically and smoothly from the Creation to the Advent, with items of particular importance being repeated occasionally in verse to emphasise their memorable qualities. There is a sustained contrast of the general and the specific, the universal and the individual, harking back to the opening passages of the prose text, where the Ages of man and the world's Ages were set down in contrast with one another. The whole has an ordered simplicity about it which belies its structural sophistication.

(b) *Structure and content of Recension II (U C)*

It has been argued in the foregoing section that the text of SAM in the MSS *R* and *P* presents a homogeneous and logical progression of theme and treatment, a balanced structure wherein prose and poetry are smoothly interwoven. The question then arises: was this the original structure of SAM? The question has been answered by Hans Oskamp thus: 'When we turn to the earliest copy of the tract that has survived, the fragment preserved in LU, it becomes clear even from the one leaf we have before us, that, as in so many cases, two distinct text traditions are in existence, which differ from each other because one of them has incorporated poetry and prose fragments related to the subject of SAM.'[25]

It is obvious, though the point bears repeating, that the original text of SAM (as established by source-analysis) was a Latin one, comprising various excerpts from the Vulgate, Jerome's commentary on Genesis, and other Latin texts. The compiler of this Latin version may or may not have been the same man who drew up the first Irish version of SAM, though we have no means of proving this conclusively either way.[26] Inasmuch as this Irish version of SAM came into existence as a close translation of a Latin prose text, it is literally true that it probably did not at first contain verses as well; but this is no ground for disputing that the Irish SAM *as originally conceived* was intended to be a prose-verse work of the kind represented by the present edition. Such a mode of composition we know to have been integral to the Irish literary tradition, as *Lebor Gabála* and the Dindsenchus amply testify. Moreover, the picture presented by the extant manuscript evidence (including, we may say, that of *Leabhar na hUidhre)* reinforces such a theory.

Oskamp's reasons for believing that the text of SAM preserved in

[25]'On the author of *Sex Aetates Mundi*', p. 128.

[26]It may be surmised that the text of Isidore's *Etymologiae* that provided the material for §4a of the edition, and which is written in *R* on the upper margin of fol. 41^r, was the same text as that used by the original compiler of the Irish SAM.

U best represents the archetype of the work are mainly codicological. He recalls at the outset[27] that in his account of the history of *Leabhar na hUidhre*[28] he had been driven to conclude that 'apart from the leaves lost in LU after the medieval signatures were written down, a lost leaf *zero* must be assumed, because the four leaves after the present first leaf of the manuscript were not enough to hold the missing parts of both SAM and *Lebor Bretnach*.' In his subsequent paper on the author of SAM, however, Oskamp revised this earlier conclusion on the basis that '*A*'s copy [of SAM in *U*] did not contain the poems which are interspersed in the Rawlinson version.'

This much we may accept as valid surmise, on the basis of the evidence from *U* alone. The *U* version of SAM may or may not have contained some or all of the poems now preserved in the manuscripts of Recension I; we have, however, no way of knowing for certain. But the assumption on Oskamp's part that these poems did not occur in *U* is then made the basis for the theory that the poems were *a later addition* by the scribe of *R*, and that *U* in consequence best represents the archetypal text of SAM; the wider variety of manuscript evidence available to us, however, makes it clear that such is not the case.

We saw above, in section 2 (b), that Rawlinson B 486 *(C)* is a representative of the second *(U C)* recension of SAM. A glance at the concordance of manuscripts shows that it contains substantially the same text as *R P*, the manuscripts of Recension I; but *C* also illustrates the tendency which finds proportionately greater expression in the work of later copyists, a habit of drastically pruning the SAM text by omitting certain prose and verse sections and by removing other sections from their context.

The *C* text begins, like *R* (significantly enough), with the prose prologue (§1) – though the details of the prologue have been garbled and the crucial words ascribing the whole work to Dublittir ua hUathgaile are altered, It would be as well at this point to cite this *C* version of the prologue as illustration of the way in which the later copyists alter the readings of their exemplars:

> INcipit Panecte. Tunnscnaid na sencaide n-eolach for Penacte tre Gaeilg andso sis .i. do ardgabhalaibh in domain ⁊ do craebhaibh cobneasa claende Nae ⁊ in uile cenealaib in domhain, do nuimir bliadan na n-aes, de randaibh clande Nae fo in domhan uili arceana.

There follows a gap of five-six lines after this in *C* between the prologue and what follows, doubtless because the exemplar from which the scribe was working contained at this point the two introductory poems *Cétna-amser bethad bind* (§2) and *Cétaimmser in bethad bind* (§3).

[27]Art. cit., p. 129.
[28]Cited in note 12 above.

The scribe of *C* may even have intended writing an abbreviated version of the poems, but he seems to have thought better of it and he left the lacuna unfilled; what follows of SAM then begins with §4, *SEX SUNT AETATES MUNDI* (sic), etc. The subsequent folios contain a large part of SAM as it occurs in *R P* (Recension I); it has omitted such passages as the alternative account of Sedechias's captivity (§55), doubtless because the author (like the scribe of *R*) thought the passage something of a digression *(etaraisnéis)*. Also omitted were the section on Methuselah (§15) and its verse summary (§16), presumably because the *C* scribe thought this merely a rehash of the preceding section. He did preserve intact, however, the poem *Gairthigern ainm in bérlai* (§7) at a place in the text exactly corresponding to that which it holds in *R P*.

Omitted also were the mystical interpretation of the Ark (§19) and the apocryphal story of Lot and his two daughters (§§35–37); but though *U* at this point substitutes for §§35–37 a single stanza (§35a) on Aran son of Thara, this stanza too is wanting in *C*. I believe the compiler of Recension II omitted the sections concerning Lot's daughters deliberately, out of prudishness; he also omitted the explicit lines in §33 which described Noah's nakedness, doubtless for the same reason. The confused genealogy in §35a (the verse on Aran) suggests that it was an ad hoc composition simply inserted to fill the gap left by the elimination of §§35–37; its omission from *C* would suggest also that it was added first in *U* and not in the archetype of Recension II.

The other omissions in *C* may be set down to the fact that most of the material jettisoned was written in the exemplar in elaborate columnar tables, and such sections as the list of Disciples (§66) did not lend themselves to easy transcription in his large, awkward hand. The general tendency seems to have been to eliminate all duplicating or overlapping material, and to abbreviate some other sections. Most important though, for the purpose of establishing the text tradition of SAM, is that §43, the poem *Dá mac deëc Iacóib,* has been removed entirely from its context by the scribe of *C* and annexed to the end of the work, where it follows immediately on the section concerning the naming of the continents. The *C* version of SAM is also the oldest manuscript that contains the various glosses on the main prose text gathered as a separate item at the end of the work. We may surmise that others of the poems in his exemplar were excised by him from their places in the prose text, either with a view to collecting them together (as he did with the glosses) or of adding them elsewhere in his manuscript.

If we recall then that *C* and *U* are textually identical, but that *C* in its *structure* is essentially the same as the *R P* version of SAM, then we are driven to conclude that *U C* represent a second, altered recension of SAM and, furthermore, that *C* better represents the archetype of that second recension than does *U*. This second recension in turn provided the basic text for Recension III *(Lc B)*, as we shall see below in section 3 (c).

In fact, it may be stated as axiomatic that the scribes of all the manuscripts that postdate *R* felt themselves at liberty to alter the structure and format of their exemplars as they saw fit. For it is a demonstrable fact that almost all of the sections which occur in Recension I but which are wanting in the SAM texts of later manuscripts can be found at some point in those later codices – either as items incorporated into later works, or as isolated *disjecta membra*. Thus, when Oskamp writes that 'one of the reasons for maintaining that the incorporated poems are later additions is that they occur only in *R*,'[29] we may say that not only is this not so (witness the *C* text), but it distorts the evidence of the manuscripts themselves.

Let us take the example of the two introductory poems in SAM, *Cétna-amser bethad bind* (§2) and *Cétaimmser in bethad bind* (§3): Oskamp states that 'it is obvious that at least the preceding poems did not occur in LU. That they did not belong to the archetype is indicated by the fact that they do not occur in Lc.' Now it has already been shown that the best representative of the second *(U C)* recension *(C)* contains §1 of SAM, the prose prologue. It has been suggested also that the gap in the manuscript between the prologue and the subsequent prose text (§4) clearly implies that *C*'s exemplar also contained the two introductory poems (§§2, 3); that they may have been extrapolated from the exemplar and kept aside for inclusion at some later stage (or in some other text) is suggested also by the evidence of other manuscripts as well. Bearing in mind the rather poor quality of *C*'s copy, it is not impossible that he omitted the poems out of sheer inertia.

It is literally true that, as Oskamp stated, the *Lc* SAM does not now contain the two introductory poems, but on fol. 267^{v}a 25 ff. of that manuscript there occurs a short passage, following on the poem *Athair cháich, coimsid nime,* which is a miscellany of jumbled notes concerning the first Age of the world, the Deluge, the ages of Adam, Seth, and Enos, and other related material. Fol. 267^{v}b 2 ff. reads as follows:

> O Adam co dilind in chetais, ise seo am in lin bliadan fil innti cheadus .i. se bliadna caecad ar se chedaib ar mile, amail asbert in file:
>
> Cétaimser in bethad bind
> ota Adam co dilind,
> se bliadna caecad, rad ngle,
> ar se chetaib ar mile.

[29]'On the author of *Sex Aetates Mundi*', p. 129.

The stanza quoted is the first one in §3 of SAM, and we may assume that the scribe(s) of *Lc* had available a text of SAM which contained verse and that those verses included at least one of the two introductory poems which Oskamp claimed were not in the archetype. How much of that verse stood in the exemplar of the *Lc* SAM we cannot say for certain, but the above cited instance is not the only one in which verse that properly belongs to a text of SAM occurs sporadically also in another context.

The text of §7, the poem *Gairthigern ainm in bérlai,* actually occurs twice in *Lc,* once in the SAM text itself and again in *Auraicept na nÉces.*[30] In this case §7 stands as comfortably in the Auraicept as it does in SAM, but the same cannot be said of some of the other items that occur scattered throughout the various codices. The question naturally arises then 'whether the Rawlinson version is just a compilation of a couple of poems and some prose fragments, more or less related to one another'.[31] Oskamp states his case bluntly: 'It will be clear,' he says, 'that the incorporated poems deal with a small part only of the subject matter of SAM: they may, therefore, be poetical reactions to the preceding prose. *It is much more likely,* on the other hand, *that they were already in existence when the scribe of R or his forerunner added them to the original. This,* as we shall see, *is supported by the fact that many of the intercalated poems are found on their own elsewhere*' [italics mine].

The notes and commentary appended to the present edition of SAM show clearly that the poems incorporated in the text form an integral part of the whole work and find their most natural setting within that context. *Pace* Oskamp, the poems definitely are 'reactions' to the prose and can be shown to derive from the same material as was used in the compilation of the prose text, in some cases even adding a significant detail, which shows that the author of the poems and the writer of the prose text were one and the same person.[32]

A case in point is the material in SAM on the mystical significance of Babylon and Jerusalem (§§60–62): the context in which these sections stand is provided in Recension I by the passage that opens the fifth Age (§56) and which recounts the most famous happenings of that Age – the destruction of Babylon and the return of the Jews from captivity to the new Jerusalem, mystically interpreted as the journey of the souls from hell back to heaven. The first two sections (§§56, 57) set the historical context and describe the physical dimensions of the city of Babylon; this material is then rendered into verse in §58. Then §59 relates the passions of the four chief Exilic prophets, as a

[30]See George Calder (ed) *Auraicept na n-Éces, the scholars' primer* (Edinburgh 1917), p. 178; my friend Dr. Anders Ahlqvist tells me that the poem probably occurs in most MSS of the Auraicept C recension. The poem also occurs twice in *B*, once in the text proper and again in §70.

[31]The words are Oskamp's, art. cit., p. 129.

[32]See the notes to §§36, 37, and 70 below.

prelude to the mystical account of the return from the captivity; the last of these prophets is Daniel, whose significance in relation to the theme of Babylon as a symbol of hell needs no elaboration. It is in this context then that the poem *Secht coícait huide co mbríg* (§61) occurs, with its prose introduction (§60) and epilogue (§62).

The recensions of these texts that occur in other manuscripts besides *R* and *P* are utterly devoid of such a contextual setting as we have seen them to have in Recension I of SAM. To be sure, texts of the poem are to be found in *Lc* and *LB* (Leabhar Breac), but *Lc* has jettisoned the prose introduction and epilogue, and *LB* has dropped the introduction. The RIA MS 23 O 48 *(Liber flavus Fergusiorum)*, fol. 34 [45]^{r}b 4–7, has preserved the epilogue alone, though the scribe seems not to have noticed the incongruity of its first few words when parted from the preceding poem.

All these texts, however, are basically identical with that of Recension I: the poem itself, with elaborate interlineal glossing, occurs along with the account of the prophets, though not immediately following on one another as in *R P*. The significant difference is that in *LB* these items are separated from the preceding text by a blank half-column, and are followed immediately by *Páis Longinus,* with which they have no connection. In *Lc,* on the other hand, the same material occurs incorporated into a miscellany of texts, secular and religious (and the Book of Rights), which again has no textual relation to it. The practice of extrapolating items and attaching them to other, formally unrelated, texts is clearly exemplified by the *Liber flavus,* where §62 (the prose epilogue to the poem *Secht coícait huide co mbríg)* is found in a miscellany of items on the subject of the merits of the *Beati* (Ps. 118). In *LB* the material preceding the texts here under discussion has the heading *Do bungenelaig na nApsdal,* and concerns the origins and missionary activities of the Apostles and the places of their deaths;[33] the same text occurs in *Lc,* fols. 166^{v}d 10–167^{r}a 28[34] and it seems clear that later scribes had in mind to collect all available material concerning the prophets and the Apostles and to bring them together in one place.

We must ask ourselves then, whether this material is integral to SAM and derived by later copyists from that text, or whether (as Oskamp thinks) these poems had an independent existence outside of SAM. Oskamp's case is clear: 'The two poems that occur separately, *Gairthigern ainm in bérla* [§7] in *Lc,* and *Dá mac deëc Iacóib* [§43] in Laud 610, are (at least for our purpose) less interesting. They confirm by their separate occurrence that the poems incorporated in SAM in the Rawlinson manuscript are later additions'.[35]

[33]See Martin McNamara, *The apocrypha in the Irish Church* (Dublin 1975) p. 85 No. 74 B.

[34]Not noted by McNamara.

[35]Art., cit., p. 130.

But the poem *Dá mac deëc Iacóib* (§43) does *not* occur in Laud 610; in stating that it could be found there on fol. 42b Oskamp was simply following Meyer, who made the statement in his introduction to the facsimile edition of Rawlinson B 502.[36] Meyer also stated in his introduction that the poem *Gairthigern ainm in bérlai* (§7) occurs also in Laud 615, fol. 116 (foot of page). Collation has established clearly that the foliation cited by Meyer has reference (in the case of §43) to *R* and not to Laud 610, for the poem *Dá mac deëc Iacóib* is found in *R* on fol. 42vb 39–50. Moreover, Meyer made an identical slip in regard to Airbertach mac Cosse's metrical version of the Old Irish treatise on the Psalms, the first three stanzas of which were said by him to be in Laud 610;[37] Meyer subsequently gave the correct manuscript reference in *ZCP* 1 (1897) p. 497, but it seems abundantly clear that at some stage in his work he confused his notes on the Rawlinson and Laud manuscripts. Oskamp, however, seems not to have examined Laud 610 and was not aware of the existence in Rawlinson B 486 *(C)* of another text of the poem *Dá mac deëc Iacóib* (§43), which in that codex has been removed entirely from its SAM context and appended to the end of the text.

There is clearly little support then for Oskamp's categorical statement[38] that 'the fact that these poems do not occur in the other surviving versions of SAM makes it obvious that they are later interpolations. They existed independently of the text as the manuscripts testify, and they were added to it by the scribe of *R* or his forerunner'. For we have seen that the independent occurrence of certain sections of SAM argues nothing for their independent *origin;* and the fact that they do not occur in *Lc* says nothing about the archetype of SAM, for it will be shown below that *Lc* and *B* (Recension III) derive from a text of the second *(U C)* recension, not from the original archetype.

Thus far then we have been concerned to show that the separate occurence in later manuscripts of certain fragments of the SAM text outside that context is in itself no proof of a separate origin for these fragments.[39] We have seen that the opposite is in fact implied by the combined evidence of the various manuscripts. In no case can it be demonstrably proved that a poem in SAM had a previous existence outside the context of that work; on the contrary, the evidence of the *C* text (i.e. the more complete text of Recension II) shows that already

[36]Kuno Meyer, *Rawlinson B 502. A collection of pieces in prose and verse in the Irish language compiled during the eleventh and twelfth centuries* (Oxford 1909) p. v; the error was passed on by Oskamp to McNamara, *Apocrypha*, p. 34 No. 24.

[37]*Irisleabhar na Gaedhilge* 7 iii (1896) p. 130; cf. Pádraig Ó Néill's article (cited above in note 6), p. 40.

[38]Art. cit., p. 132.

[39]The question of the poem *Dá mac deëc Iacóib* (§43), which is ascribed in *RP* to one Oéngus mac Suibni, will be taken up in section 4 below.

at a very early stage in the text tradition fragments of SAM were being either eliminated altogether or else incorporated into other compositions, sometimes even excerpted with a view to being added to a separate collection of more or less related material.

A striking example of how the archetypal SAM text was subsequently altered and excerpted is afforded by the manuscript history of what, in Recension I, are marginal and supralineal glosses on the main text. These notes and additions, culled mainly from the Chronicle of Eusebius-Jerome or from the *Etymologiae,* record such things as the first person to do certain things: build an altar, marry two wives, etc., as well as providing alternative forms and derivations for many of the names of peoples and places mentioned in SAM. These notes find their obvious and natural setting in the SAM text as represented by *R* and *P;* the versions in *U* and *P* show some of these glosses being incorporated into the body of the prose, but in all subsequent recensions they appear collected together to form a single prose text.

In *Lc* and *C* this new creation follows immediately on a very truncated version of the sixth Age in SAM, but it precedes the poem *Rédig dam, a Dé, do nim* (§70).[40] In the Book of Ballymote *(B),* on the other hand, the new text is separated entirely from the body of the SAM text by some two column lengths. This trend reaches its apogée in *Ld,* where the glosses are found (fol. 24^{v}b) separated even from those three paragraphs on the naming of the continents (§69) which accompany them in all the other manuscripts; the tract on the naming of the continents does actually occur in *Ld,* but on fol. 14^{v}b 14–18 of that codex.[41]

These texts then, while they sometimes occur in the manuscripts 'independent of SAM', are no evidence for the independent composition of the poems in the work. They are clearly abstracted from a text of SAM and we are able to monitor (more or less precisely) the changes which they undergo at the hands of later copyists. We may now call on one final witness to show that MSS *R* and *P* reproduce the original first recension of SAM and that the texts of the second *(U C)* recension and subsequent texts all represent later developments of that first recension. Our final witness is the NLI MS. G 2–3 *(G),* the 'Ó Cianáin miscellany'.[42] The Ó Cianáin miscellany is another of those manuscripts which contain a seemingly random selection of

[40]In fact, *C* has now only a few fragmentary lines of the poem.

[41]The occurrence in *Ld* of the poem *Gairthigern ainm in bérlai* (§7), the tract on the naming of the continents (§69), and the combined glosses, suggests that it may once have contained a substantial copy of SAM; the fact too that the glosses in *Ld* are followed by a tract on the origins of the various alphabets, which occurs also in *C* in the same relative position, further suggests that the *Ld* text of SAM (if there was one) may have been of the second *(U C)* recension. I believe that *Ld* may also once have contained a copy of the *Lebor Bretnach;* see above, p. 11.

[42]See note 10 above, and the description of the MS., p. 53.

excerpts from SAM (it contains §§3, 9, 10, 11, 69, and the glosses all gathered together), and its compilatory characteristics follow the pattern of the other manuscripts we have just been discussing.

Speaking of the poem *Ádam ocus Eua án* (§11), which is found in G 3, Carney suggested that the text of *R* (fol. 41^{r}b 1–10) was 'possibly the immediate exemplar';[43] we might expand that remark to cover the other SAM items in G 3 as well. Ó Cianáin elsewhere in the manuscript says that he has copied from the Book of Glendalough,[44] but the sequence of texts in *G* seems to me to indicate that *R* was his immediate exemplar. There is no doubt that the scribe of *G,* in those pages where he copies the SAM items, was trying to imitate the script and decoration of an eleventh- or twelfth-century codex; we can deduce from this that *R* is, in fact, the Book of Glendalough. It may be said for the present that the evidence in favour of such a deduction, though incidental and only cumulative, is strong.

The *G* text opens with an abbreviated version of §9, on the children of Adam, and follows immediately with the poem *Ádam ocus Eua án* (§11), omitting the list in §10 (doubtless because the scribe thought it superfluous to the list in the poem). More interesting though is the fact that *G* also contains the poem *Cétna-amser bethad bind* (§2) – but in fact all but this first line of the poem is taken, not from §2 but from §3, the poem *Cétaimmser in bethad bind*! We may therefore assume that the scribe gratuitously omitted the body of the first introductory poem (§2) and felt it sufficient to copy only the second; but the fact of his preserving the line *Cétna-amser bethad bind* proves that, in fact, his exemplar contained both poems. Thus the argument for that exemplar having been *R* is reinforced, and since *G* is the oldest text of SAM after *R* and *U* (though *C* may, in fact, be coeval) it gives us an important insight on the text tradition of SAM in the uncertain period between the twelfth and the fifteenth century. It is doubly significant that the version of §3 in BL MS. Egerton 1782 has made exactly the same change – it opens in fact with the first line of §2; but the implication of this parallelism between the texts of *G* and *E* is extremely difficult to work out.

(c) *Structure and content of Recension III (Lc B)*

The SAM texts in *Lc* and *B* are essentially the same, though minor variations between them are sufficient to indicate that they are not identical, nor one copied from the other. For example, *B* seems to follow the version in *U C* more closely than does *Lc,* inasmuch as it contains the stanza on the death of Aran (§35a) which *Lc* does not have; *B* likewise in §39.2 follows the correct reading of *R P* : *.i. ó gein Abráim*

[43]'The Ó Cianáin miscellany', p. 127.

[44]See Carney, art. cit., pp. 125–7; Nessa Ní Shéaghdha, *Catalogue of Irish MSS in the NLI* 1 (1967) pp. 12–18.

i tír Caldeorum, where *Lc* (following *U)* has: *ó gen Abráim co gobáil rígi do Dauíd i tír Chailldeorum. B* furthermore makes some additions to the SAM text that do not occur in *Lc;* for instance, in §49 additional details about Saul and Hisposeth have been culled from the account in Kings. But on the whole the two versions in these manuscripts may be said to comprise a distinctive third recension whose basic text follows that of Recension II *(U C),* with the addition of extraneous material from Isidore's *Etymologiae* and (perhaps) a version of the *Lebor Bretnach.*

Now we noted above in section 3 (b) that the poem *Gairthigern ainm in bérlai* (§7) actually occurs twice in *Lc,* once in the SAM text proper, and once in *Auraicept na nÉces.* The poem occurs also in the body of the text in *B* (as attested by the TCD transcripts) but it is incorporated as well into the text of the poem *Rédig dam, a Dé, do nim* (§70) in that manuscript. More significantly, however, *B* preserved the poem *Ádam ocus Eua án* (§11) which is not now in *Lc.* In other words, the archetype of Recension III must have had the poem also, a further indication that the original SAM text is best represented by the MSS of Recension I. The *Lc* version has incorporated after §5 a poem in seven stanzas beginning: *Sé bliadna caécud imalle,* which gives the *anno mundi* reckoning according to the Vulgate (A.M. 3952);[45] the same poem occurs also in *B* (fol. 10^{v}), but separate from the SAM text proper. The last stanza of the poem dates it to A.D. 1126, which may be the time at which it was added to Recension III (though this can be nothing more than surmise). The *Lc* version shows some similarity with texts of Recension I inasmuch as it follows §10 (the list of Adam's sons) with a poem *Dá mac ar chaécait co mbroit,* which differs from §11 of the edition only slightly; it is ascribed in its final stanza to one Mugrón Tuama dá Gualann, a poet otherwise unknown. We have seen already that *B* preserves §11 as in Recension I.

The concordance of manuscripts shows how Recension III differs from the other two recensions; it will suffice here to remark on some of the details. In §14 (a list of leaders of the first Age and the lengths of their lives) *Lc* gives the number *iar Septín chéadus,* but the figures are actually those of the Vulgate (with only minor errors of transcription). The two sections following (§§15, 16) have been omitted from *Lc* and *B,* perhaps because they had already been eliminated from the exemplar of the second recension, from which *Lc* and *B* seem to have derived their texts at one or more removes.

The mystical interpretation of the Ark clearly proved too much for the compiler of Recension III, as it had done also for the compiler of Recension II; but §20 (on the dates of Noah's entry into and embarkation from the Ark) has been preserved, albeit in a garbled

[45]Edited by MacCarthy, op. cit., pp. 259–60.

form. The *Lc* and *B* versions, however, have jettisoned the poem *Mathusálem, Noé cen lén* (§21), as the compiler of Recension II had done before them. The texts in *B* and *Lc* run more or less in parallel. Both texts add a section beginning *Cid 'ma n-apar Gallogréci re síl Gomér,* taken from Isidore *(Esuidir suí)*; *B* has a longer version of the text and seems to have longer extracts generally from the *Etymologiae* than does *Lc.* The *Lc* version adds a short note after §25.23 *(Albanus)* which seems to derive from a text of the *Lebor Bretnach;* this is wanting in *B*. The *Lc* version also incorporates §69 (the naming of the continents) after §26.2, and this too is wanting in *B*.

After §28.4, however, *B* reads: *Mesram immorro ciniuda imda leis,* and proceeds then with a long addition on the Greek races and kingdoms, *amail ad-bert Essuidir ⁊ Cuilmen* (i.e. Isidore's *Etymologiae)*; the same material is found in *Lc,* but after §29.17, where it more comfortably belongs. Here too there is added genealogical material related to the *Lebor Bretnach.*[46] The *Lc* version of SAM follows this long digression by an account of Sem's offspring (§31), which the *B* version seems unaccountably to have dropped. It is clear from the wording in *Lc*: *Luidi mac Sém, is uada atáit Luidi,* etc. (=§31.11) that the exemplar contained the passage which in *R* occurs as a gloss *(.i. na Lidetai, etc.)*; this tends to reinforce the general impression that *Lc* (more than *B)* seems to be following an exemplar similar in many ways to Recension I.

The *B* text, for its part, also dropped the account of Iachtan's offspring (§32), again without any obvious reason; but both manuscripts take up again in tandem with the account of the leaders of the second Age (§35). Here, however, the *B* version follows with the stanza on the death of Aran (§35a), but *Lc* does not have this, showing again that it follows more the pattern of Recension I than of II. Both manuscripts, of course, lack the account of Lot and his daughters that follows at this point in Recension I.[47]

Both manuscripts of Recension III have omitted §43, the poem *Dá mac deëc Iacóib* ascribed to Óengus mac Suibni. We saw already in section 3 (b) how the poem had been dislocated in MS. *C* of the second recension, and we must presume that it was finally dropped altogether (intentionally or otherwise) by the copyists of Recension III, presumably because its details were already embodied in the preceding section of the SAM text. Both versions are identical then up to the end of the fourth Age (§54); omitted from both manuscripts, however, is the passage on Sedechias's captivity (§55), which we saw was also dropped from Recension II.

[46]See NLI MS. G 2, fol. 3a (an intercalated leaf), which has similar details. *B* also inserts a single stanza on the Assyrian king Assur, which is not in *Lc.*

[47]*B* adds a stanza after §38.6 *(Huss mac Nachoir)* beginning: *Nachor, Nachor mar,* which is wanting in *Lc.*

In the narrative of the fifth Age all but §57 of the first recension has been omitted in *Lc* and *B*, but *B* adds one stanza about Daniel's prophecy of the downfall of Babylon, and follows that with an elaborate description of the gateway to the city that is not found in *Lc*.[48] What follows then in *B* is a prose account of Cyrus's capture of Babylon, taken from Orosius's *Historia contra paganos* II 6 (not in *Lc)* and this in turn is followed by a synchronistic passage relating the period of the Fir Bolg in Ireland and the events of the Jewish exile.

The sixth Age then follows in highly abbreviated form, omitting §§64–68 of the present edition, and the text closes with the story of the naming of the continents and the collected glosses, and finally Dublittir ua hUathgaile's poem *Rédig dam, a Dé, do nim* (§70).[49]

We may now summarise our conclusions about the manuscripts of Recension III:

(i) The texts of SAM in *Lc* and *B* are to all intents and purposes the same, though they differ from one another sufficiently for us to be able to say that neither is a direct copy from the other;

(ii) The version of SAM presented by these two manuscripts derives, in all probability, from a text of Recension II which looked like *C* but which was probably one stage further removed from the archetype of that recension;

(iii) That the version of SAM in *Lc* and *B* is the result of successive stages of dislocation and dismemberment of a more complete text seems fairly obvious, especially as we know that the scribes of both manuscripts preserved outside the context of SAM itself many of the sections that are now missing from their versions of the text.

There are no good grounds for Oskamp's claim[50] that §§58–62 of the edition are a later addition to the SAM text made by the scribe of *R*. His remark that 'the subsequent occurrence of the account of the deaths of the prophets and the poems in *Lc* and *R*, suggests that the two manuscripts have a common source in which the two episodes had already been brought together' simply begs the question, for the 'common source' was undoubtedly a complete text of SAM, as it appears now in Recension I.

It is not possible, on the available evidence, to say for certain when this third recension came into existence. There is a possibility that a text of Recension II had already in the early twelfth century travelled westwards across the Shannon, perhaps even in the company of the

[48] I have not been able to establish a source for this passage.

[49] *Lc* inserts between the collected glosses and ua hUathgaile's poem a genealogy of Joseph and a summary of the six Ages with their durations; the summary occurs in *B* fol. 10ᵛ [cf. MacCarthy, op. cit., p. 261], and in *C* fol. 65 [35]ʳa 1 ff. In *B* the summary is separate from SAM but the collected glosses and the passage on the naming of the continents (§69) occur *after* ua hUathgaile's poem.

[50] Art. cit., p. 133.

text of Orosius's *Historia* and Isidore's *Etymologiae* which had been utilised in the original compilation of the archetype. If we could be sure that the poem *Sé bliadna caécud imalle* was added to the exemplar of Recension III at its inception, then we would have a *terminus ante quem* for that version of SAM in the final stanza of the poem, which dates it to A.D. 1126. But we have no way of knowing when that poem was added to Recension III, and we are consequently without solid grounds for a dating of it.

(d) *Miscellaneous excerpts from SAM in later texts*

We saw above in section 3 (b) how various fragments of the SAM text occur scattered throughout the later medieval collections in Irish manuscripts. In *LB*, for instance, we encountered a good recension of §§59–61 (on the theme of Babylon and the Jewish captivity), and the same could be said of *Lc* and *B* as well. But besides these occasional occurrences, which have been extrapolated from SAM and collected together with other items of similar theme and type, there are also instances where the details of the SAM narrative have been incorporated entirely into new works. In the text of *LB* known as *Stair chloinde Israhél* (fol. 113[a] 39 ff.), for example, the history of the Israelites opens with the second Age and proceeds then to recount the deeds of Noah, Sem, and the chief events of the Age. The initial synchronistic details of the *Stair* are clearly based on SAM, as we can see from the opening passage:

> Incipit do stair chloinde Israhel inso siss, amail at-beir in Scriptuir.
>
> In oes tanaise in domain immorro, da bliadain nochat for dib cetaib fil innte. Noe mac Lamiach didiu ise cetna oirech na haisse sin. Se cet bliadan robo slan do Noe in tan tanic in diliu, ocus tri coicait bliadan boi ina bethaid iar ndilind, etc.

The text follows closely that of SAM §22, and the details that follow in *Stair chloinde Israhél* also derive from SAM §§35, 35a, and 38; the occurrence of the stanza on Aran would be proof enough, if proof were needed, that SAM was being directly drawn upon. The borrowing extends even to an identical arrangement of the material in columnar order, as is the case in the SAM texts, and it seems clear that the scribe/compiler of *LB* had a fairly substantial text of SAM at his disposal, which he obviously felt himself at liberty to dispose of as he wished, either by extrapolating such items as §§59–61 and collecting them together with other more or less related texts, or by incorporating certain passages of the SAM narrative into wholly new works, where he apparently thought their contents to be more appropriate.[51]

[51]This is not to imply that the scribe/compiler of *LB* was himself the author of *Stair chloinde Israhél*, but the remark applies equally to him and to his forerunners.

The same process of extrapolation and incorporation into new compositions is clearly at work also in the Book of Ballymote tract entitled *Leabhar comaimsearachta Flaind Mainistrech* (fol. 6^{r}a 1 ff.).[52] This tract opens with the words *Adam primus pater fuit, Eua cétmáthair na n-uile,* and the subsequent seventeen lines comprise a verbatim excerpt from SAM §13.[53] This tract draws further on §§17, 18, and 22 and then breaks off into a synchronism of the Persian and Greek kings with Parthalón and the Fomóire, whose origins are independent of SAM. Furthermore, the Ballymote tract has a twin in the Book of Uí Maine (fol. 104^{r}a 1 ff.), though the *M* recension seems to have fewer direct borrowings from SAM than the *Leabhar comaimsearachta.*

Such borrowings could be demonstrated in numerous other Late Middle Irish pseudo-historical compositions; the process is best exemplified perhaps in the tract known as *Leabhar na nAos* 'The Book of the Ages', which occurs in manuscripts too numerous to mention.[54] But by the time of texts like *Leabhar na nAos,* however, the original purpose of the SAM narrative – a history of Salvation and of man's journey towards redemption – has long since been forgotten. The SAM material now serves only as prefatory matter, a general introduction to collections of political tracts and genealogies. We are fortunate in being able to witness the beginning and the end of a tradition.

Having thus reviewed the manuscripts and recensions of SAM we are now in a position to make some general remarks about the text and its historical development. I believe I have shown that the archetype of SAM was conceived as a prose-verse text, the kind of text that we are familar with through *Lebor Gabála* and the Dindsenchus. A detailed comparison of all the early manuscripts has convinced me that, Oskamp to the contrary notwithstanding, the texts of Recension I *(R P)* represent the most homogeneous and balanced version of SAM and the one which is closest to the archetype. I believe too that I have shown that the sections of SAM occurring outside that context in the various codices are devoid of any real context in their new surroundings, and that the very nature of these items was such that it is impossible to believe they were composed for any purpose other than that which they serve in SAM. I do not believe that in Rawlinson B 502 we have 'just a compilation of a couple of poems and some prose fragments, more or less related to each other'. On the contrary, SAM is almost unique in being one of the very few Irish texts whose archetype and sources can be established almost entirely,

[52]The title is by a later hand than that of the main text; the work has no connection with Flann Mainistrech.

[53]See McNamara, *Apocrypha,* p. 30 No. 17.

[54]Cf. Tadhg Ó Donnchadha (ed) *An Leabhar Muimhneach* (Dublin 1940), esp. pp. 1–31.

as such, then, its importance for the history of the language and the literature cannot be exaggerated.

4. THE DATE AND AUTHORSHIP OF *Sex Aetates Mundi*

In Rawlinson B 502 *(R)* the body of the prose text of SAM is preceded by a prose prologue (§1) and two introductory poems, *Cétna-amser bethad bind* (§2), and *Cétaimmser in bethad bind* (§3), each of nine stanzas. The first of these poems gives the mundane chronology for the Ages of the world according to the figures in the Septuagint[55] version of the bible *(do réir int Septín)*, while the second gives the alternative reckoning according to the figures in the Vulgate *(debi na Fírinni Ébraide frisin Sechtmogait Tintúdach)*. The text of the prose prologue (§1) is as follows:

> Panechte *INcipit* .i. tintúd Duiblitrech huí hUathgaile forsin Pandecht Cirine tria Goédeilg in so sís: Do ardgabálaib in domuin ⁊ do chroébaib coibniusa in domain ⁊ dia hilchenélaib ⁊ do numir a mbérla ⁊ do aíssib a n-airech ⁊ dia n-anmannaib ⁊ do aéssaib in domain ⁊ do numir cacha aésse.

The wording of the prologue clearly implies that Dublittir ua hUathgaile was responsible for all that follows in the body of the SAM text, of which the prologue is intended to be a very brief summary. The SAM text is followed immediately by the poem *Rédig dam, a Dé, do nim* (§70), a verse rendering of the preceding text, which is accompanied in *R* by the rubric: *Duan Dublittrech in so forsin Panechte.* It is clear from the wording both of the prologue and of the rubric that Dublittir ua hUathgaile's claims to authorship cover the whole SAM text, and not merely the final poem (§70) and the two introductory ones. The poem *Rédig dam, a Dé, do nim* accompanies the SAM text also in *P B Lc* and *C* (fragments only), and occurs separately in *L; P* has the rubric *Duan Dublitrech huí hUathgaile in so forsin Panechte,* and the other manuscripts (except *C,* which has only fragments of the poem) preserve more or less similar forms of the ascription. The closing stanza of the poem confirms ua hUathgaile's authorship:

> Missi don chuachmaig ón chill,
> hua hUathgail a hUsenglind;
> rom-ruca sech saébi snéid
> torud Aéne ind ríg roréid.

Since the poem *Rédig dam, a Dé, do nim* is a rendering of the preceding SAM prose text and draws as well on material which was not included in the prose but which must have been available to the prose writer, we see that the words *forsin Panechte* apply to the whole SAM text,

[55]Oskamp, art. cit., p. 127, states wrongly that the first poem gives the Vulgate chronology.

both prose and verse, and that the manuscripts clearly intend to suggest the translator/compiler was Dublittir hua hUathgaile.

We are able to provide a rough floruit and a location for this Dublittir from the information supplied by a late eleventh- or twelfth-century Irish charter recorded on fol. 248^{v} of the Book of Durrow.[56] The charter records the cession to the community and monastery in Durrow of a small *erles* ('enclosure') called Ind Ednán, in recompense for an *erles* of theirs which had been granted by the monastery of Killeshin (Glenn Uissen) to the Dál Cais. I give here the witness-list of the charter; the names will help us date Dublittir's floruit:

> IS siat so dano anmand na slánta féin .i. Dublittir hua hUadgaile in fer légind ⁊ Dúnchad hua hUadgaile ⁊ Saírgal ua Suibne ⁊ a mac .i. Saírbrethach, ⁊ Artgal mac Culinnáin ⁊ *fratres eius,* ⁊ Maél Choluim mac Cortáin ⁊ *fratres eius* ⁊ Amalgaid hua hAirudáin ⁊ *fratres eius;* i n-amsir dano Muridaich meic meic Cormáin do-rattad ⁊ Muircertaich Uí Briain, ríg Érend, etc.

Now Muirchertach ua Briain, during whose reign the transaction took place, succeeded his father Toirdelbach on the latter's death in 1086. In 1116, according to the Annals of Inisfallen, he seems to have retired to the monastery of Lismore and he died three years later. Best noted that, according to the annals (AU, LCé), Muirchertach mac meic Gormáin died in 1103,[57] and the Muiredach mac meic Cormáin of the charter (king of Uí Bairrche) is termed *ordán ⁊ aireachas ⁊ prímh athlaoch Laighen* 'the ornament and glory and chief ex-layman of Leinster', in the notice of his death in AFM, s. a. 1124.[58] This Muiredach then (grandfather of bishop Find ua Gormáin, according to a misdated obit in AFM, s. a. 1085) was in monastic retirement at the time of his death; if we can assume that he succeeded Muirchertach mac meic Gormáin (his brother?) on the latter's death in 1103, then the charter could be dated to ca. 1103 x ca. 1124.

The mention in the charter of Gilla Adomnáin ua Cortén as *priest* of Durrow at the time also suggests a date around this period, for Reeves, in his chronicle of the coarbs of Columcille,[59] assigns his incumbency of the abbacy at Kells to the years 1128–38. Against a dating of the charter in the 1120's, however, is the fact that AFM, s. a. 1045, record the death of Cathusach ua Corcráin, coarb of Killeshin, along with that of Cathusach ua Cathail, abbot of

[56] First edited by Richard I. Best 'An early monastic grant in the Book of Durrow' *Ériu* 10 (1926–8) pp. 135–42; reproduced in Arthur A. Luce & others (ed) *Evangeliorum quattuor codex Durmachensis*, 2 vols (Lausanne/Freiburg im Br. 1960). Vol. 1, fol. 248^{v}, has the plate, and Vol. 2, pp. 30–1, has Best's transcript.

[57] Art. cit., p. 140 n. 1.

[58] His genealogy is given in *R* 117a = M. A. O'Brien (ed) *Corpus genealogiarum Hiberniae*, p. 10.

[59] William Reeves (ed) *Adomnan's Life of Columba* (Dublin 1857) p. 404.

Glendalough. Though, as Best pointed out,[60] there must be some confusion of date in one of the sources, his suggestion that the obit resulted from a misreading of the Roman numerals m.xc.u. (1095) would, if correct, imply a date for the charter before 1100, for the guarantor of the Durrow charter is Cathasach ua Corcráin, *airchennech* of Killeshin.

Now Dublittir ua hUathgaile, who is listed in the Durrow charter as *fer légind* of Killeshin, probably succeeded Conchobar ua hUadgaile (†1082 AFM) in that position. He and Dúnchad ua hUadgaile (a brother or cousin) were of the Uí Uathgaile, whose genealogy occurs in *R* 121 bc (*Corpus,* p. 50), and their grandfather was, presumably, the Uathgal mac Soérgaile who is there recorded among the Uí Bairrche. We may say then that the Durrow charter can be assigned outside limits of ca. 1082 x ca. 1116, i.e. the presumed date of Dublittir's apointment as *fer légind,* and the retirement to Lismore of Muirchertach ua Briain.

We see then that Dublittir ua hUathgaile's floruit can be placed roughly in the last quarter of the eleventh century and the first quarter of the twelfth. Such a date would accord well with the language of SAM, which is Middle Irish of a consistent standard throughout. Thus the historical and linguistic facts can be said to lend weight to the manuscript claims of Dublittir ua hUathgaile to the authorship of SAM. It can be said of the ascriptions of texts in Irish manuscripts generally that, when they do not apply to mythical or prehistoric figures, they tend to be reasonably faithful. So that in the case of contemporary texts which were transcribed into our great eleventh- and twelfth-century codices at the time of their composition or shortly thereafter, such manuscript ascriptions must be taken at their face value.

The prose prologue (§1) in *R* unequivocally states that Dublittir ua hUathgaile was the translator/compiler of SAM. This ascription, as we saw above in section 3 (b) above, was also copied into MS. *C* of the second recension; but *C* has substituted for the name of ua hUathgaile the more general term *in senchaid* 'the historian'. But the wording of the prologue in *C* clearly derives from a text identical with that of *R,* as the following will show:

> *Incipit* Panecte. Tunnscnaid na sencaide n-eolach for Penacte tre Gaeilg andso sis .i. do ardgabhalaibh in domain ⁊ do craebhaibh cobneasa claende Nae ⁊ in uile cenealaib in domain, do nuimir bliadan na n-aes, de randaibh clande Nae fo in doman uili arceana.

We know that *C* was copied from a good eleventh- or twelfth-century codex and there can be no doubt, in my view, that *C*'s exemplar of this second recension carried the ascription to Dublittir in wording identical or almost identical with *R*. The archetypes of both Recension I

[60]Art. cit., p. 141.

and Recension II, therefore, contained the prose prologue (§1), and both (we may be sure) ascribed the SAM text to Dublittir ua hUathgaile.

It is clear that from its inception the SAM text was much in favour with scholars and copyists. But it is equally clear that these copyists (like some modern commentators!) had difficulty with the word *Pandecht/Panechte,* in the prologue and in the rubric to ua hUathgaile's poem. In doubt about its meaning, their natural reaction was to drop the word from the text, leaving only the name of ua hUathgaile. Thus the poem *Rédig dam, a Dé, do nim* (§70) in the Book of Leinster *(L)* has the rubric *Dubliter hua Uathgaile cecinit,* and the copies of the poem in *B* and *Lc* also dropped the words *forsin Panechte.* The later copyists clearly did not understand that *Pandecht* (Lat. *Pandecta)* was a technical term denoting all the books of the bible, and that Dublittir's SAM text had derived its details from the books of the Old and New Testament. Having jettisoned the word that connected the prose text and the poem *Rédig dam, a Dé, do nim,* then, the way was clearly open for a separation of the two; the result was that the poem occurs in *L* without the body of SAM.

Oskamp, however, sees the facts in a different light.[61] He maintains that 'it must have been the superscription and the last quatrain of *Redig dam a de do nim* which supplied the scribe, who added the introductory passages in *R*, with the necessary information. One might even assume two stages: in the first stage the two poems were added; the first of them was entitled *Incipit panechte.* Another scribe glossed this with *.i. tintud Dublitrech etc.,* a fact which he deduced from the poem and its superscription; a third scribe incorporated this gloss.'

Now Oskamp believes (as I do) that the poem *Rédig dam, a Dé, do nim* (§70) is an integral part of the SAM text. But he believes also (what I do not) that the prose prologue (§1) and the poems *Cétna-amser bethad bind* (§2) and *Cétaimmser in bethad bind* (§3) are the additions of the *R* scribe. He maintains that the first poem (§2) had the rubric *Incipit panechte,* despite the fact that the poem could not by any stretch of the imagination be said to be an account of the events in the Old and New Testaments; besides, the poem already has a rubric *Do réir int Septín* which clearly takes up from the final words in the prologue: *do aéssaib in domain ⁊ do numir cacha aésse, do réir int Septín.* The verses that follow are exactly what the rubric says they are – a summary of the Ages and their duration, according to the figures in the Septuagint version of the bible.

Even if we did not know that *C* (and therefore the archetype of the second recension) contained a prologue (§1) identical or almost identical with that of *R,* Oskamp's scenario would be far from convincing. He

[61]'On the author of *Sex Aetates Mundi*', pp. 130–1.

sees the SAM text in *R* as coming into existence in the following way:

1. Prose text [=§§4–69];
2. *Rédig dam, a Dé, do nim* [§70] is added;
3. *Incipit panechte* and the two poems [§§2, 3] are added;
4. *forsin panechte* is added to the superscription of Dublittir's poem [§70];
5. The gloss on *panechte* is added [i.e. *tintúd Duiblitrech,* etc.];
6. The gloss on *panechte* is incorporated.

Allowing for the incongruity of the scenario (Nos. 3–6 have no manuscript support), the time-scale involved in such a complicated process of accretion would be much too long to allow for the appearance of such a composite text in a manuscript as early as *R*. But the evidence of *R* and *C,* the most complete texts of recensions I and II, shows clearly that the prologue as it stands in *R* is the prologue to the archetype of SAM; this original prologue ascribed the translation/compilation of SAM to Dublittir ua hUathgaile, and the rubric to his poem *Rédig dam, a Dé, do nim* implied that this was regarded by ua hUathgaile as a verse rendering of his own prose SAM text. There is a need, therefore, to correct the impression given by Oskamp that 'if the text, as it has come down in *R,* represented the archetype, it would be rather illogical that the man who is supposed to be responsible for the entire tract should be mentioned as the author of one poem only', i.e. *Rédig dam, a Dé, do nim.* For we have established that the prologue mentioned ua hUathgaile as the author of the whole tract, and the separate ascription to him of the poem *Rédig dam, a Dé, do nim* simply means that his claims extend to both prose and verse; the argument that the prologue and introductory poems were later additions to SAM rests on no firmer ground than conjecture.

If it is accepted that SAM (both prose and verse) was the work of Dublittir ua hUathgaile, then we must account for the presence within the text of the poem *Dá mac deëc Iacóib* (§43), which is ascribed to one Oéngus mac Suibni, a poet otherwise unknown. Now it has been remarked by Oskamp[62] that the SAM text in *R* is the work of a scholar, not just a scribe: '*Sex Aetates Mundi* in Rawl. B 502 is a text that "has been worked on"'. What would be more natural than that Dublittir ua hUathgaile, *fer légind* of Killeshin and an undoubted scholar, should enlist the aid of a colleague in the scriptorium?; and if so, might we not identify the Suibne of the Durrow charter with the father of Oéngus mac Suibni? Without further information, of course, such an identification can only be conjecture, but the content of Oéngus mac Suibni's poem shows clearly that he was working directly on the material immediately preceding it in SAM, §42; for such co-

[62]Ibid., p. 133.

operation to have existed at so early a stage of the text tradition strongly implies that the two authors worked together in the same monastery.

The ascription of SAM to Dublittir ua hUathgaile brings us face to face with the current controversy concerning the date and provenance of *Leabhar na hUidhre (U)*. Until recently, it was generally accepted that *U* was the work of three scribes, the second of whom was identified as being Maél Muire mac meic Cuind na mbocht (†1106). Because Maél Muire died at Clonmacnois, and because he was the scribe of most of the manuscript, it was generally assumed also that *U* was a Clonmacnois codex.[63] The discovery that hand *H* of the manuscript was also to be seen glossing the Annals of Tigernach in Rawl. B 488[64] was seen as additional support for the ascription of *U* to the scriptorium of Clonmacnois.

In recent years, however, this view has come under detailed scrutiny and attack by Tomás Ó Concheanainn, who, in a paper on 'The reviser of *Leabhar na hUidhre*',[65] upset the accepted doctrine by suggesting that Maél Muire was not to be identified with hand *M* of the manuscript (who was responsible for the bulk of what survives in *U*), but with hand *H*, the so-called reviser and the man who glossed the Rawl. B 488 copy of the Annals of Tigernach. If Ó Concheanainn were right, then the work of *H* would have to be dated ca 1100, and the two scribes *A* and *M* would accordingly have to be pushed farther back into the eleventh century. So far, however, the new theory has not found general acceptance.[66]

For my part, although there is not space enough here to discuss the question at length, I must make it clear that I believe the 'traditional' view of *Leabhar na hUidhre* to be the correct one. That is to say, I believe that hands *A* and *M* worked actively together and that the latter is to be identified with Maél Muire mac meic Cuind na mbocht. That these two scribes cooperated with one another in the initial stages of compilation seems to me clearly indicated by the fact that *A*, besides writing three tracts himself, wrote the opening sections of two others, which were then completed by *M*.[67] I further believe that Best's original estimate of the hands, that they 'appear to belong to the same school

[63]See esp. Oskamp 'Notes' (cited in n. 12) and the literature cited in the description of the MSS below, p. 51.

[64]Richard I. Best 'Palaeographical notes 1: The Rawlinson B 502 Tigernach' *Ériu* 7 (1913) pp. 114–20.

[65]*Éigse* 15 (1973–4) pp. 277–88.

[66]The only other scholar to commit himself to Ó Concheanainn's theory in print is David Dumville ' "Scéla lái brátha" and the collation of Leabhar na hUidhre' *Éigse* 16 (1975-6) pp. 24-8, at p. 24: 'Now, following Ó Concheanainn's convincing *coup*, *H* will be dated to ca 1100'; Dumville's various papers on the subject (listed above in the section on the MSS) provide a useful commentary on the controversy, but they do not materially affect the arguments either way.

[67]See Oskamp 'Notes' pp. 117–22.

and are, I think, of the same period' has yet to be disproved, and certainly has not been refuted by subsequent writers.[68] The argument for the contemporary working of the scribes provided by art-historical analysis of the manuscript[69] seems to me to further strengthen the case for the traditional view. I am not convinced by Ó Concheanainn's revised identification of the hands in *U*, but believe his arguments to have been more than adequately answered by Oskamp.[70]

In consequence of these arguments, therefore, I see no good reason to depart from the traditional view that *U* is to be dated ca 1106. That it should contain a version of Recension II of SAM at so early a date need not surprise us at all, for there are numerous other texts in *U* which exist in different recensions and which *U* preserves in inferior copies to those of later manuscripts.[71] The solitary folio of *U* that contains the SAM text has been sufficient to enable us to say that the version it preserves belongs to the second recension; the textual readings are not obviously inferior to those of the manuscripts in the first recension *(R P)*, but they already show the features which are characteristic of the later versions.

Taking all this evidence into account then we may suggest that SAM was composed perhaps ca 1090. The textual tradition indicates that the work enjoyed an early and widespread popularity and it was a common text in the twelfth-century Irish codices. The fact that the best and most complete copy of SAM is contained in Rawlinson B 502 raises the question, whether this might not, in fact, be Dublittir ua hUathgaile's own fair copy, and *R* in consequence the product of the Killeshin scriptorium.[72] The codex is clearly of south-Leinster provenance and the terminal names in the genealogies suggest a time of compilation ca 1130; such a date might not be outside the bounds of ua hUathgaile's known floruit. Even if the codex were not the work of ua hUathgaile himself there would still be reason to suggest that it derived from Killeshin, for the text of SAM in *R* is so pure that it must stand practically at the head of the manuscript tradition

[68]In his introduction to the RIA's 1929 diplomatic edition of *U*, p. xvii, Best remarked that 'the script of *H* contains no elements so markedly different from the other two hands as would enable one to assign a later date to it on purely palaeographical grounds'; but he then mentioned Thurneysen's claim that the hand was thirteenth century and added: 'this may be so'. Ó Concheanainn, art. cit., p. 278 n. 3, points out the weakness of Thurneysen's arguments.

[69]Françoise Henry & Geneviève L. Marsh-Micheli 'A century of Irish illumination' *PRIA* 62 C 5 (1962) pp. 101–64, at pp. 114–16.

[70]'Mael Muire: compiler or reviser?' *Éigse* 16 (1976–7) pp. 177–82.

[71]Cf. Dumville, art. cit., p. 24 n. 5, and Edgar M. Slotkin 'The structure of *Fled Bricrenn* before and after the *Lebor na hUidre* interpolations' *Ériu* 29 (1978) pp. 64–77.

[72]Cf. Francis J. Byrne, *A thousand years of Irish script. An exhibition of Irish manuscripts in Oxford Libraries* (Oxford 1979) p. 13, No. 4: 'It [sc. *R*] was written at a Leinster monastery, probably Killeshin, Co. Laois'.

and may be a copy of ua hUathgaile's own text. The motivation for preserving the ascription intact would therefore be obvious, since SAM would have been the work of a former *fer légind* in the monastery.

But, unfortunately, we have no real, solid evidence on which to base such an ascription to Killeshin. We know of no such Irish codex as *Lebar Glinne hUissen* and it would be hard to think of such a fine manuscript as *R* passing down through history without mention, if such were in fact its name. Of great Irish books there was, apparently, no end in the twelfth century, but there was no Book of Killeshin. *Sed quis in scriptis incertis exactitudinem praestabit*?

As an illustration of how I see the text tradition of SAM the following stemma gives a schematic picture of the manuscripts, their probable dates, and their interrelationship with one another. The sigla are those of the foregoing discussion and are the same as the sigla of the edition and of the MS. concordance; the only additions are MS. Y (the archetype of Recension II), and MS. X (the archetype of Recension III), neither of which appears to have survived; TCD MS. H. 2. 4 *(T)* and its copy TCD MS. H. 1. 15 *(N)*, and the Mullingar MS.

STEMMA CODICUM

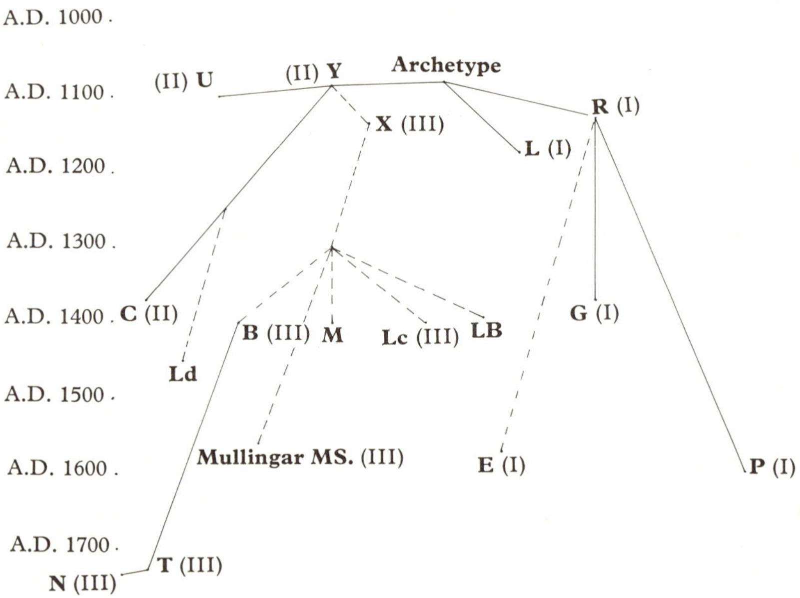

(a) The *Sex Aetates Mundi* and *Lebor Bretnach*

In his great study of the Historia Brittonum[73] and its origins, Heinrich Zimmer stated categorically that the *Sex Aetates Mundi* was one of the texts on which Nennius, writing in the year A.D. 796, had drawn.[74] This is not the place to scrutinise Zimmer's theories about the *Historia Brittonum,* and I have not the courage to drag the reader through the morass of articles about that work,[75] but it must be said that Zimmer's theories are all based on the evidence of the late derivative Recension III of SAM and are therefore of no value.

But though Zimmer's theories about SAM cannot stand, his theory that the *Lebor Bretnach,* the Irish translation of the *Historia,* was made by Gilla Coémáin (flor. ca A. D. 1072) has been taken up and expanded by Oskamp, who sees in the *Lebor Bretnach* and SAM the work of one and the same scholar. As an alternative to Dublittir ua hUathgaile's authorship of SAM, Oskamp proposed that Gilla Coémáin be credited with it; but he argued from a basis which he admitted had been sidetracked in his article – the ascription to Gilla Coémáin of the *Lebor Bretnach.* The arguments adduced by Anton G. van Hamel in his edition of LB[76] are reasonable grounds for dating the work to the second half of the eleventh century, which means that hand *A*'s copy of the tract in *Leabhar na hUidhre (U)* is quite close to its date of origin.[77]

Oskamp's argument is, that since SAM and LB seem to have come into existence at roughly the same period, and since they are found together at the beginning of *U,* then they were possibly copied from the same exemplar and even, perhaps, written by the same man.[78]

It must be stated clearly that there is no textual evidence to suggest that SAM and LB are in any way interdependent. The only passage where the two texts overlap (§26) could very easily have been independently derived by both works from the original source.[79] The most significant point in favour of Oskamp's thesis is the fact that LB omitted the section *de sex aetatibus* that occurred in the

[73]*Nennius vindicatus. Über Entstehung, Geschichte und Quellen der 'Historia Brittonum'* (Berlin 1893).

[74]'Eine Abhandlung über die *Sex aetates mundi* war das dritte irische Denkmal, welches Nennius a. 796 benutzte' (p. 225); the other two alleged sources were the Lives of St. Patrick and *Lebor Gabála.* In the following discussion Zimmer made it quite clear that by 'eine Abhandlung' he meant our text.

[75]See the article by Dumville, cited in n. 3 above, pp. 13–14 ff.

[76]*Lebor Bretnach, the Irish version of the Historia Britonum ascribed to Nennius* (Dublin 1932).

[77]Note, however, that this fact need not necessarily imply that the *U* copy stands at the head of the text tradition; see the article by Dumville cited in n. 3.

[78]Art. cit., p. 137.

[79]I believe that the text in *Lebor Bretnach* was taken from SAM but at what date, I cannot say; see the commentary on §26 below, p. 149.

original Latin version. While I do not quite understand the reason offered by him (p. 139) in explanation of this omission, there is no doubting that the omission was a deliberate one.

But the foundation of the Oskamp view rests on the assumption that LB was composed by Gilla Coémáin – an ascription which Oskamp made no effort to defend or support, and which has been vigorously attacked by David Dumville.[80] Dumville's main reason for questioning the ascription to Gilla Coémáin is that it occurs only in a pair of related manuscripts, the Book of Uí Maine *(M)* and TCD MS. H. 2. 17 *(H)*.[81] We may remark in passing that there are, in fact, three rubrics for the LB text in *M*, not two, as previous writers seem to have assumed. One is found on fol. 91 [35]^{v}a 74 (last line) and reads: *Sequitur sencus Breatan annseo sis;* the other two follow on fol. 91 [35]^{v}b (top of col.) and read: *Sequitur leabur Breatnach*[82] and *INcipit de Britania airte quam Nenius construxit, Gilla Coemain ro-impai i Scotic.*

But there is, in fact, another ascription to Gilla Coémáin which may be said to lend support to Oskamp's view; it occurs in the Genealogies of Saints in Laud 610 and seems to be independent of the ascriptions in *M* and *H*. I give here the relevant passage direct from the manuscript:[83]

> Cairnech mac Luítheich meic Lugdach meic Dalann meic Ithachair meic Ata. Is amlaid sin ínnísus Gilla Caemain i stairib na mBretnach *quod* do Bretnaib Cornn do ⁊ is uime at-berar Cornech fris.

The same passage occurs in the Genealogies of Saints in *M* (fol. 107 [51]^{v}c 41 ff.), but the fact that it concerns the origins of St. Cairnech shows that the material is independent of the *M H* recension of *Lebor Bretnach,* for the Cairnech saga material does not occur in that recension.[84] It would seem then that two separate recensions of LB ascribed that text to Gilla Coémáin; we know he was alive ca A.D. 1072 and the language of the tract would not be inconsistent with a late eleventh-century dating. It is possible that the ascription to Gilla Coémáin passed from one recension of the text to the other but without the complete evidence which only a thorough-going modern edition of the tract can provide we cannot say for sure that he was the author.

[80]See especially the article cited in n. 3 above.

[81]Ibid., pp. 261, 269–70.

[82]In a hand later than that of the main text.

[83]The text published by Grosjean in *Irish Texts* 3 (1931) p. 97 is not accurate.

[84]See Dumville, art. cit., p. 267 and n. 78.

THE MANUSCRIPTS

Listed below are only those MSS that were utilised in the construction of the present edition; excluded therefore are *Lc, B, T, N,* and the MSS that only preserve fragments of SAM incorporated into other texts. The sections of SAM in these latter MSS have, of course, been discussed in the chapter on the text tradition (pp. 18–19), and their respective extents are tabulated in the Concordance.

It has not been felt possible to provide full descriptions of the MSS, and though my views on some of them derive from my own researches I have listed in the bibliographies only such printed material as I thought helpful to the reader of this volume. There has been no attempt to make these bibliographies exhaustive.

R *Oxford, Bodleian Library, MS. Rawlinson B 502 (Arch.F.d.28).* Dating from the period ca A.D. 1130 and compiled probably at Glendalough. Our text is found in the second vellum part (fols. 40^{v}–5^{r}) following *Saltair na Rann.*

Bibliography: Kuno Meyer, *Rawlinson B 502, a collection of pieces in prose and verse in the Irish language, compiled during the eleventh and twelfth centuries* (Oxford 1909) [Full photographic facsimile]; Françoise Henry & Geneviève Marsh-Micheli 'A century of Irish illumination (1070–1170)' *PRIA* 62 C 5 (1961–3) pp. 134–6; F. J. Byrne, *A thousand years of Irish script. An exhibition of Irish manuscripts in Oxford libraries* (Oxford 1979) p. 13, No. 4; Pádraig Ó Riain 'The Book of Glendalough or Rawlinson B 502' *Éigse* 18 (1981) pp. 161–76.

U *Dublin, Royal Irish Academy, MS. 23 E 25 (1129).* The celebrated *Leabhar na hUidhre,* dating to the period ca A.D. 1100 and compiled probably at Clonmacnois. The present first leaf of the MS. is all that remains of our text.

Bibliography: R. I. Best & Osborn Bergin (edd) *Lebor na hUidre, Book of the Dun Cow* (Dublin 1929) [Full diplomatic transcript]; H. P. A. Oskamp 'Notes on the history of Lebor na Huidre' *PRIA* 65 C 6 (1967) pp. 117–37; Tomás Ó Concheanainn 'The reviser of Leabhar na hUidhre' *Éigse* 15 (1974) pp. 277–88; Our text was edited from this MS. by Edmund Hogan, *The Irish Nennius from L. na Huidre & homilies and legends from L. Brecc.* RIA Todd Lecture Series 6 (Dublin 1895) pp. 1–10, but he confused the work with the *Lebor Bretnach* that follows it in *U.*

P *Dublin, National Library of Ireland, MS. G 131 (Phillipps 17082)*. Dating probably from the early 17th c., the exact provenance of this MS. is unknown. It was written by members of the O'Clery family. Our text occupies pp. 3–28, and was probably copied from *R*.

Bibliography: Nessa Ní Shéaghdha, *Catalogue of Irish manuscripts in the National Library of Ireland* 4 (Dublin 1977) pp. 51–6.

C *Oxford, Bodleian Library, MS. Rawlinson B 486.*
Dating probably from the period ca A.D. 1370, the MS. almost certainly derives (at least in this part) from Lorrha (Co. Tipperary), though it was subsequently at Cluain Plocáin (Ballymulconry, Co. Roscommon) and then passed into the possession of Sir James Ware *ex dono Caroli Conway xxiiii*^{to} *Junii 1625*. It contains material from a late 11th or early 12th c. codex, possibly to be equated with *Lebar Ruadáin Lothra,* and specific mention is made also of *Liber Tíre dá Glas,* from which other items were copied. Our text occupies fols. 67^{r}–74^{v}.

Bibliography: Charles McNeill 'Reports on the Rawlinson collection of manuscripts' *Analecta Hibernica* 1 (1930) pp. 141–2; F. J. Byrne, *A thousand years of Irish script,* p. 21, No. 11.

L *Dublin, Trinity College, MS. H. 2. 18 (1339).*
The Book of Leinster, or *Lebor na Nuachongbála,* compiled ca A.D. 1150–1200, probably at Terryglass. Only the last section of our text (§70) is found in the MS.

Bibliography: R. I. Best, Osborn Bergin & M. A. O'Brien (edd) *The Book of Leinster, formerly Lebor na Nuachongbála,* 5 vols (Dublin 1954–67) [diplomatic transcript, incomplete]; William O'Sullivan 'Notes on the scripts and make-up of the Book of Leinster' *Celtica* 7 (1966) pp. 1–31.

LB *Dublin, Royal Irish Academy, MS. 23 P 16 (1230).*
The *Leabhar Breac,* compiled ca A.D. 1400 at Cluain Leathain (unidentified), by Murchad Ó Cuindlis (who also collaborated on the writing of *Leabhar Mór Leacáin).* The MS. was in the keeping of the MacEgan family of Dún Doighre in the 16th c., whence it received its traditional name, *Leabhar Mór Dúna Doighre.* The MS. preserves only seven sections of our text.

Bibliography: Eugene O'Curry & others, *Leabhar Breac, the Speckled Book* (Dublin 1876) [Full facsimile of a transcript made by Joseph O'Longan]; Kathleen Mulchrone & Elizabeth Fitzpatrick, *Catalogue of Irish manuscripts in the Royal Irish Academy* 26–7 (Dublin 1943) pp. 3379–3404; Tomás Ó Concheanainn 'The scribe of the Leabhar Breac' *Ériu* 24 (1973) pp. 64–79.

G *Dublin, National Library of Ireland, MSS G 2–3.*
These two manuscripts originally formed one volume, of 14th c. date, compiled by Ádhamh Ó Cianáin (in part at least) from an exemplar belonging to or perhaps written by his teacher, Seaán Mór Ó Dubhagáin (†A.D. 1372), poet to the O'Kellys of Uí Maine. The four sections of our text in the MS. were probably copied from *R,* and *R* in turn is probably to be identified with *Lebar Glind dá Lacha,* cited also as a source by Ó Cianáin.

Bibliography: Nessa Ní Shéaghdha, *Catalogue of Irish MSS in the NLI* 1 (Dublin 1967) pp. 12–28; James Carney 'The Ó Cianáin miscellany' *Ériu* 21 (1969) pp. 122–47.

Ld *Oxford, Bodleian Library, MS. Laud Miscellany 610 (Arch. F.c. 30).*
Compiled at various locations, mainly during the years A.D. 1453–4. It contains only two sections of SAM and some of the glosses.

Bibliography: Myles Dillon 'Laud Misc. 610' *Celtica* 5 (1960) pp. 64–76; 6 (1963) pp. 135–55; Anne & William O'Sullivan 'Three notes on Laud Misc. 610 (or the Book of Pottlerath)' *Celtica* 9 (1971) pp. 135–51.

CONCORDANCE OF MANUSCRIPTS

The concordance that follows is intended to show the extent of the SAM text in each manuscript and the manner in which the various manuscripts are interrelated. Each section of the text is tabulated by folio/page and line reference, showing the place of the section in terms of the whole work and, further, in the codicological context of the individual codices. The intention is to show the user which manuscripts have the most complete versions of SAM, and which are the manuscripts that have suffered displacement of SAM sections. The primary purpose is to indicate that *R* has the most complete text, closely followed by *P*, and that these two copies provide the basis for comparison.

Where certain sections of SAM are contained in other texts it has not been possible to indicate that fact in the concordance. All such stray items, however, have been discussed in the section on the text tradition, and the reader may speedily locate the material from the references cited there. The references in the concordance are to the folio numberings of all manuscripts; except in the cases of *U*, *T* and *N*, where the reference is to page numbers, it has not been possible to include facsimile paginations. The use of asterisks after certain sigla indicates that the text in those particular sections is, for one reason or another, fragmentary. The sigla are as follows:

R	Rawlinson B 502
P	National Library of Ireland MS. G 131
U	*Leabhar na hUidhre*
C	Rawlinson B 486
B	The Book of Ballymote
Lc	The Great Book of Lecan
LB	*Leabhar Breac*
Ld	Laud Misc. 610
G	National Library of Ireland MS. G 3
L	The Book of Leinster
T	Trinity College Dublin MS. H. 2. 4 (1295)
N	Trinity College Dublin MS. H. 1. 15 (1289)
E	British Library MS. Egerton 1782
M	The Book of Uí Maine

It should be noted that, in the case of the Book of Ballymote *(B)*, whose text is now acephalous, the full version can be recovered by reference to TCD MS. H. 2. 4 (1295) [*T*], which was copied by Richard Tipper from *B* in 1728, when that codex still contained the now lost first folio. The second TCD MS., H. 1. 15 (1289) [*N*], was, I think, copied by Tadhg Ó Neachtain from the Tipper transcript, not (as the Catalogue states) directly from *B*. Hence, for the first twenty-three sections of SAM, the reader should read down the columns *T N* to see which of those sections were contained originally in *B*.

It should also be noted that no account is here taken of the numerous late copies of §70, the poem *Rédig dam, a Dé, do nim,* that occur independently in MSS. They are all derived from Recension III of SAM and need be collated only for the purpose of editing that Recension.

	R	P	U	C	B	Lc
1	40^{v}b 15–19			67^{r}a 1–9		
2	40^{v}b 19–37					
3	40^{v}b 38–41^{r}a5					★ 267^{v}b 5–7
4a	41^{r}marg. sup.					
4	41^{r}a 7–14	3, 1–6		67^{r}a 15–24		22^{r}a 1–40
5	41^{r}a 15–19	3, 6–10		67^{r}a 24–b9		22^{r}a 42–b27
6	41^{r}a 20–3	3, 10–14		67^{r}b 9–18		22^{r}b 28–38
7	41^{r}a 24–7	3, 14–17		67^{r}b 19–26		22^{r}b 34–8 269^{r}a 11–15
8	41^{r}a 28–32	3, 17–20		67^{v}a 1–10		22^{r}b 39–46
9	41^{r}a 32–8	3, 20–5		67^{v}a 11–23		22^{v}a 1–12
10	41^{r}a 39–49	3, 26–4, 4		67^{v}b 1–16		22^{v}a 15–32
11	41^{r}b 1–10	4, 5–14				
12	41^{r}b 11–14	4, 15–17		67^{v}b 16–23		22^{v}b 31–6
13	41^{r}b 14–29	4, 17–5, 3		68^{r}a 1–b6		22^{v}b 1–23
14	41^{r}b 30–9	5, 3–12		68^{r}b 6–16		22^{v}b 23–33 267^{v}b 7–21
15	41^{r}b 31–40	5, 4–12				
16	41^{r}b 41–51	5, 12–24				
17	41^{v}a 1–8	5, 25–6, 4		68^{r}b 17–^{v}a9		22^{v}b 34–23^{r}a3
18	41^{v}a 9–14	6, 4–9		68^{v}a 10–23		
19	41^{v}a 14–23	6, 9–16				
20	41^{v}a 24–37	6, 17–27		★ 68^{v}a 23–b12		23^{r}a 4–15
21	41^{v}a 38–47	6, 27–7, 8				
22	41^{v}a 48–b1	7, 9–12		68^{v}b 13–21		23^{r}a 16–20
23	41^{v}b 2–10	7, 12–20		68^{v}b 22–69^{r}a18		23^{r}a 21–35

LB	Ld	G	L	T	N	
		24^{r}a 34–^{v}b26				E 44^{r}b 1–21
				1, 1–4	1, 1–7	
				1, 5–8	1, 8–11	
				1, 8–11	1, 11–14	
	116^r marg. inf.			1, 12–15	1, 15–18	
				1, 16–19	1, 19–22	
		18^{v}a 9–20		1, 19–24	1, 22–7	
		18^{v}a 20–b20		1, 24–7	1, 27–31	
		18^{v}b9–29		1, 28–37	1, 32–41	
				1, 38–40	2, 1–3	
				1, 40–2, 10	2, 4–16	M 104^{r}a 1–24
				2, 10–15	2, 16–22	
				2, 16–23	2, 23–31	M 104^{r}a 25–
				2, 23–7	2, 31–7	M ★ 104^{r}a –39
				★ 2, 28–32	★ 2, 38–43	
★ 113a 43–8				3, 1–4	3, 1–4	
				3, 4–11	3, 4–13	

	R	P	U	C	B	Lc
24	41^{v}b 10–29	7, 20–8, 4		69^{r}a 18–^{v}a11	★ 2^{r}a 1–16	23^{r}a 36–b23
25	41^{v}b 30–42^{r}a1	8, 5–19	★ 1a 1–13	69^{v}a 12–b24	2^{r}a 16–54	23^{r}b 23–^{v}a27
26	42^{r}a 1–13	8, 19–28	1a 13–31	69^{v}b 25–70^{r}a24	2^{r}a 55–b11	23^{v}a 28–b6
27	42^{r}a 13–19	8, 28–9, 2	1a 31–40	70^{r}a 24–b12	2^{r}b 11–19	23^{v}b 6–13
28	42^{r}a 20–32	9, 2–11	1a 41–b12	70^{r}b 12–^{v}a11	2^{r}b 19–22	23^{v}b 14–41
29	42^{r}a 33–49	9, 11–22	1b 12–34	70^{v}a 11–b11	2^{v}b 15–34	23^{v}b 42–24^{r}a4
30	42^{r}a 50–b9	9, 22–8	1b 34–2a2	70^{v}b 12–71^{r}a2	2^{v}b 34–48	★ 24^{r}a 5–16
31	42^{r}b 10–23	9, 29–10, 13	2a 2–17	71^{r}a 3–27		24^{v}a 22–42
32	42^{r}b 24–35	10, 13–21	2a 17–31	71^{r}a 28–b12		24^{v}a 43–b8
33	42^{r}b 35–43	10, 22–7	2a 31–9	71^{r}b 12–21	2^{v}b 48–59	24^{v}b 8–26
34	42^{r}b 43–^{v}a8	10, 27–11, 8	2a 40–b13	71^{r}b 22–^{v}a15	2^{v}b 59–3^{r}a20	24^{v}b 26–46
35	42^{v}a 8–20	11, 9–16	2b 14–27	71^{v}a 16–b3	3^{r}a 20–36	24^{v}b 47–25^{r}a5
35a			2b 27–30		3^{r}a 34–7	
36	42^{v}a 20–5	11, 16–20				
37	42^{v}a 26–37	11, 21–12, 2				
38	42^{v}a 38–49	12, 3–11	2b 29–43	71^{v}b 3–19	3^{r}a 37–50	25^{r}a 6–15
39	42^{v}a 50–b15	12, 12–26	★ 2b 43–	71^{v}b 19–72^{r}a17	3^{r}a 50–b10	25^{r}a 16–31
40	42^{v}b 16–25	12, 26–13, 2		72^{r}a 18–b2	3^{r}b 11–19	25^{r}a 31–41
41	42^{v}b 25–34	13, 3–9		72^{r}b 2–15	3^{r}b 19–29	25^{r}a 41–b7
42	42^{v}b 34–8	13, 9–11		72^{r}b 16–21	3^{r}b 30–48	25^{r}b 7–11
43	42^{v}b 39–50	13, 11–24		72^{v}a 8–b3		
44	43^{r}a 1–39	13, 14–29		72^{r}b 22–^{v}a21	3^{r}b 29–42	25^{r}b 11–27
45	43^{r}a 1–27	14, 7–17		72^{v}a 21–b15	3^{r}b 52–^{v}a6	25^{r}b 28–41
46	43^{r}a 28–36	14, 17–23		72^{v}b 16–73^{r}a2	3^{v}a 7–16	25^{r}b 42–^{v}a1

LB	Ld	G	L	T	N
				4, 5–27	4, 13–41
				4, 28–36	4, 42–5, 7
				4, 36–5, 4	5, 7–14
				5, 5–6, 26	5, 15–7, 11
				6, 26–38	7, 11–26
				6, 39–7, 3	7, 37–44
				7, 8–13	7, 45–8, 5
				7, 13–25	8, 5–21
3a 56–b4				7, 25–34	8, 21–34
3b 4–6				7, 38–9	8, 34–6
3b 7–18				7, 40–8, 6	8, 37–9, 4
				8, 7–18	9, 5–18
				8, 19–23	9, 19–24
				8, 24–30	9, 25–32
				8, 30–2	9, 32–5
				8, 32–41	9, 5–10, 6
				8, 42–9, 6	10, 6–15
				9, 6–11	10, 15–22

	R	P	U	C	B	Lc
47	43^{r}a 37–40	14, 23–6		73^{r}a 3–8	3^{v}a 15–19	25^{v}a 2–4
48	43^{r}a 38–46	14, 27–9		73^{r}a 9–18	3^{v}a 16–25	25^{v}a 5–20
49	43^{r}a 48–b2	15, 1–10		73^{r}a 16–25	3^{v}a 25–41	25^{v}a 8–20
50	43^{r}b 3–23	15, 11–16, 1		73^{r}a 26–b17	3^{v}a 41–54	25^{v}a 21–34
51	43^{r}b 24–43	16, 2–17		73^{r}b 18–^{v}b1	3^{r}a 54–b18	25^{v}a 34–b13
52	43^{r}b 43–50	16, 17–24		73^{v}b 1–28	3^{v}b 18–30	25^{v}b 14–27
53	43^{v}a 1–11	16, 25–17, 5		74^{r}a 1–19	3^{v}b 20–39	25^{v}b 28–39
54	43^{v}a 11–18	17, 6–12		74^{r}a 19–b3	3^{v}b 38–43	25^{v}b 39–49
55	43^{v}a 19–33	17, 12–24				
56	43^{v}a 34–43	17, 25–18, 4		74^{r}b 3–18	3^{v}b 44–53	26^{r}a 1–11
57	43^{v}a 43–b11	18, 4–18		74^{r}b 18–^{v}a16	3^{v}b 53–4^{r}a8	26^{v}a 12–27
58	43^{v}b 11–44^{r}a5	18, 18–20, 4				
59	44^{r}a 6–20	20, 5–17				193^{r}a 18–35
60	44^{r}a 20–5	20, 17–21				
61	44^{r}a 26–37	20, 22–21, 4				193^{r}a 37–b7
62	44^{r}a 38–45	21, 5–11				
63	44^{r}a 45–51	21, 11–16		74^{v}a 17–b3	4^{r}b 1–12	26^{r}a 28–33
64	44^{r}b 1–6	21, 16–21				
65	44^{r}b 7–11	21, 21–5				
66	44^{r}b 12–32	21, 6–22, 8				
67	44^{r}b 13–21	22, 16–20				
68	44^{r}b 33–42	22, 9–16				
69	44^{r}b 42–^{v}a3	22, 20–23, 2		74^{v}b 5–22	5^{v}a 40–7	26^{r}a 34–46
70	44^{v}a 4–45^{r}b19	23, 5–28, 24			4^{r}b 13–5^{r}a24	26^{v}a 22-27^{v}a24

LB	Ld	G	L	T	N
				9, 11–15	10, 22–5
				9, 13–20	10, 23–30
				9, 24–8	10, 35–11, 5
				★ 9, 33–10, 1	★ 11, 6–16
				10, 1–14	11, 16–32
				10, 14–22	11, 32–44
				10, 23–9	11, 45–12, 7
				10, 29–32	12, 7–10
				10, 33–9	12, 11–19
				10, 39–45	12, 19–29
181b 1–19					
181b 20–31					
181b 32–55					
				12, 1–8	13, 23–31
	14^{v}b 6–28			19, 1–7	20, 16–23
			141b 27-143a39	12, 9–16, 22	13, 32–17, 42

TEXT

The edition of the *Sex Aetates Mundi* that follows is basically a transcript of the text in Rawlinson B 502 *(R)* and represents Recension I of the text. Besides the published facsimile of *R,* I also used photographs of *R* and of Rawlinson B 486 *(C),* and collated the text fully with all the manuscripts in Dublin libraries. Apart from emendations, therefore (all of which are noted), and the usual editorial conventions, the version of the text here presented is as it appears in *R.* Thus the orthography and arrangement follow that manuscript as closely as possible, even to the extent of retaining the characteristic punctuation of point (.) and point with comma (.,); the numbering of sections is, of course, editorial, and Latin words and passages are marked by the use of italics.

Contractions have, in all cases, been silently expanded; any doubt about the manuscript reading may be easily dispelled by consulting the published facsimile of *R.* Words are separated according to the usual modern practice; all preverbs and adverbs are hyphenated, and the hyphen is also used to separate stressed words from enclitics. Since long vowels are only rarely marked in *R* the acute accent has been added where necessary (no use is made of the macron); and the acute accent on diphthongs is marked regularly over the second vowel *(Goídil, saér,* etc.); where hiatus is required by the metre it is marked by diaeresis. Roman numerals that occur in prose passages have been expanded, except where such expansion would distort the sequence of words in the text; numerals in columnar tables have been left without expansion, for obvious reasons.

The orthography of *R* has not been regularised, only the minimum of emendation being made to ensure easy comprehension. Hence spellings like *tíctain* and *at-ract* have been retained, as they represent an orthography that was valid for early Irish. In some cases, where lenition has been felt to be required, the mark of aspiration has been indicated by [h] in the edition; but the mark of lenition over *s* and *f,* and the punctum over *n* in nasal clusters, have not been restored when wanting in *R.* In the Latin passages the spelling *hautem* has been used throughout to indicate the use in the manuscripts of the abbreviation *h*ʳ. But in all such cases the intention has been to follow as faithfully as possible the scribal practices of the primary manuscript (whose text is very good), not to impose modern orthographical standards.

The apparatus criticus is based on the substantial variant readings of manuscripts other than *R*. While all of the manuscripts have figured in the discussion of the text tradition, and are tabulated in the Concordance, it has been thought best to cite in the apparatus only the texts of Recensions I and II, with the occasional addition of some fragmentary texts in good codices like Laud 610 and *Leabhar Breac*. The text of Recension III requires a separate edition, in my view, in order to indicate accurately the manner in which it differs from the texts of the other recensions.

The variant readings are given with a minimum of editorial punctuation and references are always to the line-numbers of each individual section of the edition. Besides the variants from manuscripts, reference is also made in the apparatus to a number of sections in SAM which were edited individually by various scholars; I give here a list of these articles with the sigla used to denote them in the apparatus:

KM Kuno Meyer 'Mitteilungen aus irischen Handschriften' *ZCP* 3 (1901) pp. 17–20 (§§1–3, 58, 61);

OB Osborn Bergin 'A mystical interpretation of the Beati' *Ériu* 11 (1932) pp. 103–6 (§§60–62);

Osk H. P. A. Oskamp 'On the author of *Sex Aetates Mundi*' *Studia Celtica* 3 (1968) pp. 127–40 (§§1, 61);

IT Paul Grosjean 'List of Apostles and Disciples (with a marginal note on the persecutions)' *Irish Texts* 4 (1934) pp. 1–2 (§§65–67).

An asterisk beside a siglum indicates that the text of the section concerned is incomplete in that manuscript (or edition, as the case may be), either for codicological reasons or because of editorial practice.

Words or passages enclosed in arrow brackets are glosses on the main text in *R*. Glosses in *R* which were damaged by the binder and are not now complete have been restored by reference to the other manuscripts, without indicating loss of text in the edition; however, variant readings for these glosses are noted as in all other cases. Otherwise, editorial additions or corrections have been marked by the use of square brackets and the only section which has been inserted is §35a which, though it does not figure in the manuscripts of Recension I, occurs in *Leabhar na hUidhre* (the oldest surviving witness to SAM) and has been included for that reason.

[SEX AETATES MUNDI]

1. Panechte *INcipit* .i. tintúd Duiblitrech huí hUathgaile forsin Pandecht Cirine tria Goédeilg in so sís:
Do ardgabálaib in domuin ⁊ do chroébaib coibniusa in domain ⁊ dia hilchenélaib ⁊ do numir a mbérla ⁊ do aíssib a n-airech ⁊ dia n-anmannaib ⁊ do aéssaib in domuin ⁊ do numir cacha aésse.

2. Do réir int Septín in so.,

(1) Cétna-amser bethad bind
ó thús domuin co dílinn;
dá cét cethracha imma-lle,
dá bliadain is dá míle.

(2) Is d'aés tánaissi, ní tár,
ó dílinn co Abrahám;
noí cét, ó chianaib, is cet,
dá bliadain is dá fichet.

(3) Ochtmoga bliadan co mblaid,
fiche bliadan do bliadnaib,
cét ar thrí mílib na-mán,
ón chétchrut[h]ad co Abrám.

(4) Ó Abrám co Tempul ṅDé
noí cét bliadan, buan in ré.
Do réir riagla is lór a fat,
cethri bliadna ochtmogat.

(5) Atát cóic bliadna is cóic [c]ét
ó Abrám, ní himmarbréc,
cor' dluiged Muir Romuir ruad
ria Moíse cona mórṡluag.

(6) Ó Moísi co Tempul trén,
cethri chét bliadan at-bér;
a noé sechtmogat fri sein —
is ceirtidde in chomáirim.

---

1. R C KM] 1 INcipit panecte. Tunnscnaid na sencaide neolach *C* 2 for penacte, *with* Cirine *om. C* tre Gaeilg *C* sís *om. C* 3 c. c. claenda Nae *C* 4 in uile cenealaib in domhain ⁊ do nuimir bliadan na naes *C* 5 De randaibh clainde Nae fo in domhan uili arceana, *with* dia n-anmannaib – aésse *om. C.*
2. R KM] 21 moṙsluag *(sic) R* 25 ceirtidde] -de *subpuncted re KM.*

(7) A cúic sechtmogat, trí chét,
ó ro-toglad Troé na trét;
iar n-aís Moíse, iarair lat,
in chúiced bliadain tríchat.

(8) Trícha ocus cethri bliadna
ar ocht cétaib coémriagla,
ó Abrám co togail Troé,
cen imroll, cen immargoé.

(9) Ó ro-toglad Troé na tor
coro-chumtaiged Tempol,
do bliadnaib, ní saéb in sét,
oénc[h]oéca ar oén fri oénchét., Cétna.,

3. Debi na Fírinni Ébraide frisin Sechtmogait Tintúdach in so sís.,

(1) Cétaimmser in bethad bind,
óthá Ádam co dílinn,
sé bliadna coícat, rád ṅglé,
ar sé cétaib ar míle.

(2) INd aimser thánaisse trán,
ó dílinn co Abarám,
a dó nóchat, guth ṅgluair ṅgrinn,
ar dá cét ṁbliadan ṁbláithbind.

(3) IN tress amser, fég co fír,
óthá Abrám co Dauíd;
a dó cethrachat, cen ail,
ar noí cétaib do bliadnaib.

(4) IN chethramad chubaid chóir,
ó ṡhain co brait ṁBabilóin;
trí bliadna sechtmogat sain
ar chethri cétaib coémaib.,

(5) IN chúiced ón brait bláith bil
co gein Meic Dé i mBethil;
a noé ochtmogat fil ann
ar cóic cétaib cain cumaṅg.

---

3. R G KM] 2 cedna aimsear beathadh bind *G* [= §2. 2] 3 ota *G* 6 In aimsear tanaisdi thran *G* 7 oda *G* 8 gluair grind *G* 11 o Abaram *G* Daibhith *G* 14 cethramad cubaidh coir *G* 15 ṡhain *linked to* Dauíd (11) *by construe mark R* braith *KM note* 19 maic *KM* 21 .cccc. *G* 23 laithi mbratha

(6) INt sessed ó gein Críst chóir
co lathe brátha bágmóir;
ní fitir nech acht Dia dil
cid bias isind aimsir-sin.

(7) INt sechtmad, is gním glan glé,
i comsíniud friu huile;
ó Abél, fír[ḟ]ial a dath,
cosin fírian ṅdédenach.

(8) INd ochtmad ó ṡhain imach,
is í-side int sírsaéglach.
Innisimm, is ní bréc dam,
ná bia crích ar a cétmad. Cétaimmser.,

(9) Críst ar cara ro-chaín cess,
Críst, co rala frim arddless!
[Críst] ron-cuinnig ó chéin chain,
Críst, ar cuinnid iar cétaib.
Cétaimser in bethad binn.,

4a. ⟨[*Sex sunt aetates hominis.,*]
Prima aetas hominis infantia, in septem annis finitur. Secunda pueritia, usque ad quartum decimum annum. Tertia adolescentia, usque ad uiginti octo annos. Quarta iuuentus, usque ad quinquagesimum annum. Quinta senio, a quinquagesimo anno usque ad septuagesimum annum. Sexta senectus, quae nullo annorum tempore finitur. Senium uero pars ultima senectutis.,⟩

4. *SEX AETATES SUNT MUNDI, id est* ó Ádam co dílinn in chétna-aés. Ó dílinn co Abrám ind aés tánaisi. Ó Abrám co Dauíd in tres aés. Ó Dauíd co brait ṁBabilóne in chethramad aés. Ó brait co Críst in chóiced aés. Ó Críst co bráth int [s]essed aés., Ó Abél mac Ádaim co martra hEle ⁊ Enóc fri bruinni ṁbrátha int sechtmad aés. Ó bráth immach ⁊ lathi brátha fodeissin ind ochtmad aés, *ut supra diximus.,*

---

mbithchoir *G* 26 o Aibial *G* 27 o mac Adaim teachnair (?) *G* 28 lia rin amser o shen amach (?) *G* 30 Agus laithe bratha buan *G* 31 ni rofitir gach roshluagh G 32 isi sen in tochtmad oll *G* 33 romsaera ara rochomlond *G* 34 rochan *G* 35 durala agun airleas *G* 36 rochuindingh o chliú *G* 38 Cedna *G*.

4a. R] *Opening, and some words in marg. supra, damaged by binder; see Commentary.*

4. R P C] 1 sunt aetates *C* 2 cet *C* in taes taniste *C* Dabith *C* 3 cethramad *P* ceathram/adh/ *C* 4 Crit *(sic) C* coidedh *(sic) P* O Christ *P* Crit *(2°) C* ó Abél – diximus (7) *om. C* 6 laithiu *P* ut s. d. *om. P*.

5. IS fissi cia lín bliadan techtas cech aés cenmothá in n-aés ṅdédenaig, ar ní fil crích furri hi lleth frinni chétus. *Et* cateat airig cecha aíssi ⁊ cadeat a saégla na n-airech-sin? *Et* ciaso aés dona haéssaib sin inro-rannad in domun hi trí ⁊ cateat anmann na rann-sin ⁊ can assaro-gabsat anmann.,

6. Cinnas ro-gablaigset clanna Noé, *et* cia lín cenél n-écsamail i tarrasatar? *Et* cia lín bérla techtait, ⁊ cid arro-imdaigthe na bérlai, ar is oénbérla fo-gabam díb ar thús .i. Gairthigern a ainm in bérlae-sin .i. bérla frisin n-apar bérla na nÉbraide indiu, *ut poeta dicit.,*

7. (1) Gairthigern ainm in bérlai
ro-buí ic Mac Dé[a] dagṡegdai
ocus oc síl Ádaim huair
ria cumtuch in Tuir Nebruaid.

(2) Caro-llen bérla nEbra
ic lucht in domuin delbda,
hed bas ainm iar ṁbráth na ṁbern
don bérlu gnáth: Gairthigern. Gairthigern.,

a) .i. oc Ádam

8. Ocus cia aimser inro-imdaigthe na bérlai? Ocus innat lia na cenéla oldát na bérlae? Cia lín cenél ⁊ citni cenéla ná fuillet numir cenél acht a ṅgabáil i fothechdas na cenél ata coibniusda dóib? Cia lín cenél ⁊ citni cenéla ro-claémchaset anmann sech a cétairec?

9. IS sé seo lín bliadan fil isin chétna aís cétamus .i. sé bliadna coícat ar sé cét ar míle. Ádam dano cétna-aire na haéssi-sein. IS fissi hi sunn cia lín do chlainn ro-thusmistar Ádam. Ní annsa: coíca mac ⁊ coíca

---

5. R P C] 1 fissca *C* bliadan] br *written first*, r *eras.*, .i. bliadan *add. supralin. R* mblia- *C* techtus *P* gach aes dibh *C* 2 deidenach *C* crich airithi fuirr seine *C* frinni *on* friuni ? *R* cetus *P* caidhe iat airichch *(sic) C* 3 caidhe saeghal *C* cach hoirigh dibh *C* cia haes *C* 4 ina randadh *C* a tri randaibh *C* doman *P* caidhe *C* 5 a nanmanda *(2°) C*.
6. R P C] 1 rogabhsat *C* cenél: gñ *R hic et passim* ceneal *C* 2 tarrastar *C* bertla *(sic) C* roteachtsat *C* ra- *P* cia lin mblia- roteachtsat a cemenda *add. C* ar rohimtaigtea *C* 3 rofhoghain daibh *C* Gairtighernd *C* .i. bérla *om. C* 4 risa nabhar in *C* Abhraidhe *C* amail isbert in file *C*.
7. R P C Ld] 1 Garthigern *Ld* Gartighernd *C* 2 roboi *Ld* dobai *C* daighergna *P* 3 uair *Ld C* 4 re ndenam *C* ccumtach *P* cumtach *Ld* an tur *P* Nemruaid *Ld* Neamhruaidh *C* 5 Cia *P Ld C* rolen *Ld* rolin *C* 6 o lucht *Ld* 7 ed *Ld* eadh *C* na mbenn *Ld* na meand *C* 8 berlae *P* berla *Ld* graith *C* Gartigern *(1°) Ld* Gartighearnd *C*.
8. R P C] 1 Et (1°) *C* imdaightea *C* anait anait *(sic) C* 2 berladha *C* caidhe iat *C* fuillet in nuimir *P* a nuimir na cenel *C* 3 fchtes *(sic) C* at comneasa *C* ciada *C* 4 -caemchlaset *P* -claechmotseat *C* a nanmanda *C* airech *C*.
9. R P C G] 1 Is sé – na haéssi-sein *(2) om. G* cetna *P* cet *C* cetus *C*

ingen, amal do-fedat stairscríbnidi na Román. Acht ní áirim Cirini acht triur do macaib Ádaim .i. Caín, Abél, Séth. Mad iar n-arailib senchaidib *hautem,* is lia clann Ádaim *quam* ind numir at-chuadammar do macaib chétus, ar it hé in so a n-anmann.,

10.	Caín	Abilón	Orth	Feth	Naath
	Abél	Sarath	Eth	Gusmus	Narchon
	Séth	Saliath	Horam	Nemath	Heth
	Cám	Silith	Gad	Pan	Ceth
	Camur	Séig	Tigri	Peor	Silath
	Cumul	Gismus	Teo	Pennán	Sile.,
	IUdas	Gessmus	Thul	Alluriath	
	IUdas	Lagor	Pin	Mediath	*De quibus*
	Leui	Ligor	Pille	HÁm	*poeta dicit.,*
	Ubull	Liuiath	Fomor	Balad	
	Aboll	Lón	Fór	Borad	

11. (1) Ádam ocus Eua án,
coa mbaí in maicne chaém chomlán;
coéca lín a mac sunn sain,
dias ar choícait d'ingenaib.

(2) Caín, Abél, Séth, ní saéb,
Cám, Camur, Cumul cnesschoém.
Iudas, Iudas, Leui lór,
Ubul, Abol, Abilón.

(3) Sarath, Saliath, Silith, Séig,
Gismus, Gesmus co nglanchéill.
Lagor, Ligor, Liuiath, Lón,
Orth, Heth, Oram, Gad glanmór.

(4) Fomor, Fór, Feth, Gusmus glé,
Tigri, Teo, Thul, Pin, Pille.

.ui. b. l. ar .dc. ar .i. *R* .ii. b. xl. ar .cc. ar .iim. *P* ui. blia- .l. ar da .c. ar mile *C*, *which add. verse:* O Adhamh co dilind a ngenair iar setaibh .ui. blia- .l. ar da .c. milibh aireach *C* na haimsire *C* 3 do clainn *P* -thusmiustair *P* do tuismestar *G* rotuismeadh *C* 4 -fetat *P* indisid *C* adfedat *G* scribindeadha *C* ni tachmaigheand canoin *C* 5 Caidhin *C* Ma *G* 6 na deigheolcaibh *C* hautem *om. C* quam] inas *C* ind numir *om. C* in uimir *G* anubhramhar *C* 7 do macaib chétus *om. C* cetus *P* anmanda clainde Adhaimh *C.*

10. R P C G] 1 Abiuth *C* Nath *C* 2 Gusmus *om., but add. after* Gessmus *C* 5 Cammur *P* Peor, Pennan *reversed C* 6 Pennan *add. supralin. G* 7 Gesmus *P* Alluriath, Ham *reversed C* 8 Medbh *C* De quibus – dicit (9) *om. P* decibus feota dicit *G* 10 Balad, Borad *reversed G.*

11. R P C] 1 Eba *C* 2 combui *P* mbi *C* caem comlan *C* 5 Aibhel *C* 7 Idas *(2°) C* 8 Ubull Aboll *P* 9 Sarrath Sabiath *C* 12 Gadh *(bis) C*

Alluriath, Mediath, is Hám,
Nemath, Pan, Peör, Pennán.

(5) Heth, Ceth, Silath, Sile slóg,
Balad, Borad, Naath, Nachor.
Cianos-labram tiar is tair
'siat-sain anmann mac nÁdaim. Ádaim.,

⟨*Hironimus: Tot filii Adae quot sunt dominici dies in anno, id est .lii. Tot filiae Adae quot sunt lingae, id est .lxxii.,*⟩

12. Ocus níro-clannaigset acht triur dona maccaib *tantum:* Caín, Séth, Sile .i. sóssar mac nÁdaim secip cruth. It hé seo a trí mná, ⁊ trí ingena dano do Ádam iat-side .i. Pip ben Chaín, Olla ben Séth, Pithib ben Sile.

13. *Adam primus pater fuit* ⁊ *Eua prima mater fuit.,*
Caín dano a prímgeinni, ⁊ is leis cétna-ro-chumtacht cathir .i. Enocham *ciuitas*. Ocus do-rat in n-ainm sin fuirri ó anmaimm a meic prímgeinni .i. Enóch a ainm-side, ⁊ is leis do-rigned cétar ⁊ cétbuain.

Abél immorro, in mac tánaisi do Ádam, is hé-side in cétna-fírian ⁊ in cétna-martír ro-buí do síl Ádaim. Laméch ⟨.i. *bigamus*⟩ mac Mathusaél meic Manuel meic Hirad meic Enóch meic Caín meic Ádaim, is hé-sin toísech tuc dá mnaí .i. Adda ⁊ Sella, *ut Hironimus dicit* ic tráchtad for Geneiss rechta.

Ruc dano Adda dá mac do Lamiach: IAbal ainm in chétmeic ⁊ is hé-side ro-chlecht ar thús buachaillecht ⁊ bith hi fássaigib la hindilib. IUbal in mac aile, is é-sside toísech ro-clecht cruit ⁊ orgán.

Ruc dano Sella mac aili don Lamiach cétna .i. Tubal Cain a ainm-side. Rop hé-side in cétgoba ⁊ in cétcherd ⁊ in cétsaér. Ocus ruc Sella ingin *post* .i. Nemma, siur Tubail Cain. Enóch mac Iaréth, di clannaib Séth, is é cétna-litterda ro-buí riam.,

---

15 Am *C* 18 Natha *C* 20 siatt *P* Adam *(2°) P* 21 Hironimus] *Haec omnia om. C.*

12. R P C] 1 -clannuigset *P* nír clandaighseat *C* triur dibh ina ama *(sic) C* tantum *om. C* 2 sosar na clainde *C* faidhein *add. C after* mná 3 Pib *C construe marks connecting* ben (Chaín) *with* b. (Séth) *and* b. (Sile) 4 ⁊ Sile sosar na mac sin *add. C* [= §10. 6].

13. R P C] 1 cetmathair na nuile *C* 2 -geine *C* -cumdaigedh *C* 3 Enocham ciuitas *om. C* ciuitatem *R* anmun *C* 4 leis *linked to* Caín (2) *by construe-mark R* is la Cain beus *P* -raineadh *C* 5 Abel mc̄ in mc̄ *R* A. in mac *P* i sidhein cetfhiren *C*, *with* ⁊ cetsacart ⁊ cethogh *add. after* martír ⁊ Mathusalem *P* 7 meic Manuel – Ádaim *om. C* Hiarad *P* do claind Cain *add. after* Matha sael *C* 8 toisiuch *P* ut Hironimus d. – rechta *om. C* 10 Eadha *C* 11 -clecht ar tus *P* toiseach rocleacht *C*, *with* thús *om.* beith *C* 12 mac tanaisti *C* 13 Lamhfhiach *C* Tubal Chain *P* 15 iar sin *C* Tubal Chain *P* Iared *P* 16 cet *C*.

14. Is iat-so airig na cétna-aéssi cona saéglaib, iar Séth chétus.,

Saégul Ádam acccc.xxx Saégul Enos acccc.u.
Saégul Séth ac.xii. Saégul Malalel acccc.
Saégul Cainán acccc.x. Saégul Enóch accc.lxu.
Saégul IAréth acccc.lxu. Saégul Laméch, acclxxuii
Saégul Mathusálem accccIxix *id est pater Noe.*

15. Cestnaigit araili hi sunn do chomsaégul Mathusálem immale fri Ádam ⁊ d'éis Ádaim co dílind ⁊ do chomsaégul Sém meic Noé la Mathusálem., Teora bliadna cethrachat ar díb cétaib do Mathusálem hi comaimsir fri Ádam. Sé bliadna fichet ar secht cétaib dó dar éis Ádaim co dílind. Noí [bliadna] sescat ar noí cétaib a saégul uli. Ocht bliadna nóchat do Sém mac Noé *hautem* i comamsir fri Mathusálem. Dá bliadain ⁊ cóic cét do Sém *post diluuium.,*

16. *De Mathusalem ⁊ de Sém hoc carmen.,*

(1) Teora bliadna cona mblaid,
cethrachat ar díb cétaib
baí Mathusálem gaéth glan,
i comaimsir fri Ádam.

(2) Sé bliadna fichet, fír sain,
ar secht cét do chainbliadnaib
co dílind dó 'na bethaid
dar éis Ádaim ḟírbrethaig.

(3) Noí ṁbliadna sescat iar sain
ocus noí cét do bliadnaib,
rob hé-sain huile cen fell
saégul maith Mathusálem.

(4) Ocht ṁbliadna nóchat, nír bḟann,
baé Sém mac Noé na niamclann
i comaimsir cen nach ṁbrath
fri Mathusálem saéglach.

---

14. R P C] 1 aireach na cetaisi *C* cona a *(sic) C* chétus *om. C* 2 saégul] s. *passim R, om. passim P, add. after numl. passim C* dccccxxx *(1°)*, dcccc.u. *(2°) P* 3 dc.xii *(1°)*, d ccc.xc./at/ .u. *(2°) P* 4 dcccc. x. *(1°)*, ccc.lxu. *(2°), with something eras. before 1st digit P* 5 d cccc lxii *(1°)*, .dcc. lxx.uii. *(2°) P* 6 d cccc .lx. ix. *(1°) P* id est pater Noe *om. C.*

15. R P] 4 secht cétaib] .acc. /aib/ *R* 5 Acccc.lxix. a.s.u. *R* .dcccclx.ix a saeghul uile *P* 6 Mathusalam *P* 7 diluium *P.*

16. R P] 2 brig co mblaid *P* 11 ⁊ no cet *R* et *P* 15 bui *P* 18 D.b. ⁊ .ccccc. *R* D. b. et .cccc. *(sic) P* 20 cen terbrud *P.*

(5) Dá bliadain ar cóic cét cain
ro-baé Sém mac Noé nertglain
ce[n] terbrud fo rethaib renn,
'na bethaid d'éis na dílenn.

(6) Críst ro-chum in domun ṅdúr,
cen homun is cen imthnúd,
co rísiur nem niamda hi-tá,
iar testugud na teora! Teora.,

17. Ro-forcoṅgair Dia trá for clannaib Séth náro-chummascdais fri clanna Caín ⁊ náro-clannaigdis friu ⁊ ná tucdais mná díb. Tarmideochatar dano clanna Séth in forcital-sin ⁊ tucsat ingena clainni Caín, ar ba mór a caémi, ⁊ ro-clannaigset friu dar sárgud Dé. Conid de-sin ro-geinset torothuir in domuin .i. fomoraig ⁊ luchorpáin ⁊ cech n-écosc torothorda ṅdodelbda ro-buí for doínib.

Ót-chonnairc Dia *hautem* tíctain dóib dar a thimna ro-chinnistar na doíni do huili-dilgenn, conid [d]ó tucad in díliu darsin domun, do bád[ud] clainni Caín.

18. Ó thucad didiu in díliu ro-báid na huili doíni ⁊ indili acht Noé cona tríb maccaib ⁊ cona cethrib mnáib, ar is hé int oénḟírén fríth do clannaib Séth cen chummasc fri clanna Caín. Conid hé-sin fescor na haéssi-sin, ar ro-baé matan ⁊ fescor cacha haéssi.

Cethracha lá ⁊ cethracha aidchi ro-buí in díliu ic ferthain. Coíca ar cét lá ro-baé cen sergcud, conid annsin tuc Dia na gaétha do súgud na n-usce.

19. Cestnaigthir *hic* do thomus ⁊ do figuir ⁊ do eterchert na háircce: *Arca graece, Secreta latine interpretatur* .i. deirrit. *Longuitudo hautem árcae perseuerantiam perfectionis significat* .i. feidligthetu na fuirbthitad tóirnes a fat. *Latitudo eius latitudinem caritatis significat* .i. forleithi na deiṡeirce tóirnes a lethet. *Altitudo eius altitudinem spei significat* .i. arddi ⁊ áithi na freiscisen fil ó duini co Dia tóirnes a hailt .i. a hairddi,

---

17. R P C] 1 tra Dia *C* narachummasctais for *P* nara cumaiscdais fria clandaibh *C* 2 nara- *P* 3 nir dechadar *C* forcétul *C* 4 ba leor *C* a chaemi *R* et ra- *P* 5 -genedar *C*, *with* torothuir – .i. *om.* lubprucain *C* cach *C* 6 dodelbda *om. C* -bai *C* 7 im̄ *C* tichtain *P* tiachtain *C* tara a *(sic) C* -chinniustair *P* -cindestar *C* 8 na daine uile do dilgeand *C* conid o *P* 9 do badad *P* baghadh *C*.

18. R P C] 1 do baidheadh *C*, *with* indili *om.* tucad *P* díliu] in dili *P* -u *eras.* (?) *R* 2 tri mnaib *P* a tri hingeanaibh *C* -firian *P* ase Nae aenfhirenach *C* 4 dobai maitan ⁊ sescor in gach aes dibh *C* c̄ahaaessi, *with 2nd* -a- *sublin. R* 5 roba *C* 6 seargadh *C* gaeth *C*, *with* na *om.* sugad *P* ⁊ na nuisceand *C*.

19. R P] 3 árcae *linked to* eius (4, 5) *by construe-mark R* feidligthetu] *on* fu- *R* 9 tóirnes *om. P*.

id est unum cubitum, id est, uniuersalem catholicam fidem significat .i. oénchubat a hairdi .i. oéndatu ⁊ huilidetu inna hirsi catholicda fon huili ṅdomun tóirnes in sin.

20. *Interrogatio hic.,* Cia haés ésci ⁊ cia lathi sechtmaine ⁊ cia lathi mís gréne do-chuas isind áirc ⁊ tícht essi? Ocus cia bliadain, hi commun nó i n-emblesim? Ní annsa: hi sechtmaid fichet ⟨.i. Maii⟩ do-chuas inti ⁊ tícht essi, ⁊ is sí tarrasair for Sléib Arméniae. *Terticim Kalendas* Iúin do-chuas inti ⁊ sechtmad id Maii tícht essi, ar aí lathi mís gréne. Can asa thucthar sin? Ní annsa: ar is oénlathi déc fil etir sechtmad id ⁊ *treticim,* ⁊ iss ed ón beres bliadain gréne do bliadain éscae, ar it cethri lathi coícat ⟨.i. ar tríb cétaib⟩ [fil] i ssuidiu ⁊ is ed ón fil etir *treticim* ⁊ sechtmad id hi cind bliadna.

Oéndiden *hautem* do-chuas inti. Can asa tucthar sin? Ní annsa: ar is i n-oéndiden tarmthecht Ádaim. Cubaid dano ciambad inti natíssed dígal forsin ṁbith. Cest: cia lathi sechtmaine tícht essi? Ní annsa: .i. Mairt. Can asa tucthar sin? Ní annsa: ar is hi *treticim kalendarum* Iúin do-chuas inti. Secht lá déc ⁊ bliadain de-side ro-buí Noé 'sind áirc. Hi sechtmaid déc dano mís Maii ro-thinscan in díliu ferthain. Sé cét bliadan dano aés Noé tan tánic in díliu.,

Cethrur dano i[s] siniu aés adid-fét in Scriptúir i sund, is cui[n]dtesta.,

21. *De Adam ⁊ de Iareth, de Mathusalem ⁊ de Noe hoc carmen instruitur.,*

(1) Mathusálem, Noé cen lén,
Ádam ocus Iäréth,
cethrur sain cen bini ṁbróin
hi[s] sine ad-fét in Chanóin.

(2) Trícha, noí cét do Ádam,
is ed ad-fét co grádmar;
coíca, noí cét, caín in fiach,
ro-chaith Nöé mac Lamiach.

(3) Sesca, noí cét, dá bliadain,
má beith nech fora iarair,
ar cach taidbsine ní chél,
forair aimsire Iaréth.

---

20. R P C] 1 Interr. hic *om. P* 2 Ocus] ⁊ *abbrev. R* Ocus – i n-emblesim *om. P* 3 sechmaid *(sic)* .xx. et, *gl.* .i. Mai *P* 4 ⁊ tícht essi *om. P* 8 coícat (.l.) *gl.* .i. ar trib cetaib *P* 13 is *om. P* 14 conid .xuii. laa *C* -bai *C* 16 Secht mbli- dano roba slan do Noe *C* in tan *C* darin ndomhan *add. after* díliu *C* 17 Cethrur – cuindesta *om. C* i siniu *P*.

21. R P] 1 ⁊ *(1°) om. P* Mathusalam *P* 6 his sini atfet *P* 7 Tricha /a/ n.c. *P* 11 do bliadnaib *R* da bliadain *P*

(4) Noí ṁbliadna sescat, noí cét,
ní gó do neoch adid-fét,
ní baégul a rád co tenn,
saégul sen-Mathusálem. Mathusálem.,

22. *De secunda aetate incipit.,* INd aés tánaisi dano hit dá bliadain nóchat ar díb cétaib fil inti. Noé dano is hé cétna-hairi na haéssi-sein. ⟨*Noe primum altare fecit post diluuium.,*⟩ Coíca ar tríb cétaib bliadan ro-baé Noé i mbethaid iar ṅdílinn, conid coíca ar noí cétaib a aés uili.,

23. Ro-bennach Dia do Noé cona maccaib ⁊ at-bert friu: "Forbrid ⁊ imdaigid ⁊ línaid in talmain ⁊ benfat-sa mo chardes immole frib ⁊ ní thibér dílinn iarmothá darsin ṅdomun cotici in crích coitchinn. Do-bér dano comartha mo charaitraid dúib isin nem ⁊ in céin at-chichestar in comartha sin ní bia scichlim ná forba for clannaib Noé. IS sé in so immorro in comarda .i. sámaigfet mo ḟidbocc isin nem" .i. tuag nimi, conid hé-sin senchas na tuagi nimi .i. a tabairt do chomarthu do clannaib Noé iar ṅdílind hi comarthu a n-oéntad fri Dia i céin at-chichestar i[n] stuag nime. Conid follus de-side ná rabi in stuag nime ria ndílinn.

24. Do clannaib Noé in so sís.

Ro-thuisim Noé trí macu ria ndílinn, conid uadib-side génatar na dá cenél sechtmogat iar ṅdílinn. IS amlaid so *hautem* ro-sílsat na cenéla .i. secht cenéla fichet díb ó Ṡém, trícha immorro ó Chám, a cóic déc ó Iaféth; conid dá cenél sechtmogat sin uli ⁊ conid dá bérla sechtmogat tuctha dóib *post* ic tairmesc in Tuir Nemruaid. Conid hi cind deich ṁbliadan iar tain ro-thepestar Foénius Forsaid bérla na ṅGoédel asna díb bérlaib sechtmogat, coro-taselb dia daltu, do mac Agnomain.

ISs ed ro-imdaig *hautem* numir na cenél sech numir na mbérla: ar itát isind Affraic ilchenéla im oénbérla ⁊ iss ed fot-era sein, ná rabatar acht dá cenél sechtmogat tall in tan ro-imdaigthe na bérlai

---

22. R P C] 1 De sa *(sic)* etate nacipit *(sic) C* hit *om. C* .i. o dilind co hAbraham .942. *add. manu recentiori P* 2 ar .cc. *R* ar .dcccc. *P* fil inti *om. C, but adds:* O dilind co hAbramh a ngenair iar setaibh. da blia- bailc tochat nochat *(sic)* ar dibh .c.aibh aireach *C* na haimsire *C* 3 et is lais doronad altoir cetus ier ndilind *P* .l. ar .cccc. aib *R P* 4 robui *P*.

23. R P C] 1 cona tri maccaib *C* F. ⁊ imdagudadh ⁊ in talamh do linadh *C* 2 bainfead *C* amaille *C* 3 nocho tiber *C* iarmothá *om. C* cotici *om. C* caich *add. after* coitchend *C* 4 -cithear *C* 5 scithlim *C* for bar clannaib co brach *C* 6 saithfeat *C* 8 combia Dia ina naentaid friu *add. after* dílind *C* 8–9 aireat athcithear *C* 9 istuag nimi *P* na raibi *P* nocha raibe de side *C* in tuag nimi *P* 10 re nidind *(sic) C*.

24. R P C] 1 De *C* andso, *with* sís *om. C* 2 uatha sin *C* rogeineatar *P* rogenedar *C* 5 ó Iaféth] o *supralin. R* .u. dec do cenelaibh dIafeth *C* da blia- *(sic) C* 6 post] iar sin *C* Nembroth *P* Nemhrun *C* 7 iar sin *C* Fenius Forsaidh *C* 9 do Gaedeal *add. after* mac Agnomain *C* 10 Ro haimdaigheatar

⁊ ciaro-imdaigset na cenéla *post* ní tharta i n-áirim cenél n-écsamail acht a lécud hi fothechdas na cenél n-aile ata coibniusta dóib; condat lia na cenéla iar tothucht indáit na bérlae, cian combat lia iar numir; ar ciaro-bátar ocht meic ic Iaféth, acht ciniud trí mac díb ní thabair in numir na cenél.

Ocus cia ainmnigtir sé meic ic Sém, ní thabair in árim acht ciniud dá mac díb *tantum*. Ocus cia ainmnigtir cethri meic ic Cám, ní áirim[thir] acht ciniud trí mac díb; ocus ní amlaid bátar na meic aile uili cen genimain uadaib, acht níro-génair uaidib ní armad diṅgbála sluind ceníuil do thabairt. *Et* is amlaid bas follus sein dia n-innister cech mac do Noé fo leith, cona clannaib, for oénlíne uili.,

25. Do clannaib Iaféth meic Noé in so sís.,

IAFéth didiu et Olibana a ben, ro-thechtaiset ocht maccu.,

.i. Gomér
Magoch
Madue
IaUban
Tubal
Masoch
Tiaras
Masseca

Gomér is uad ataat Galatacdai ⁊ is inunn iat-side ⁊ Galli. A ainm aili dóib Gallogréci. Magoch, is uad atát Scithecdai. Madai, *a quo Medi.* Iaban, *a quo Ioni sunt* ⁊ *a quibus nominatur Ionicum mare,* ⁊ is uadib ro-génatar Eolldai ⁊ *a quibus nominantur Iolici* ⁊ is uaidib ainmnigthir in cúiced bérla na Gréci .i. bérla Eolla. Tubal, *a quo sunt* Hiberdai ⁊ Hespannai ⁊ Celtiberdai., Masoch, is uad Capadocdai. Tiaras, *a quo* Traicecdai., ⁊ *septem filios habuit*. Clanna Gomér meic Iaféth .i. Ascenez *filius* Gomér, *a quo sunt Régini.* Eripham *filius* Gomér, *a quo Paplagoni*—cenél doíni filet i slébib Riphi, *qui et Colchi sunt.* Togorma *filius* Gomér, átát na Frigitae. Trí meic sin Gomér meic Iaféth.

Dá mac Magoch meic Iaféth meic Noé .i. Baath ⁊ Íbath. Mac don Baath Foénius Forsaid, *a quo sunt Scithi* ⁊ *Gothi*. Foénius Forsaid didiu mac Baath meic Magoch meic Iaféth meic Noé, *et reliqua.* Íbath dano, in mac aili do Magoch, mac dó-side Elonius nó Alanius. Trí

C hautem *om. C* 12 ni ribhatar *C* no himdaigtea *(1°) C* -himdaigtea *(2°) C* 13 in aiream i cenel *C* 14 is comhneasa *C* 15 berladha *C* 16 acht ciniud no m̄c *(sic) P* cineadh *C* díb *om. C* 18 ainmnightar *P* ainmnigtear *C* .u. meic *C* ni tabhar aireamh *C* 19 nama *C* ainmnigter tri *C* 19–20 ni airimthir *P* ni tabhar in aireamh *C* ocus] et *P* da mac *C* 21 uaithigh *C* uaithibh *C* 22 ainm cenel *C* dia nainmnigter *C* 23 cach mac do macaibh Noe *C* uili *om. C.*

25. R P U* C] 1 meic Noé in so sís *om. P* De claind Iafeth meic Noe no iarna fir *C* 2 -techtsat *C* mc̄a *P* 3 Gomer, Maghog, Madai, *etc. in long lines C* Talatacdai *C* 4 A *om. C* 5 Madai *gl.* nó ue (i.e. nó Madue) *R* Madue *P* is uada atait Medhi *C* Iauan *C* is uadha atait Ionnai, *gl.* on ainm in Muir Ionnai *C* 6 Ionicum mare *R* Ionic- marae *P* Eolldai *linked to* uaidib (7) *by construe-mark R* 7 is uaithib ainmniter *C* 8 is uada atait *C* 10 Thires *C* 11 ⁊ septem – habuit *om. C* 12 filius Gomer *om. (bis) C* Regni *P* otat Regini *C* 13 cenél – sunt (14) *om. C* 14 Togorma] *LU begins here* filius Gomer *om. U C* otát Frigiae *U* 16 Magog *U* 17 Baath mac do side *U* B. mac do sein *C* Fenius *U C* Scithecda *U* athair na Sceithecdai *C* Forsaid *om. U C* 18 Baaith *C* Ibad *U* 19 nó Alanius *om. C* 21 Gebidus *C* meic aca-side .i. Armon, Negua, Hissicón. Cóic meic ic Armon .i. Gothus, Uolegothus, Cebidus, Bargandus, Longobardus. Negua dano trí meic leis .i. Uandalus, Saxus, Bogardus. Hissicón dano cethri meic aice .i. Francus, Romanus, Albanus, .i. ótá ind Albain airtherach isind Assia móir., Britus, ó ráter inis Bretan.

26. IS annsin ro-rannad in domun i tríb rannaib .i. Eoraip, Affraic, Assia. Sém i nAssia, Cám i nAffraic, Iaféth i [n]Eoraip. Ocus is hé cétfer do síl Iaféth tánic i nEoraip .i. Alanius mac Íbaith meic Magoch meic Iaféth meic Noé. IS amlaid tánic Alanius ⁊ a trí meic leis .i. Armon ⁊ Negua ⁊ Hisicón, conid hi fus ro-clannaigset na meic at-chuadammar.

Saxus mac Negua meic Alani meic Íbath meic Magoch meic Iaféth meic Noé, is uad atát Saxain. IAban dano mac Iaféth meic Noé, cethri meic aca-side .i. Elisa, Tarsis, Cethim, Dodanim. Tarsis, *a quo sunt Tarsi* ⁊ Cilecdai. Cethim, *a quo sunt Cethi,* ⁊ uadib-side ainmnigthir prímchathir na Cipricda .i. *Citheum.* Dodanim dano, uad-side *Rodii* ⁊ is uadib-side ro-fodlait insi in mara Tirritae frisin n-abbarar Muir Toirrén, cona chenélaib écsamlaib ⁊ cona mbérlaib.

27. IS iat-sin cóic prímchenéla déc clainni Iaféth cona fochenélaib. Ro-selbsat sin feranna imdai isind Assia, ó Sléib Imai ⁊ ó Sléib Thúir co sruth Danai ⁊ condici in Scithia; ⁊ ro-selbsat in nEoroip n-uili condici in n-acian muridi funita insi Bretan, ⁊ in nEspáin n-uilidi co huilinn talman.

Do chlannaib Iaféth meic Noé condici so cona prímchenélaib ⁊ cona fochenélaib⁊ cona n̄gablaib ⁊ cona ferannaib etir Assia ⁊ Eoroip. *Finit.,*

28. Do clannaib Cáim meic Noé in so sís hi fecht-sa.,
Cám dano ⁊ Oliua a ben, cethri meic leo .i. Chuss, Futh, Mesrom *et* Channán. Chuss, *a quo sunt Chussi;* Etheopacdai a n-ainm-side indiu.

Burgandus *U C* Longubardus *U* 22 les *U* 23 Albanus *gl.* is uada raiter Albain en Eorpaip *(sic) C* .i. ótá – móir *om. C* Albannai i nAsia *U.*

26. R P U C] 1 and sain *U* dorandad *C* i tri *U* 2 Iafed *U* Iafeth rogab *C* Ocus] Et *P* 3 Alanius *gl.* is uad raiter Alania i nEoraip *U, after* Noé Neua *G* 5 -chlannaigset *U* macau *(sic) C* na macu *R P* 8 atát *om. U C* 10 is uad ⁊ Celtecdai *(sic) U* is uad Cethei *U* ainmnigther *U* ainm caithir *C* 11 cathir na Ciprecda *U* 12 ro- *om. P* frisin nabb-ar *R* inse Mara Torren *U* Torrian *C.*

27. R P U C] 1 .xu. primchenela *R U P* .u. primcenel dec *C* Iaféd *U* 2 sin *om. U C* 3 Tanai *U* cnuice *C* ro ṡelbsat *U* 4 coruice *C* naicen *C* muridi *om. C* fuineta *U* fuineata *C* 4–5 co huilinn talman *om. U C* 6 De *U* co cnuicie sin *C* primgñ, fogñ *R* 6–7 ⁊ cona fochenélaib *om. U* 7 cona ngabalaib *U P* gabhalaib *C* ⁊ a f. *U* Finit *om. U C P.*

28. R P U C] 1 De chlannaub Cam *U* in so – fecht-sa *om. C* 2 *ref. marks under* Chuss, Futh, Mesrom *and et R* Futh, Mesrom *reversed C* et] *sic R* ⁊ *abbrev. U* 3 uad side Chusi *U* uadha sein *C* Ethiopia *U* a haim *(sic)*

Mesrom, *a quo Aegiptus.* ⟨La Mesrom do-rónad altóir *prius* i nAffraic iar ṅdílinn⟩. Futh, uad Affracdai nó Libitai; *Futhei* a n-ainm-side fecht n-aili riam ⁊ is uad ráter sruth Futh.

Cannán, is uad Cannánai; is hé a ferann-side ro-gabsat meic Israhél iar ṅdilgenn ⁊ iar n-inarba na Cannána. Chus mac Cáim, secht meic leis .i. Saba, *a quo Sabei.* Ebila, *a quo Getuli* filet i ndíthreib na Affraice. Sabatha, *a quo Sabatheni* .i. a senainm sin; *Astabari hautem* a n-anmann indiu. Recma, Sabata, Acha, Nebroth. Is leis-side cétna-ro-chumtacht in Babilóin, ar ciaro-chumtaiged la Nín mac ṁBéil iar tain, in tan ro-gab rígi na nAssarda, is la Nebroth cétna-roacht múr Babilóne.,

29. *Babilonia, id est confussio* .i. cummasc, iarsindí ro-cummasctha na bérlae isind luc sin. Sessach *hautem* a ainm cáduis. *Et* is la Nebroth ro-cumtaiged Arach *ciuitas;* ainm aili di Edissa. IS leis ro-cumtacht Achad *ciuitas* ⁊ Cabanna *ciuitas*—is é a ainm-side indiu immorro, *Seleucia, a Seleuco rege* ro-ráded. I mMaig Sennáir ataat sin uli. *Doram* dano ainm aili do Maig Sennáir.

IS do síl Nebroith atát Assardai, iar fairind; nó is do síl Sém meic Noé int Assúr .i. Assúr mac Sém meic Noé. *Et* is ann ro-génair Assúr, i mMaig Sennáir ⁊ is leis ro-cumtacht Ninue *ciuitas* ⁊ Tala ⟨*ciuitas*⟩ ⁊ Resen ⟨*ciuitas*⟩ .i. cathir mór fil etir Ninue ⁊ Tala.

Dá mac ic Recma mac Chuis meic Cáim meic Noé .i. Saba ⁊ Dodam, *a quibus gens Ethiopiae in orientali plaga.* Saba mac Recma *per* SIN *scribitur,* Saba mac Chus *per* SAMECH *scribitur.*

---

side *U* 4 Mesrom – Aegiptus *inserted after* sruth Futh *P* laiside doronad *P* is uadha *C* is uad Egiptus *U* Egipti *C* 5 Futh. is uad *U C* (Fuith) nó Libitai = *gloss U om. C* Fuithe *C* 7 Cannai *P* ferann-side *gl.* ro aittrebh; ro-gabsat *om. P* iar tain *add. after* Israhél *U* iar dain *C* 8 íar dílgend na Cannanna ⁊ iarna n-inarba *U* iar ndilgend na Candanach ⁊ iarna n-indarba *C* .íííí. meic *C* 9 is uad S. *U* is uadh *C* uad side Getuli *U* uadha sein Getule *C* fil *C* i ndithruib *U* i ndithrumaibh *C* na hAfraice *U* 10 a quo S. – Sabatha *add. in marg. with ref. marks P* is uad S. *U* .i. a senainm sin *om. U C* hautem] im̄ *U C* a n-ainm *U* 11 Recina is uadha Sabatha *(sic) C* cétna *om. U C* ro-chumtacht] *sic R* -cumtaiged *U* -cumdaigheadh *C* 12 ar tús *add. after* Babilóin *U* ar *om. U C* -cumtaiged *U P* mac mBel *P* 12–13 in rogabhastar *C* 13 na *om. U C* Asár *U* Assar *C* is la Nebroth – Babilóne *om. U C.*

29. R P U C] 1 id est] I÷ *R* .i. *U C* confussio] *sic R P C* confusio *U* interpretatur *add. after* c., *gl.* combuaidred interpretatur *C* cumasc *U om. C* iarsinní *U om. C* -cumaiscthea *U* -cummosctea *C* 2 Sessach – cáduis *om. U C* caduius *R P* Et] *sic R* ⁊ *abbrev. U C* Neamhrath *C* 3 Arach *gl.* .i. cī *C* ciuitas *om. U C* Edisa *U* ro-cumtacht] *sic R* -cumtaiged *U* -cumtaigeadh *C* ciuitas *(1°) om. U* 4 Achad ciuitas *om. C* Cabann *U* ciuitas *(2°) om. U C* a hainm *U C* immorro *om. U C* a Seluco *P* Feiliuia *C* ond ríg Seleucio *U* cuid righ Sseliu o ro naded *(sic) C* 5 Doram – Sennáir *(2°) om. U C* 6 Sennáir *(1°) linked to* S. *(2°) by construe marks R* 7 Is – .i. (8) *om. P* de *(1°) U* Nemhruaidh *C* atát – fairind *om. C* 8 Asúr tát Asardai *U* de ṡil Séin *(sic) U* mac Séin *(sic) U* Et *om. P* Assúr *om. U P* 9 A. *before* is ann *C* Sennar *U* Senair *C* is leo *C* ro-cumtacht] *sic R* -cumtaiged Ninues *U* -cumdaigedh *C* 10 ciuitas *om. U C* eter *add. betw. cols. U* Tala *and* Resen *gl.* cī *R P* 11 Rema *C* Chuius *R P* Chus *U* Cuis *C* 12 a quibus – plaga *om. U* a quibus –

Clanna Mesrom meic Cáim meic Noé .i. Ludim, Anamim, Labaim, Neptaim, Petrosim, Chesoloim. Is uadaib-sain ro-génatar na Filistindai ⁊ Capturindai ⁊ ciniuda imda aile erili, ⁊ nídat cínte ⁊ nídat derba indiu, ar ro-cloémchoisset attreba ⁊ anmann.,

30. Do clannaib Cannáin meic Cáim meic Noé in so sís iar n-urd.,

Cannán	Sidon ⟨.i. *primogenitus*⟩	Gergessius	Aradius
mac Cáim	Cetheus	Euheus	Samarius
meic Noé,	Iebusseuus	Aracheus	Amatheus,
.xi. meic leis	Amorreus	Sineus	*qui fuit iunior.*

Sidon, is uad ainmnigthir prímchathir na Foénice ⟨.i. Sidon⟩. Aracheus, is leis ro-chumtaiged Arachas .i. cathir fil for agid Tripolim, i fail Slébe Lebain. Aradius, *a quo Aradii,* ⁊ is iat-side ro-selbsat in n-inis dianid ainm Aradum; muncenn cumuṅg eturru ⁊ trácht na Foénice. Samarius, *a quo Samarii,* ⁊ is leis ro-chumtaiged Samair, in c[h]athir. *Finit* de Chám.

31. Do clannaib Sém meic Noé in so sís hi fecht-sa.,
Sém mac Noé, Olla a ben. IS dia síl na hÉbraidi huili. Cóic meic aice .i. Elam ⟨.i. *primogenitus*⟩, Assúr, Arfaxad, Ludim, Saram, Elam, *a quo sunt Elamitae;* toísig Persidis ⁊ Siriae iat-side. Assúr, *a quo sunt* na Assardai iar fír, ⁊ is leis ro-chumtacht Nínue ⁊ Tala ⁊ Resin, *ut supra diximus.* ⟨Assiri *ab* Assúr mac Sém meic Noé. Siria *hautem* ó Assirim

---

scribitur *(2°) om. C* 13 scribthair a ainm *(1°) U* scribthair a ainm side *(2°) U* 14 Mesram *U* Mesraim *C* Luidima *C* Nanñ (*for* Anamin) *C* 15 Nepthaim *U* Neptalim *C* Pethrosim *U* Petnosim *C* Chesloim *U* Cesloim *C* is uad side *C* 16 Capturim *U C* erili *om. U* arceana *C* nitat achinti *U* nidat achindti *C* nídat derba *om. U C* 17 -chloemcoiset *U* do claechloseatar *C* attreba ⁊ *om. U C.*

30. R P U C] 1 De chlannaib Cannan *U* in so sís iar n-urd *om. C* iar n-urd *om. U* 2 Cannán, *etc. in long lines C* Sidon *gl.* .i. primogenitus *R P* primogenitus eius (ə) *C* .i. primogenitus *om. U* Gergesius *U, reversed with* Eutheus Arcadius *U* 3 Chetheus *P* Euceus *C* Samarus *C* 4 Iebuseus *U* Iebusscus *(sic) C* Amatheuus *U* 5 Ies *U* Ammorreuus *U* qui fuit iunior *om. U C* 7 .i. Sidon *add. after* Foénice *P* ainmnigther *U* in chathir .i. Sidon isind Foenici *U* 8 -cumtaiged *P* les ra cumtaiged *U* Arachius *U C* ar agid *U C* 9 slebe Leuain *U* sleibhe Labhain *C* Aratius *C* is uad atat *U* is uadh atait *C* Aradai *U* Arauií *C* 10 in n-innis *U* in n-indsi *C* dian ainm *C* Ardam *C* muinchend *U* munced *(sic) C* 11 na Foénice *illeg. U* iar sin *add. after* Foénice *C* is uad atat Samari *U* otat Samharii *C* -cumtaigeth *P* -cumtaiged *U* Samaria *U, gl.* .i. c. 11–12 in – Chám *om. C* in chathir *P* 12 Finit de Chám *om. U P.*

31. R P U* C* Ld] 1 De *U C* hi fecht-sa *om. U* sís – fecht-sa *om. C* 2 a ben-side *U C* na Ebraide *U* na hAbhraighe *C* uli *U* meic *add. supralin. U* 3 Elam *gl.* .i. primogenitus *R P* primogenitus *om. U* Assúr – Elam *(2°) om. U* Luidhi *C* Alamh *C* 4 is uad E. *U* is uadh atait Elamitea *C* Asur *U* is uad atat Asardai *U* is uadha atat A. *C* 5 na *om. U* Asardai *U* ro-chumtacht] *sic R* -cumtacht *P* -cumtaiged *U* -cumdaighedh *C* Ninues *U* Inuineas *(sic) C* Thala *U* Tala ⁊ /nó/ Siren *(sic) C* ut supra d. *om. U C, with* .i. cathir mor fil eter Ninue ⁊ Thala *add. U* .i. cathair fil itir Ninues ⁊ Tala *C* 6 Assiri – meic mac Daddain meic Iaxain meic Abráim⟩., Arfaxad, is uad atát *Caldei* ⁊ is leis ro-chumtacht ind rígcathir .i. Igbathanis, ⁊ do-rigni a múru do chlochaib cetharochraib. Sechtmoga cubat i n-ailt in múir, trícha a láit. Cét cubat i n-airdde a tor; is í-sin prímchathir Med indiu.

Ludim, *a quo Lidia* ⟨.i. na Liditai ⁊ ro-gabsat na cenéla-sin raind móir isin nAssia óthá sruth nEofrait cosin n-ucht nInnecda ind aceoin móir ocind orint airtheraig⟩., Saram, is uad atá Siria. Is í ardchathir na Siria, Damaisc. Arfaxad mac Sém meic Noé, mac dó-side Sala. Mac do Sala Éber; is uad-side ainmnigter Ébraidi .i. ó Éber mac Sala meic Arfaxad meic Sém meic Noé. Dá mac ic Éber .i. Fallec ⁊ Iactan. Fallec .i. *diuisio,* ar is 'na aimsir ra-fodlait na bérlai.,

32. IAchtan mac Éber meic Sala, trí meicc déc oca, *ut numerantur.,*

Elmodad
Saleph
Asarmoth
IAre
Aduram
Aduzal
Decla
Ebal
Abimel
Saba
Ofir
Euila
IObab

Ataat cethri [cenéla] sescat dia síl-sain isind India ⁊ is iat ro-gabsat huili-ferann na hIndia ⁊ araill mór dind Assia .i. óthá sruth nEofrait aniar conici in n-acian n-airtherach. Clanna Saram meic Séim meic Noé .i. Us, is uad atát Traconitidi ⁊ is leis ro-chumtaiged in Damaisc; etir Palestina ⁊ Coél na Siria atá in ferann-sin. Ul, is uad atát Armiannai. Gethér, is uad atát Arcani. Mess, dianid comainm Mosoch, is uad *sunt Meones.*

Do síl Saram meic Sém meic Noé dóib-sin uili ⁊ isin nAssia atát.

33. Do senchus na fomorach ⁊ na luchorpán ⁊ na torothur in so sís., Fechtas ro-buí Noé inna thabernacuil ina chotlud iar n-ól fína meisc

---

Abráim *om.* *U P C* o Assur *Ld* Siri *Ld*, *with* hautem *om.* Assurim *Ld* 7 atát *om.* *U* 8 ⁊ is leis – indiu (10) *om.* *U C* 9 trícha] .xx. *R P* 10 cubat *om.* *P* 11 Lidia *connected by ref. mark to marg. gloss R* Lidi *U*, *with one letter eras. after* L Ludi *C* úad atá Lidia *U* .i. na Liditai – airtheraig (13) *om.* *U C*, *follows* Lidia *P* 13 Sarum *U* ha hardchathir *(sic)* *U* a h- *C* 14 na Siria *om.* *U C* Damascus *U* Damocscus *C* Arafaxat *U C* Sela *U* 15 Mac do side *U* Ebraide *U* Ebraighe *C* 16 Arafaxat *U C* Falec *U C* Iactan] *sic R U* Iachtan *C* ⁊ Iactan *om.* *P* 17 Falec *U* Salec *C* .i. fodail .i. *add. after* diuisio *U* .i. fothail *C* ro- *P U C.*

32. R P U C] 1 Iactan *U* mac Éber – Sala *om.* *C* trí meicc déc] *sic R* .xiii. meic *U* aci *U* acco *C* ut numerantur *om.* *U C* 2 .lxiiii. d.s. *R* Atat .iiii.xl. *(sic)* cenela *U* a .lx.iiii. *P*, cenéla *om.* Atait cetri ceneal .xl. *C* 3 ra- *P* gabait *U C* ule feranna *U* fearanda *C* Indiae *U* ⁊ araill – Assia *om.* *U C* 4 Asarmo *U* nEofrait *om.* *U C* anair *C* 5 n-airtherach *om.* *U C* Saraim *C* 6 atait *C* Conititi *(sic)* *C* les *U* 7 Aducal *C* ro-chumtaiged] -chum̄ *R P* -cumtaiged *U* Damhasc *C* Pasilisitina *(sic)* *U* Coelensiria *U* Colensiria *C* 8 a ferann *U C* 9 Arcannai *U C* Mes *U C* dianid – Mossoch *om.* *U* danadh *C* 10 Abimael *U* is úad atat Meones *U* is uadh atait M. *C* 11 De sil Samar *U* 12 Offir *C* i n-Asia *C* 13 Ebila *C.*

33. R P U C] 1 De senchas na torothur .i. na luprucain ⁊ na fomorach inso sís *U* Do senchus na torothur ⁊ luchrupain ⁊ fomhorach annso sis *C* 2 -bai *P*

⁊ sé lomnocht, co tánic a mac ’na dochum .i. Cám ⁊ co faca amal ro-buí ⁊ co nderna gáire imme ⁊ coro-innis dia brát[h]rib .i. do Iaféth ⁊ do Sém, ⁊ do-deochatar-side ⁊ a ndrommann rempaib arnád ḟaicidis féli a n-athar ⁊ in ball diaro-thusmit a colla saindílsi, ⁊ do-ratsat a étach thairis.

34. At-ract *post* Noé asa chotlud ⁊ ro-failsiged dó Cám dia ḟochuitbiud ⁊ rom-mallach *post* ⁊ ro-bennach in diis n-aili. Conid hé Cám de-side cét[d]uine ro-mallachad iar ṅdílinn ⁊ conid hé comarba Caín iar ṅdílinn ⁊ conid huad ro-génatar luchorpáin ⁊ fomoraig ⁊ goborchinn ⁊ cech écosc dodelbda archena fil for doínib, ⁊ conid aire tucad dilgenn for Cannánaib, ⁊ tucad a ferann do macaib Israhél hi comarthu na mallachtan cétna, ar ropa do síl Cáim do Channánaib.

Conid hé-sin bunad na torothur ⁊ ní do síl Chaín dóib, amal ad-fiadat Goídil, ar níro-mair ní dia síl-side iar ṅdílinn, ar rop hé fochonn na dílenn do bádud clainni Caín; ⁊ ro-báte cid clanna Séth uli immale friu acht Noé cona trí maccaib ⁊ cona cethri mnáib, amal innises Moísi mac Amra in sein i nGenis rechta, ⁊ Dia féin do-rat in rechtsain do Moísi i Sléib Sína ⁊ is hé féin ro-scríb cona láim.

35. Is iat-so airig na haísi tánaisi iar líni geneloig Sém meic Noé.,

Noé a.e.l.	Thara, trí meic leis .i. Abraam, Nachor,
Sém a.c.	⟨*qui primus murum de lapidibus fecit*⟩.,
Arafaxat ccccxxxix.	Áran. Mac dond Áran-sin Loth. Ro-bátar
Sale acccxxxiii.	dano dá ingin ace .i. Iascha ⁊ Melcha,
Éber cccc.lxiiii.	dí ingin Árain meic Thara, sethracha do
Fallec ccxxxix.	Loth; ⁊ is inun in Iascha ⁊ Sarra. Ocus

-boí *U* -boi *C* in thabernacuil *(sic) U* ar n-ol *U* meisc *om. U* 3 ⁊ is he lomnocht *(sic) U* lamhnocht *C* a dochom *U* cuice *C* co n-aca *U* cor acca *C* -baí *U* dobai *C* 4 -dernai *C* gari imbi *U* amail dobai Nae *add. after* brátrib *C* braitrib *P* 5 do dechatar *C* a cul *U C* rempo *U* rompu *C* arnaictis *U* na haictis *C* féli *U* 6 ⁊ in ball – dílsi *om. U C* -tusmit *P* 7 tairis *U*.

34. R P U C] 1 Atrácht *U* Adaghar *C* iar sin *after* Noé *U C* asa chotlud *om. U C* -fallsiged *U* do foillsigheadh *C* 2 ⁊ rom-mallach *om. U* romallach he *C* iar sin *U C* dis naile *U* diss ele *C* 3 cetuine *R P* cet duni *U* cet duini *C* íar nilind *(sic) U C* ⁊ conid – dílinn *om. C* ⁊ conid] Ocus c. *R* nilind *U* miscathach ara drochairillib *add. after* Caín *P* 4 luchrupain *U C* goborchind *U* gaborchind *C* 5 archena *om. C* ar doinib *C* 6 clannaib Cam *U* Cannanachaibh *C* fearanda *C* comorda *U* chomharta *C* 7 mallactan *U* ar ropa – Channánaib *om. U* dona *C* 8 he sen *U* torothor *U* ⁊⁊ ni *R* de síl *U* amal a. G. *om. P* atfiadait *C* 9 na Goidil *U C* da sil sein *C* nilind *U* robae fochaind *C* 10 clann Cáin *U* -batea *U* -baitea *C* Sed ule *U* immalle *U* 11 trí *om. U* cethrib mnaib *P* 12 Ammra *U* insin Genis ind recta *U* 13 féin *om. U C* cona laim fein *U* cona a lamhaibh fein *C*.

35. R P U C] 1 Is iat – Noé *om. C* so sís airich *U* ilini *R* líni genelaig *U* meic Noé *om. U* 3 ac. *R* .a.cccc.l. *P* accccl. a saeghal *after* Noé *C* .s. *add. after each numl. C* qui p.m.f.d.l. *P* 4 sen Loth *C* 5 acccxxx *C* dí ingin *U* ace *linked* to Áran (4) *by construe mark R* aice *gl.* .i. ac Aran *P* Iascha, Melcha *reversed U* 6 Heber *U* ccc.lxui. *C* dí ingin – Thara *om. C* 7 Falec *U*

Reu cc xxxix.
Seruch cc.xxx.
Nachor clxuii.
Thara lxx.

at-bat[h] Áran riana athair .i. ré T[h]ara ⁊ is hé-sein cétmac at-bath riana athair iar ndílinn, ⁊ is ann at-bath, i nÚr *Caldeorum.*,

35a. Amal at-beir in fili Goédelach sin.

Cétmac as marb riana athair
innisfet tria bardne brecht:
Áran mac Tara meic Nachar,
iarna rachur tarin recht.

36. Dá ingin dano la Loth mac nÁrain .i. Iachether ⁊ Iachereth a n-anmann Ébraide, Achiros ⁊ Miros a nGréc, *Sadibilis* ⁊ *Adherens* a Laten. Is iat-sin ro-dáilset immarcraid fína fora n-athair, ar dáig a n-etrána, coros-torche triana mesce, co ndernae dá mac friu .i. Moab ⁊ Ammon, *de quibus hoc carmen.*,

37. (1) INgena Loith, légtar lib
a lucht in scéoil—scíthangbaid!
Do-rigset claind meblaig mbain
na demnaig fri mac nÁrain.

(2) IAchether in ben cen raind
robo siniu don minchlaind;
tuc fín dia athair im nóin
diaro-dathaig gním n-écóir.

(3) IAchereth in ben aile—
finnat uaib na senchaide!
Gním lé cen tálgud 'na tig:
sárgud a Dé 's in chlérig.

(4) Achiros a nGréc co ngráin
ocus Miros co mmidáil,
mar nos-dedlaig dagrann den
mebraig anmann na n-ingen. INgena.

Sala *U C* cccxxxix *U C* inund *U* inand *C* in *om.* *U C* 8 -bath *P* atbath *U* rena *U C* iar ndil- *add. after* athair *C* .i. ré T[h]ara – ndilinn *om. C* rana hathair *U* 9 Saruc *U* Saruch *C* 10 íar nilind *U*.

35a U Lb] 1 ise sin didiu cetmac is marb riana athair ar tus for druimm domain ut dixit *Lb* 2 Cetmac as *in text, rest add. in marg. (some letters obscure) U* is marb *Lb* 3 indisfet tre briathraib becht *Lb* 4 Nachair *U* 5 rachor asin recht, *gl.* .i. legem Moisi *Lb*.

36. R P] 1 dano *om. P*.

37. R P] 3 doronsat *P* 8 diara- *P* 14 et Miros *P* 21 dorignit *P*.

(5) *Sadibilis mali* maill
in ben ba siniu don chlainn;
Adherens malo—fír dam—
ba sí sósar na n-ingen. INgena.

(6) Na meic da-rignit ann sain
tria beirt n-ińglicc fria n-athair,
Moab, Ammón—co fír dam—
ba hí clannón na n-ingen. INgena.,

38. Abrám ⁊ Nachor *hautem,* dá mac Thara, tucsat dá mnaí .i. Sarra ⁊ Melcha, dí ingin a mbráthar féin .i. dí ingin Árain meic Thara. Tu[c] ém Abrám Sarra, dianid comainm Iascha. Tuc immorro Nachor Melcha ⁊ ruc Melcha ocht maccu do Nachor., It é in so a n-anmann.,

Huss
Buz
Camuel
Chaseth
Azau
Feldas
Iadilafas
Bathuel

Ó Bathuel mac Nachoir ro-génair Laban ⟨.i. *filius*⟩ ⁊ Rabecca *filia.* Huss mac Nachoir, is uad Iób ocus is dia síl Balam in druí. Camuel dano, athair *Sirorum* é-side. Caratben Nachoir .i. Roma í-sidi, máthair Tabee ⁊ Gaom ⁊ Thaas ⁊ Macha. Fodla ⁊ ilgabla mac Noé, ⁊ forba na haéssi tánaisi condici so anuas.

39. Din tress aés in domuin ⁊ dia airechaib in so sís.,
Dá bliadain cethrachat ar noí cét isin tres aés in domuin .i. ó gein Abráim i tír *Caldeorum* co gabáil rígi do Dauíd; ⟨*Casdei nunc Caldei uocantur*⟩. Gein Abraháim didiu tossach na haéssi-se iar fír. Sé bliadna ochtmogat ropo slán do Abrám in tan ro-thussim Ismal ó Agáir Égeptacdai; ⟨*Agareni a hAgar*⟩. Cét ṁbliadan immorro robo slán de in tan ro-thussim Isac ó Sarra.

---

38. R P U C Lb] 1 hautem – Thara *om. U C Lb* hautem *om. P* di mnai *Lb* 2 dí]-i *sublin. R* da ingein *C* dí ingin *(2°) om. C Lb* 3 Tuc *P C* dana comainm *C* dian c. *Lb* Iascai *Lb* 4 ruc si, *with* Melcha *om. P* .uii. maccu *R* .uiii. macu *U C* maca *P* Nachor *om. C* 5 Hus *U C (list in long line)* Is uad side [*sc.* Bathuel] *U* mac Nachoir *om. U C* -genedair *C* Lauan *gl.* .i. filius *U* .i. filius *add. after* Laban *P C* (fels̄) 6 Rabecca *gl.* .i. filia *U* filia ⁊ Rabecca *(sic) C* 6–7 do sil Huis *C* is dia ṡíl Buz⟨⟩ Balam *U* 7 pater Sirorum *C* 8 Cascht *C* Caratben Nachar *U* is i side *U* mathaiir Tabe *U* Macha *before* Gaom *C* Goom *U* 9 Azau *and* Feldas *written as one name R* Azau Feldas *C* Maachai, *with* Fodla *om. U C* ilgabla *et rel. om. C* 40 Dend ais tanaise connici so anuas *U* 11 Iadilafac *U C.*

39. R P U* C] 1 Den tres ais *U* treis *R* in domuin – airechaib *om. U C* so sis i fechtsa *U* 2 In tres aes in domain ise so lin bl- fil inti .i. .dccccxlu. *U C* *Begins* CETHRACHA, *then eras. P* ar *om. P* gen *U* 3 Abrahaim *P* i tír Caldeorum *after* Dauíd *U (U ends here)* i tír – Dauíd *om. C* 4 isse tossach *C* 4–5 .ui. bliadna .lxxx. *R P* .lxxxui ropo slan *C* 5 in tan *om. C* rotuisin Isamail *C* 6 Ag. a hA. *om. P C* ab Agar *Ld* ba slan *P* 7 Dotuisin *C*

Do-rusim dano maccu aili ó Chethura .i. ón mnaí thuc iar n-éc Sarra; ⟨*Saraceni a Sarra*⟩. Is iat-so a n-anmann-side .i. IAmbram, Iaxan, Madian, Mathan, Iasboch, Sue. Iaxan mac Abráim meic Thara, dá mac les .i. Sabba ⁊ Daddan. Clanna Daddain .i. Assurim ⁊ Lathussim ⁊ Loommim. Clann Madian meic Abráim .i. Epha ⁊ Ofer ⁊ Enóch ⁊ Abida ⁊ Elda. Clann Abráim ⁊ Cethura sin anuas. Clann immorro Ismail meic Abráim ⁊ Agáre Égeptacdai inalta Sarra in so sís, ⁊ prímgeinni Ismal do Abrám; ⟨*Ismohelitae ab Ismal*⟩.

Prímgenni Ismail in so .i. Nabioth, ⟨*a quo Nabatheni*⟩; is hé ro-gab in ferann óthá sruth nEofrait condici Muir Robuir, ⁊ is leis Nabathena—rann hí-sside hi ferunn Arabiae, i lleth fri airther.,

40.	Nabioth	Mamsan	Thema
	Dehin	Masma	Hiur
	Cedar	Dumma	Naphis
	Abdel	Massaadad	Chedma.

IS siat-sain clanna Ismail meic Abráim ⁊ is iat-sin dá thoísech déc na dá treb ṅdéc Ismail ⁊ marait a n-anmann indiu fora lessaib ⁊ fora cathrachaib. *Et* is hé ferann ro-gabsat, óthá Sliab Euilath conici Súr fil ar agaid na hÉgipti, in chonair tiagair i nAsardaib. At-bath Ismal iar sin, iar secht ṁbliadna tríchat ar cét.

41. Do clannaib Isac meic Abráim in so sís.
Tucastar Isaac mac Abráim meic Thara meic Nachor mnaí .i. Rabecca, ingen Bathuel meic Nachoir meic Thara .i. siur Labain. Ruc Rabecca dá mac do Isaac do oéntairbirt .i. Iacób ⁊ Issau.

Do-chuaid Iacób co tír Messopotamiae, co bráthair a máthar, co Laban mac ṁBathuel meic Nachoir, co tuc dí ingin Labain .i. Lia ⁊ Rachel ⁊ coro-chlannaig friu ⁊ coro-clannaig fria n-inailtib .i. Bala, inailt Racheli, ⁊ Selpha, inailt Lia. Coro-thusmiset na dá mnaí cona cumalaib dá mac déc ⁊ oéningen do Iacób .i. Dina a ainm-side.

---

9 Saraceni a Sarra *after* Sarra *P om. C* Saracini *Ld* Iamrom *C* Aexan *C* 10 Madan *C* Llutian Iasbach *(sic) C* Tarra *C* .u. *(sic)* meic occu sein *C* 11 Dathan *C* Cl. Dathain *C* Lasurim *C* 12 Abrahaim *P* Opher *C* Elda *om. C* 14 Isamal *C* .i. inailt do Sarra i sein *C* 15 ⁊ prímgeinni – Abrám *om. C* Ismail *P* Ismohelitae ab Ismal *om P C* Ismahelitae *Ld* 16 .i. *supralin. R* a quo N. *om. P C* Nabath⟨eni⟩ a Nabeoth *Ld (obscure)* 17 o sruth *C* corrighe *C* 18 hi ferunn *om. C* i lleth fri airther *om. C.*

40. R P C] 1 Nabioth *om. C numl. prefixed to each name in C* Tema *C* 2 Deni *C* Iur *C* 3 Duma *C* 4 Massa *C* Cedma *C* 5 Is iat sein tra *C* ⁊ is iat – cathrachaib *om. C* innsin *(1°) P* Abrahaim *P* 7 Et] *sic R om. C* Súr – agid *om. C* 8 sruth na hEgipti *C* i chonair *C* 9 i cind .c.xxxuii. blia- ba slan do in tan atbath *C* a aeisi *add. after* cét *P.*

41. R P C] 2 Isac *C* 3 meic Nachoir – Thara *om. C* Lauan *C* 4 da mac toisach *C* Esau *C* 5 i tir *C* Messopotamiae] –o– *(2°) supralin. R* Meastapatamia *C* 6 Lauan *C* Nachor *P* meic Nachoir *om. C* da ingein *C* Lauain *C* 7 ⁊ co – friu *om. C* 8 -thusiím in da miai *(sic) C* 9 do Iacob *after* Dina *C* nē *above line*, ia *below line add. betw.* Dina *and* do Iacob *C* a ainm-side *om. C.*

42. IS siat-so anmann mac Lia cétus,

Filii Liae,	ISachar	Dan	Gad Asser
Ruben	Zabulon	Neptálim	*Filii Racheli* .i.
Semeon	*Filii hautem*	*Filii*	IOseph
Leue	*Balae,* cumaili	*Selfae,*	Beniamín
Iudas	Racheli,	cumaili Lia,	

43. Oéngus mac Suibne *hoc carmen cecinit de duodecim filiis Iacob.,*

(1) Dá mac de[ë]c Iäcóib—
gnáthaigthe, badat cuman!
Ocht meicc na dá grádaigthe,
cethri meic na dá cumal.

(2) Sé meicc Liä lánglaine:
Ruben, Semeon, ros-cualaid,
Leue, Iudas, Isachar,
Zabulon soillsi sluagaib.

(3) Dá mac Selpha sétglaine,
cumaile Lia láne;
dá derbráthair thétraide:
Gad, Asser, imbaid áine.

(4) Dá mac inna cumaile
Bala, dos-biur i n-árim,
ar Samsón soér subaide,
ní dermat, Dan, Neptálim.,

(5) Dá mac roglach Racheli,
bátar airdirciu arttaib;
óssar bán Beniëmín,
Ioseph mór ba mó maccaib. Dá.

(6) Dí ingin áin adguidi
Labain meic Bathuail brattaig,
dí phiair báin barrbuidi:
Lia, Rachel, ocht maccaib. Dá.,

---

42. R P C] 1 It iat *P* anmanda *C* 2 *numl. add. above each name C* 3 meic Raceil *C* .i. *om. P* 4 Semion *C* Filii *gl.* meic *(bis) C* hautem *om. C* 5 Leui *C* (F.) Cealpa *C* 6 Iuda *C* Raceil *C.*

43. R P C] 1 Conid doibh rochan Oengus mac Suibni *P Rubric om. C (very obscure)* 7 Rumen Semon rocualaidh *C* 8 Leui Uitas *(sic) C* 9 Crabulon soills *(sic)* sluaghaibh *C* 10 *3rd and 4th stt. inverted in C* Selba *C* 12 cetraidh *C* 13 imbid ane *C* 15 i *slightly rubbed R* dosber *C* 17 na dermait Don Neptallim *C* 18 roglach re cele *C* 19 dadar *(sic)* airdrice *C* 22 Da ingen ain adbuidhe *C* 23 Mathuail brataug *C* 24 da fiair *C* 25 co maccaibh, *with* ocht *om. C.*

44. *Fili Ruben*
ENóch
Falluc
Esrom
Charmi
Filii Semion
Manuel
Aaod
IAmim
IAchin
Zare
Saul
Filii Leue
Gersom
Merari
Caath,
qui Abram genuit
⟨.i. *patrem Moisi* ⁊ *Aron*⟩.
Filii Iuda
Her
Onan, ⟨*qui ambo mortui sunt in terra Channan*⟩.
Sela
Phares
Zare
Filii Fares
Esrom. Amul.
Filii Isachar
Tholia
IAsub
Fili Dan
Fua
Semram
Suchaim
Filii Neptalim
IEsichel
IAssera
Fili Zabulon
Sareth
IAlel

Filii Ioseph
Effraim
Mannases
Filii Effraim
Suthula
Bechen
Techen
Filius Mannase
Machir *pater* ⟨.i. Galad⟩.
Meic imdae ic Galad,
it é-so a n-anmann,
Hiester
Elech
Asriel
Sechem
Semida
Epher,
pater Salfad.
Ocus ní bátar meic
oca acht cóic ingena.
Fili Beniemín
Bale
Azebel
Achirama
Suphaim
Filii Gad
Sephon
Aggei
Suni
Ozin
Aroth
Arialab
Filii Asser
IAmne
IEssui
Briae

---

44. R P C] 3 Fallu *C* Mannases .i. ma *(sic) C* 6 Filii *gl.* meic *C* Becher *C* 7 Ramuel *C* 8 Aodh *C* Mannasses *C* 9 .i. pater Galad *add. after* Machir *P* M. .i. athair G. *C* 10 Badar meic *C* 11 Care *C* a n-anmann *supralin. R* anmanda *C* 13 Filii *gl.* meic *C* Leue *om. C* 14 Arril *C* 16 Cath *C* 17 qui *linked to* Caath *by construe-mark R* 18 .i. patrem Moisi ⁊ Aron *om. P* Abram patrem Moisi ⁊ Aran genuit *C* Effre *C.*

45. Clanna Essau in so sís .i. Eliphaz a prímgeinne, is é for-athmentair i lLibur Ióib, *dicens: Hii sunt tres amici Iob* .i. *Eliphaz Themanites et Baalad Suetes et Sophor Amanathites,* ⁊ Thamma ainm a charatmná. Is iat-so anmann a mac archena: Rahuel, Ieuus, Hielon, Chore. *Filii Eliphaz* .i. Theman, Homar, Sephum, Gatham, Cenez, Amalech. *Filii Rahuel:* Naad, Zara, Semma, Mesta. Mac do Séir Horreus ⁊ is ai[r]e cumnigthir sunn, ar is do clannaib *Horreorum* caratben Eliphaz meic Essau. IS iat-so anuas clanna Abráim cona cinedaib.

Do-rat Abrám a chomarbus huili etir íri ⁊ indile do Isaac. Do-rat *hautem* ascada do maccaib na caratban .i. do Ismal mac Agáre Égeptacdai *et* do mac[aib] Cethurae, ⁊ ros-dedail fri Isaac *et* ros-cuir i n-airther na Aissiae, i lleth fri Innecdu.,

46. At-bath Abrám iarsin cóiced bliadain sechtmogat ar chét a aéssi ⁊ ro-adnacht isind inud dianid ainm *Spelonca duplex,* ⁊ is ann atá-side, i tír Effron meic Sooir Chethecdai, agid fri agid is Glenn Mamra. Abrám féin immorro ro-chennaig in n-inad-sin ó macaib Ceth i frithálim a adnaicthi, conid annsin ro-adnacht Abrám ⁊ Sarra a ben. *Et* dessid ordan ⁊ rath Abráim for Isaac, conid huad meic Israhél uili. Ocus Críst, iar geneloig a cholla, is co Isaac berair.,

47. Is iat-so uasal-athraig na tressi aési cona s[a]églaib.

.Saégul Abrahám	.lxxu. ar .c.
.Saégul ISaac	.clxxx.
.Saégul IAcób	.cxlui.

48. IS siat-so immorro Iudice na haéssi cétna ⁊ nocon hí a n-aés huili ármidir i fus dóib acht numir bliadan a flath[i]usa *tantum.,*

.regnauit IEssus	.xxui.	*.regnauit* Thola	.xxui.
.regnauit Gothoniel	.xl.	*.regnauit* IAhir	.xxii.

---

45. R P C] 1 Cland im̄ *C* Elifa *C* 2 dicens – Amanathites *om. C* 3 a charatmná *linked to* Essau (1) *by construe-mark R* 4 a nanmanda *C* Hieus *C* Filīi no Filii *(sic) C* 5 Elipaz *C* Cenest *C* Ama. lech *C* 6 Rauel *P C* Mesta *om. C* *stroke on* ar *compendium om. R* ⁊ cumnigther *C* Elipaz *P* Elefaz *C* 9 comhrabus *C* huili – indile *om. C* etir íri] *sic R P* etir íri ⁊ indile *om. C* 10 hautem im̄ *C* 11 Égeptacdai *om. C* et] *sic R P* ⁊ *abbrev. C* do mac *R P* do macaibh *C* -deghail *C* re hIsac iat *C* rocuir *C*.

46. R P C] 1 .i. .u. blia- ar .c. iseadh sin roba slan do do *sic* hAbramh in tan atbath, *gl.* nó .u. blia- dec ar tri .xx.ib ar .c. roba slan dAbram *C* 2 -adhnaiceadh *C* isin dunadh *C* Splonca tuplex *C* 3 in aghaidh fria *C* 4 Abraham *P* immorro *om. C* -cennaig *P* in tinad *C* 5 dia adhnacul and *C* -hadhnaiceadh *C* Abram *gl.* ⁊ a ben Sarra *C* 6 Ro suighidh rath, *with* ordan ⁊ *om. C* ⁊ conad da sil Crist iar colaind *C* 7 uili *om. P*.

47. R P C] 1 na haise sein .i. tres aess in domhain *C* do dreim dibh .i. la triar dibh *add. after* saeghlaibh *C* 2 saégul] .S *prefixed to all three names in R P, om. C* Abramh *C* .clxxx. *C* 4 .cxlu. *C*.

48. R P C] 1 *Rubric linked to* Iessus (3) *by caret-mark R* nochan e a saeghal *C* 2 huili *om. C* airmigter *C* dóib *om. C* flathasa *C* tantum *om. C* 3 regnauit] .r *prefixed to all names in R, om. P C* .xx./et/ sex. *(1°) C* xxxui

.regnauit Aod.,	.lxxx.	*.regnauit* IAphte	.u.i.
.regnauit Deborra	.xl.	*.regnauit* Esegon	.uii.
.regnauit Gedeon	.xl.	*.regnauit* Samson	.xx.
.regnauit Abimelech	.iii.	*.regnauit* Heli *sacerdos*	.xl.
		.regnauit Samuel	.xl.

49. *Saul primus rex fuit in Israhel. Regnauit quadraginta annis* ⁊ ro-mmarbad *post* Saul ⁊ a mac .i. Ionothan, i Sléib Gilbae ra Filistindaib ⁊ is hé fescur na haéssi-sin., Ro-gab Dauíd rígi Dethrebe iar sin ⁊ ro-gab hua do Saul rígi Deich-Treibi .i. Isposeth mac Ianothain meic Sauil. His í-sin in tres a aés.,

⟨Rechab ⁊ Banna, dá macc Remmoin Birothitai[c]the, roda-marbsat Hisposeth mac Ionathain meic Sauil meic Ciss meic Abel meic Seoir meic Bechoir meic Aphia meic *uiri* Emini., Samuel mac Helcanna meic Herobuam meic Heleo meic Thau meic Suph Eufratecda a Sléib Effraim, meic Elcanna meic Maath meic Massia meic Elcanna meic Iohel meic Azaria.,

Saphaneth uel Somnofaneth nomen Iosephi in Aegiptiaco. Si Ebraice nomen est, saluator mundi interpretatur. Si Aegiptiace nomen est, repertor sompniorum dicitur. Ammoebár nomen Moisi apud parentes, filius filii interpretatur⟩.

50. Aisnéis don chethramad aés in so sís i fecht-sa.,
Trí bliadna sechtmogat ar cethri cét, is í numir bliadan na cethramad aéssi. IS as *hautem* gabair tossach na haéssi-se, ó gabáil ríge do Dauíd. Cethracha bliadan ro-buí-side for Israhél .i. secht m̄bliadna ⁊ [sé] mís i Cebron ⁊ dá bliadain tríchat i nHierusálem.

Cestnaigthir hi sunn do numir clainni Dauída ⁊ do hurd a ndénma, eter Cebron ⁊ Hirusálem. It hé in so meic Dauíd i Cebron cétus: Ammon *hautem* a prímgeinni, Archinoe Israélda a máthair. Eleaab in mac tánaise, Abigáil ben Nabail Slébe Carmill a máthair-side. Abisolon in tres mac, Maacha, ingen Ptolomei *regis Gessor,* a máthair. Adimas in cethramad mac, Aggíth Égeptacda a máthair. Sophatha in cóiced

---

(2°) *C* 4 la .xxii. *(2°)* *C* 5 Aaod *P* Aoth *C* Ie *C* 6 Esegeon *C* 7 Labdon .uiii. *C.*

49. R P C] 2 marbad *P* post] iar sin *C* Saul *om. C* ⁊ a mac *et rel. after* Gilba *C* 3 Deest *compendium* (Dẓ) *in marg. betw. lines R*, *referring to passage enclosed in angle brackets* fesscor in treas aes *C* iar sin *om. P* 4 Roghab *P* Dabith *C* Isposeth mc̄ mc̄ Sauil *P* Ionothan *P* 5 His í *et rel. om. C* a *om. P* 6 Rechab – macc *still visible*, Remmoin – Aphia (8) *shorn by binder R*, *restored from P* 7 Birothitaithe *P* m̄ Ionathain *supralin. P* 8 mc̄ uri, *with* Emini *after* Azaria (11) *P* m̄ Emini *still visible in R*, *after* Azaria 10 Massia] – ssia *supralin. P* 11 Azariam *P* 15 Otholia filia – Ochozias (= §52.3–5) *add. P after* interpretatur; Roghab – aes (= 3–5) *follows.*

50. R P C] 1 Aisnéis *om. C* i fecht-sa *om. C* 2 TRi bliā. lxx. ar .ccc. *R* .U. (?) blia- .lxxx. ar .cccc. *P* IN cethramadh aes dano andso ⁊ in muimir blia- fuil inti .i. ccccIxxxui. *C* 3 hautem] im̄ *P C* gabhar tosach *C* 4 -bai *C*

mac, Abithal a máthair. Hiethram *de Agal, uxore Dauid,* in sessed mac .i. mac banrígna. Is iat-sin meic Dauíd i Cebron.

IS iat-so dano a meic i n̄Hierusálem .i. Samaa, Sabab, Nathan, Salemon. Anmann dano a ingen: Ibar, Eleussa, Nephech, Iaphia, Lisania, Elida, Elephelech. Conid a secht déc lín clainni Dauíd samlaid.

⟨Dá siar immorro Dauída .i. Saruia ⁊ Abigaheal., .i. trí meic Saruia .i. Iób ⁊ Abisai ⁊ Iasel., Amassa *hautem* mac Abigaheal.,⟩

Solam immorra, a mac, is é ro-gab dara éssi.

Isind aés-[s]i ro-thinscanad flathius na Macidónna, *et* Caranus ainm in chétríg ro-gab díb. Hi cinn secht bliadan fichet ón bliadain-sen gabála flathiusa do Macidónnaib co ndernad in cétna-Oénach Olimp la hAthanenstu. Hi cinn cóic bliadan ar chethri cét dano iar togail na Troí do-rónad-side. Sé bliadna fichet ón chétna-Oénuch Olimp corotusmed Róim.,

⟨Athalas, is é in cétna-astrolacda ro-boé⟩.

51. *Roma condita est* .i. ro-thusmed ind Róim i Sléib Palantini .i. *Palantinus mons* ainm int slébe i ndernad. In oénmad kalaind déc Mai ro-thinscanad la Romail ⁊ la Remuil .i. dá mac Rea Silueae iat-side, ingene Minituir meic Proich.

IN Rea-sin, óg uestella í-side .i. óg ro-ailed i Tempul Mairt. Acht ro-hélned chena hí ó sacurd in Tempuil, corbo torrach uad ⁊ co ruc dá mac. *Et* iss ed at-bert-si, robo la Mairt in clann ⁊ is aire-sein ro-láthe na dá mac for Tibir .i. forin sruth, i cliabán bic, ar níro-lámdas a marbad la Mairt, ar is é-side robo dee dóib-seom.

Ro-adnaiced *hautem* in máthair ⁊ sí beó, ar a hóge do milliud di. Amullius, bráthair a athar, is é rodas-adnaic. Fustulus dano, buachail ind ríg, is hé fuair na dá mac i mbrúch srotha Tibir, condas-tuc leis dochum a mná .i. Luppa dano a ainm-side. Alta-si dano na dá mac combat móra.

Ro-innised dóib *post* Amulius do marbad a máthar ⁊ dia cur féin forin sruth, co tarclamsat munter a n-aite .i. slóg na mbuachala ⁊ co ragbaiset teg forsind ríg .i. Amulius é-side ⁊ ro-mmarbsat i ndígail a máthar ⁊ tucsat rígi dia senathair .i. do Minitur mac Proich .i. athair

---

.uii. mis *C* secht *om. P* 6 Cestnaigthir – éssi (19) *om. C* 17 Dá siar – Abigaheal *om. P C* 19 .i. Dauid *add. after* éssi *P* 20 isind aissia tindscindter *C* -tinnscanad *P* 23 .ccccu. b. *R P* .u. mblia- ar .cccc. aib dano *C* 24 .xxui. b. *R P C* on cet aenach *C*, *with* Olimp *om.* 26 Athalas – ro-boé *om. P C.*

51. R P C] 1 Palestii̅ *(sic) C* Palaintini .i. Palantinus *P* Palesinus *C* 2 in .xi. kl. *R P* in undecim kl. *C* 3 Romuil *P* 4 ingeni Numituir meic Pich *C* 5 IN Rea Siluia sein *C* og uestalda *C* Mair *(sic) C* 7 Et] *sic R P* ⁊ *abbrev. C* rop la M. *C* -lathea *C* 8 fon T. *P* arna rolamhadh *C* 9 ar – dóib *om. C* 10 hautem] im̄ *P C* in máthair *om. C* 11 Amulius im̄ *C* athair *R* athar *P C* rosadhnacht *C* 12 i mbruach in tsrotha *C* co tuc *C* leis *om. P* 13 cuim a mna *C* Rosalt sein *C* 14 corsat *C* 15 post] iar sin *C* da ccur *C* 16 cor tinolsatsom *C* s. na mbuachalla *P* 16–17 corogabhsat *C* 18 a mmathar *C* da s. do Mintuir mac Picc *C* .i. *add. supralin. R* 19 rocumdaigh *C.*

a máthar ⁊ at-bath-side ⁊ ro-gab Romuil ríge ⁊ ro-chumtaiged ind Róm leis isint sessed bliadain a flathiusa, iar fairind.

52. Ríg mac nIsrahél in so fri ré na aéssi-se, cona flat[h]iusaib.

Dauíd .xl.	Ochozias *et* Otholia	Ezecheas .xxuiiii.
Salemon .xl.	⟨.i. *mater eius*. Otholia	Mannases .lu. *annis*
Robuam .xuii.	*filia* Acaib meic Ambre	IOsias .xxxi. *annis*
Abiam ⟨*uel* Abiasa⟩	*mater* Ochozias⟩ .i. *anno*	⟨*uel* Ammon .xii.⟩
.iii. *bus annis*	IOas .xl. *annis*	IOtha .iii. *bus mensibus*
Assa .xl. *annis*	Amasias .x[x]ix.	⟨*uel* Iachaz [.i. *filius*]
IOsofath .xxu.	Ozias *qui* ⁊ Azarias .lii.	Iossiae, ii[i]. *bus*
IOram .uiii. *annis*	IOtham .xui.	[*mensibus*]⟩
	Achaz .xui.	IAchim .xi. *annis*
		IOchin *qui* ⁊ Iochonias
		.iii. [*bus*] *mensibus* ⁊ .x.
		diebus
		Sedechias .xi. *annis*

⟨Tales Milessius, is hé cétfissecda ro-baé riam⟩

53. ISsind oénmad bliadain déc flathiusa Sedechias rucad in tuad Iudaide isin doíre ṁBabilónda ⁊ ro-chured dar cenn Hierusálem uili ⁊ ro-loisced in Tempul mór Solman. I cind .ccccxxx. nó .ccccxxxiiii. [ṁbliadan], amal at-berat fairenn, ó do-rigned coro-losced.

Labudsardan, toísech do Nabcodón, is hé ro-airg Hierusálem ⁊ ruc les in tuaith nIudaide uli ⁊ a ríg .i. Sedechias, co Babilóin i ndoíri ⁊ ro-bátar sechtmoga bliadan isin doíri conas-relic as Cir ocus Dair mór mac Astiages—Dair mac Arbei ⟨nó Arsabei⟩ immorro ba tigflaith Pers ar cind flathiusa Gréc—*et* coro-chumtaiged Hierusálem ⁊ in Tempul mór aridisi la Estras ⁊ Nemias. Ocus conid hé-sin forba na cethramad aéssi ⁊ tinscetal na cóicedi aéssi.

---

52. R P C] 1 Is iat so na righ rogabhsat do macaibh Israhel *C* cona flathiusaib] -aib *cut off by binder R* cona flaithiusaibh *P* flathiusaibh .i. *C* 2 Flathius Dauid ⁊ na righ so anuas *prefixed C* Achaz *for* Otholia, *with* .f. *add. hic et passim C* .xxuiiii. *om. C* 3 Otholia – Ochozias *om. P* Gotholia mr̄ *C* 4 Iaas *C* Iossias .xxxii., *with* Iossias *and* Ammon (5) *reversed C* 5 Abiassa *(sic) C* 6 Iotha uel Iachaz *gl.* .i. filius Iossiae *P* 7 Assa .xli. *C* .xl. *R P* Am meissas .xxix. *C* .xix. *R P* .iii. mis *C* 8 Ozias, Azarias *reversed C*, dr̄ *add.* 9 .xui. *om. C* 10 Eliachim qui ⁊ Iacim dr̄ .iii. *C* Acha, *with* .xui. *om. C* 12 iii menses *R P* .iii. mensibus ⁊ .x. diebus *om. C*, dr̄ *add.* 14 Sededias *R P* 15 *om. P C.*

53. R P C] 1 Isin noenmad *P* in tuath *C* 2 uili *om. P* 3 nó .ccccxxxiii. *C* 4 is and roscailedh ⁊ roloisceadh *add. after* do-rigned *C*, coro losced *om.* 5 Nabudsardan *corr.* ⟩ Labudsardan *R* Labudsardan *P* 6 in tuath, *with* uli *om. C* 7 cona as relec as *(sic) C* Cir mac Dair *C* 8 mór – Gréc *om. C* Dair mac Arsabaei *P* 9 co *om. C* ⁊ ro athcumdaigedh *C* 10 mór *om. C* La Estras ⁊ Nemias *om. C.*

54. Conid hí in chethramad aés de-side, ó gabáil ríge do Dauíd co lécud na braiti for cúlu. Isind aés-[s]e ro-churit na trí gillai 'sin sorn tened la Nabcodón .i. Sedrac, M[i]sac, Abdinago, ⁊ roda-saér Dia ón tenid-sin ⁊ ro-loisc ilmíli do muintir Nabcodóin. *Et* is annsin tucad Daniél i cuithe na leoman, iarna chosaít do maéraib ind ríg ⁊ do sacartaib na n-ídal ⁊ térna Daniél óna leomnaib ⁊ ro-chuirit sluag na maír ⁊ na sacart 'sin cuithi *post* iar sin, conas-duatar leomain in chuthi.,

55. Aisnéidit starigi na nÉbraidi Sedechias mac Iosia do dallad do muintir Nabcodóin ic Reblatha ⁊ cen a brith co Babilóin etir, amal is follus sin asind oéntaid ro-buí etir Iochin, ríg nIuda, ⁊ Euilmoradach mac Nabcodóin, ara tachur i n-oéncharcair .i. dia mbaí Nabcodón secht [ṁ]bliadna ic geilt feoir ⁊ [sé] crom tornocht etir na hossu altaidi ⁊ na halmu centai, co tucsat a aés gráda a rígi dia mac. Ó thánic *hautem* a chiall do Nabcodóin ⁊ ro-gab a rígi, ro-irgaib a mac ar rígi do gabáil dia és ⁊ do-fuc i carcair ar oén fri ríg nIuda, corba marb fodesin intí Nabcodón.

Tucsat immach munter Nabcodóin Euilmoradach asin charcair do gabáil rígi a athar, ⁊ níra-gaib co tuargabtha dó tassi ⁊ apaigi a athar—arná bad éc góach na-beth dó ⁊ ná ba rígi éluithech dano dó-som a rígi. Ocus ro-turcbait dó do thétaib ⁊ corránaib a thassi asa adnacul, conid iarum ro-gab Euilmoradach rígi, ⁊ ba cennais hé fri Iochin.,

Etaraisnéis dano sin anuas ⁊ forba na cethram[ad] aési. *Finit amen.,*

56. IN chúiced aés in so sís, cona numir bliadan.,

IS sí-seo numir bliadan na cóiced aési ⁊ in chúiced aés fodessin .i. .dlxxxix. IS sí ind aés-[s]a uili ó forbu na do[í]ri Babilónda co gein Críst. La tinscital dano na haéssi-se ro-toglad Babilóin la Cir ⁊ la Dair mac Astiages for Ballasair mac Labudsardan meic Neocusser meic Euilmoradach meic Nabcodóin meic Merach Balodan meic Balodan, *et reliqua.*

For Ballasair, ríg Caldea, ro-toglad Babilóin ⁊ ro-gab Cir rígi ⁊ do Medaib dó-side ⁊ is annsain tánic in rígi co Medaib ⁊ is hé in Cir-sin ro-léc ass in popul nIsraélda fuair isin Babilóin fora chinn, i ndoíri ic Ballasair. Ba hé a lín, trícha míli.

---

54. R P C] 2 Isind assia *C* -cuirit *P C* giallai *C* 3 Sidrach Misach et Abdenago *P* Sedrach. ⁊ Misach Abdinago *C* rodo saer *P* tuc Dia imlan ass iat *C* 4 sin – Nabcodóin *om. C* 5 iarna *et rel. om. C, with* ⁊ ni duadar na leomhain he. Finit in cethramhadh aes sin ⁊ tosach in cuicedh aes so sis *add.*

55. R P] 1 staruidi *P* 2 Babloin *P* 5 sé *om. R P* 12 dó] *supralin. R* 13 do thétaib] d *of* do *on* a *R* 15 na cetramad aeissi *P* Finit amen *om. P.*

56. R P C] 1 Quinta aetas incipit *C* 2 in domain *add. after* aési *C* ⁊ in – .i. *om. C* 3 huil *C* 4 Babloin *C* la Cír mac nDair *C, with* mac Astiages *om.* 5 mac Labudsardan *et rel. om. C* 8 ⁊ romarbhadh B. *C* righ na Callacda, *with* -toglad B. *om. C* 10 roleic *C* Rofhuair *C* fora cinn *P* ara cind *C* 11 Ba hé – míli *om. C.*

57. Robo díbrithi aichne trá la feraib in domuin in Babilóin do thogail, ara dangne ⁊ ar mét a cumtaig. Ar la Nebroth mac Chuis meic Cáim meic Noé ro-chétna-cumtacht. La Nín mac m̄Béil meic Ploisc meic Philiris Agamuil meic Feronessis meic Omulis meic Githlis meic Therris meic Assúr meic Sém meic Noé [ro-athcumtaiged], ⁊ la mnaí Nín *post* .i. Samiramis dano a ainm-side; ingen-side Zambri meic Suuil meic Buz, ríg inna India.

IS amlaid seo do-rónad múr na Babilóine .i. do aél berbthi ⁊ do bitumain, iarna cummasc, ro-chomdlúthad in múr. Cethrochair cutrumslesta a sudigud. Coíca cubat tigi a mmúir. Dá chét cubat a arde. Ccccl xxx. stadi ⟨nó sesca míli⟩ inna tacmoṅg. Cét ndorus n-umaide furri.

Iss ed at-ber[ar] i llebraib *antiquitatum,* fiche cetharriad for héraimm do thuidecht etir dá sreith do thigib for mulluch a mmúir, ar thiget. Sruth nEofrait dara lár .i. fo stuagdórsib cloch.

Conid amlaid tánic Cir ⁊ rámann leis i lláim cech oénfir, corofodlaiset in sruth i minsruthu cen fis do lucht na cathrach. Co tánic sluag Cir iar conair int srotha co rabatar ar lár na cathrach cen forclosin do lucht na cathrach. Conid amlaid-sin ro-toglad Babilóin.

58. *De Babilonia hoc carmen.,*

(1) Babilóin, ro-clos hi céin,
dind ro-chumtaig Nín mac Béil
ar sírecla slait na slóg,
cathir dírecra dímór.

(2) Cethrochair in chathir chain,
dona flathib fót n-ortain;
suairc solus, sét co nglaine,
co cét ṅdorus n-umaide.

(3) Sesca mórmíli imma-cuaird,
rob hé a tomus, nírbu duairc,
do chémendaib uird ellaig,
iar rémendaib ro-thennaib.

---

57. R P C] 2 ara – cumtaig *om. C* 3 rocumdaighedh ar tus. ⁊ ro hathcumdaighedh *C* 3–4 meic Ploisc – Noé (5) *om. C* 6 post *add. supralin. R* Nín post *om. C* la Samiradis *C* dano – India *om. C* 8 im̄ *add. after* seo *C* doríneadh *C* 9 Cethrochair – sudigud *om. C* 10 .l. cubat na tighe *C* a mmúir *om. C* Cetri .l. cumat na arde *C* 11 Is amlaidh robai se cethrachar ara cuima *add. after* tacmong *C* .lx. mili stadi *(sic) P* 12 n-umaide *om C* 13 at-berar] atb- *R* atberar *P* Iss ed – ar thiget (14) *om. C* 15 tar lar *C* .i. fo stuagdórsib cl. *om. C* 16 Conedh didiu doroine *C* rama do tabhairt *C* cacha fir *C* 17 ⁊ in sruth do lecudh *C* i min-srothu *om. C* lucht nathrach *(sic) C* Co tánic – cathrach *om. C* 19 Finit in .u.edh aes *add. after* Babilóin *C.*

(4) Coíca cubat tigi a mmúir,
annsa a thogail do nach dúil;
dá cét cubat, cumul ṅglé,
suas i n-aër i n-hairdde.

(5) Fichi cetharriad, coém dúib,
talldais for mulluch a mmúir;
gním cen nach cleith cumuing lib—
etir dá sreith do thigib.

(6) Ní dernad riam tiar ná tair
etir selbaib síl Ádaim,
foclaim, ar is caṅgen chóir,
dún daṅgen mar Babilóin. Babilóin.

(7) Tic sruth nEofrait dara lár,
de baé gleothroit is gleodál;
co nde ro-forbad a fóir
is ro-toglad Babilóin. Babilóin.

(8) Do-dechaid Cir lín a sluaig
dochum int srotha ruitruaid;
ro-scaíl, ro-fodail 'ma-sech
comba sét soraid sóinmech.

(9) Luiditar tria, bríg ṁbrotha,
innund for slicht int srotha
co dorus in tigi móir
i mbaí in rí 'sin Babilóin. Babilóin.

(10) IAr sin ro-airg cathraig Nín
cona rígraid, cona ríg
Ballasair, ba hardd a blad,
robo mac do Negussar.

(11) Negussar co luathi a hech,
mac-side Labudsardech;
Labudsardach, cruaid i cath,
ba mac Euilmoradach.

(12) Euilmoradach fodéin
ba mac Nabcodóin nárféil;

---

58. R P KM] 21 etir *KM* 24 coir *P* 25 Babilóin *(2°) om. P* 27 gleothroit] o *add. supralin. R* 29 irro- *P* Babilóin *(2°) om. P* 31 ruitruaid *gl.* rioth *P* 32 ro-fadail *R P* 34 tri *P* 38 chathraig *P* 49 ro-airggech] *sic R corr.*〉

is hic Nabcodón cen fell
ro-airggech ar thús Sálem.

(13) Ruc brait móir a cathraig ṅDé
ocus ro-mill a aidme;
ro-siachtatar lais dia thaig
laéchaib, cléirchib, mnáib, maccaib.

(14) Sechtmoga do bliadnaib dóib
i ndoíre 'sin Babilóin
co tánic Cir, comul ṅglé,
coro-fuaslaic a ndoíre.

(15) At-rubairt friu Cir iar sin:
"Éirgid dia bar tír feissin
ocus imthigid co tenn
co ríssid Hierusálem."

(16) IAr sin do-chuatar fodes
dochum a tíre cen chess,
cor' chumtaigset cathraig ṅDé,
etir aidmi ocus tige.

(17) IAr sain insaigis Cir cain
ríge for feraib domuin;
trícha bliadan baí a glóir
'sa hardrígi i mBabilóin.   Babilóin.

(18) Luid iar sin Cir lín a sluaig
cosin Scithia n-uabrig n-uair
ic iarair chána ní is sia—
ro-marb rígan na Scithia.

(19) Cethri flathiusa cen on
ar méit neirt, ba cain comol,
ro-gabsat in domun ṅdóid,
amal innises Canóin.

(20) Flathius na nAsarda n-án
co tánic Cir, mó cech mál;
flathius Med is Pers, ba glicc,
conas-tánic mac Pilipp.

(21) Flathius na nGréc, gríbda a ṅgáir,
conas-táncatar Rómáin;

Rómáin, ráid, hi rrígi iar sain
cotici déad in domuin.

(22) Inad in Tuir Nemruaid náir:
ar lár in Maige Ṡennáir
sluind, im sruth nEofrait co ṅglóir
ro-cumtacht in Babilóin. Babilóin.,

59. IMráiter sunn dano do aidedaib na prímfátha ⁊ dond lucht fo n-eblatar ⁊ dona hinadaib inra-adnaicthea.,

Ro-marb trá Mannases mac Ezechia Issias mac nAmois amlaid-so .i. a thócbáil i n-airdde ⁊ a rainn do thuirisc serrda iarna fot, co n-erbailt ⁊ coro-aidnaiced fo daraig Rogél.

Heremias *hautem* do chlochad ón phopul i nÉgipt ac Tammna ⁊ ro-adnacht icon Tammna chétna, airm i n-adnaictis foroinn, ríg ind Égeipt. Coni[d] hé-sin aided Heremiae meic Chelchiae Anothithecda.

Ezechel fáith *hautem,* ro-marbsat toísig in phopuil Israélda ar díchonderclígi a forcitail ⁊ a méit nadas-inchrechad im chol a n-écrábuid. Ron-adnaicset in popul i tír Maurim, fri adnacul Arafaxad.,

Daniél fáith *hautem* ⟨.i. mac Abda⟩, iar comlánugud a lathe in cach fuirbthetaid, at-bath isin doíre Babilóndai ⁊ ro-adnacht co honórach a oénur isind uaim rígda, ar náro-adnacht nech remi ⁊ ná adnaicfider iarum.,

60. Cestnaigthir beus hi sunn cia lín huide ro-baé do macaib Israhél ó Babilóin co Hierusálem. Ní annsa: cóic huidi sescat ar trí cét. Ar iss ed-sain fil ón Babilóin siansaidi .i. ó ifurn, hi fail cach cummasc ⁊ cach ṁbuadrech, cosin nHierusálem nemda, hi fail cach síd ⁊ cach sónmigi. Acht chena, filet sechtmoga sé passe ar chét in cach uide ⁊ dá staid ar fichit in cach pais, *ut dicitur.,*

-airggeth *KM* -airgget *P* 61 co rrisid *P* 65 etir *KM* 84 Romain raid (*zu lesen* Rōmānrad ? p. 19 n. 2) *KM* 86 Neṃbroaith *P.*

59. R P Lb KM*] 1 didiu súnd *Lb* prímḟátha *Lb* prīmflatha *(sic) KM* 2 -epleter *Lb* dona lloccaib *Lb* inra- *on* inna *R* inro hadnaicit *Lb* 3 Mannasés mac Esticia meic Amois *(sic)* amlaid so romarbad sén *Lb* Ezechiass mac nAmois *(sic), with* Issias *om. P* 4 co nerbailt de *Lb* 5 -adnacit *Lb* roda raigel *gl.* .i. p. (?) *Lb* 6 prímfáith *add. after* Heremias *Lb* hautem] uero *Lb* roclochad é side *Lb* 7 roadnaicthea na Foraind .i. riga Égepti *Lb* 8 conid hé *P* conid hi *Lb* oided Eremias meic Selicie Anothigecda *Lb* 9 Exeche (?) primfaith didiu *Lb* in *om. Lb,* fessin *add. after* Israélda 10 fora meit ro hinchrechad a col ⁊ a peccad impu *Lb* 11 -adnaicset *Lb* i tír] in tir *R P* in Abrim *Lb* 12 Danel primfaith tra *Lb* a bethad *Lb* 12–13 cech forpthetu *Lb* 14 arna roadnacit *Lb* nech riam *Lb* 15 iarum *om. P* dia essi *Lb.*

60. R P Lb OB KM Osk] 1 Cestnaigther didiu beos *Lb* -boi *Lb* do maccu *Lb* 2 coic huide *Osk* uidi *om. Lb* for trib cetaib *Lb* 2–3 ise sin *Lb* 3 siansidi *Osk* siansaide *Lb* i fil cech écumsanad ⁊ cech mbuaidriud *Lb* 4 ṁbuadrech] *punctum om. KM* i fil cech *Lb* cech sonmige *Lb* sonmigi *KM* 5 .clxxui. passe *R P* .uii. (?) paissi .lxx. ar .c. *Lb* cech uide dib *Lb* didiu *add. after* filet *P* 6 fichet *R* for fichet *Lb corr.*⟩ fichit *KM* cach huidi *R corr.*⟩ c. pais *OB* cech páis *Lb* passe *P* ut dicitur *om. Lb Osk KM.*

61. (1) Secht coíca[i]t[a] huide co mbríg,
a cóic déc cen immarrím,
ó Babilóin[b] duiscthi drenn[c]
co cathraig[d] Hierusálem.

(2) Sechtmoga sé passe ar chét[e]
in cach uidi[f], adbul mét;
do-rímet[g] ecnaide[h], is glé,
acht sain cenél[i] cech phasse.

(3) Dá staid ar ḟichit[j] cen chleith
in cach oénphais díb fo leith;
co rúinib screptra nach diss,
formae ueteris legis[k].

(4) Cóic paisse fichet[l] ar chét
in cach oénstaid[m]—sluinti sét;
fort-gellat fellsaib, ní fann,
mundi per geometricam.

(5) Argamaint seo remi-tét
ind ochtmad sailm déc ar chét;
scrútad co léir in cach than
cech ecnaid ro-chlunithar.

(6) Dauíd, do réir Ríg nime
in rígḟáith, in rígḟile,
ro-fég in rúin-se co rath
triasin spirut sechtṅdelbach. Secht coícait.,

(Glosses)
a) .i. cóic huidi sescat ar .ccc. sain uile. b) .i. ó iffurnn. c) .i. crithnaiges détu. d) .i. co nem in sein. e) .i. lín fers na biate in sein. f) .i. in cach cémmim don biait. g) .i. áirmit *(Lb)*. h) .i. eolaig *(Lb)*. i) .i. pais stairidi ⁊ pais siansaide. j) .i. dá lebur ar .xx. na fetarlaice. k) .i. na dá lebor ar ḟichit. l) .i. ochtmad rann in míle. m) .i. in cach oénlibur.

---

61. R P Lb OB KM Osk] 1 coicat *R P* .l.at *Lb* 2 a cóic déc] *sic R P* .xu. *Lb* immarīm *OB KM* imarim *Lb* 3 dúscid drend *Lb* 5 sech/t/moga .uii. (?) paissi *Lb* 6 cech uide *Lb* 7 dos- *Lb* *glosses* g *and* h *om. R P* ēcnaide *KM* 8 na paisse *Lb* 9 ar fichet *Osk* stait ar .xx.it *Lb* c. cleith *Lb* 10 cech *Lb* 11 c. rúnib *Lb* nachdiss *Osk* dis *Lb* 13 paisi *Lb* 14 cach oenstait *Lb* sluinnte *Lb* 15 -gellait fellsaim *Lb* 17 reme- *Lb* 18 in dochtinad *(sic) Osk* in tochtmad salm *Lb* at chet *Osk* 19 co lléir *Lb* cech tan *Lb* 20 -clunither *Lb* 21 rér *Lb* 23 na rúnsi *Lb* 24 tresan *Lb* sechtdelbach, *with* S.L.u. combr ⁊rl *add. Lb.*
Glosses: a) *om. KM* uide *Lb* sin uli *Lb* b) iffern *Lb* c) .i. dett *Lb* d) in sein *om. Lb* e) biaite *OB Lb* f) in *om. Osk* cech *Lb* cemimm *OB Lb* g) *om. R P* h) *om. R P* i) staraige *Lb* j) da lebar ar xxit na petarlaice *Lb* k) lebur *Osk* fichet *Osk* xxit *Lb* l) ochtmud *Osk* rand *Lb* m) in cach *om. Lb* énlebar *Lb*.

62. IS sé-seo trá huidi beres ind anim hi céin bíthir ic gabáil na biaiti .i. céim cacha fersa .i. sechtmoga sé ar chét. Ocus atá tothucht na dá lebur ar fichit in cach fers isin bia[i]t, conid aire do-beir in biat anmain a hiffurn hi cind bliadna, ar is sí chuibdigthir sech cech n-airnaigthe frisna dá lebur ar fichit na fetarlaice .i. a comlánius uili in cach oénfers ⁊ dá coibtel ar fichit inti fo numir apgitrech na nÉbraide.

Conid hé Dia de-side ro-lín fáithsine ṅDauída triana n-uidib-sium ⁊ ní hiat-som féin rodas-orddaig.,

Conid amlaid sin ro-forbad in chúiced aés.

63. *De sexta* [*a*]*etate incipit.,*

Sexta aetas haec est. IS sí int sessed aés, ó gein Críst co bráth. Ní fil numir bliadan árithi forsind aés-sa i lleth fri do[í]nib chétus, cia beith i lleth fri Dia. Ar ní fil isin scribtúir, iar ṅdíriuch-scríbunn, bale asa tíssed, cia beith do thoíb inti chena ní asa ṅgabtha numir bliadan na [a]éssi-se.,

Ab initio mundi, iuxta Septuaginta Interpretes, .u. milia .cxc. Secundum uero Ebraicum .iii. milia .dccclii. Ab urbe condita .dcclii.

64. IS tria Críst ro-génair ó Mhaire óigingin i tossuch na sessed aéssi, isin dara bliadain cethrachat flathiusa Cessair Auguist, ro-saérait lucht na cóic n-aés remi-deochatar in cach n-immarbus, ⁊ do-rochratar i nÁdam.

Hi cóiced bliadain déc flathiusa Tibir Cessair immorro ro-basted Críst ó Iohain Babtist in nEnnon, *iuxta Salem,* hi tríchatmaid bliadain a a[é]ssi ḟodessin. *Et* is í-sin bliad[a]in ro-thog apstalu ⁊ desciplu .i. dá apstal déc ⁊ dá deiscipul sechtmogat.,

65. *Haec sunt nomina Apostolorum.*

Petrus Simon	Pilippus	IAcobus Alphei
Andreas	Bartholomeus	Tatheus
IAcobus Zebedei	Tomas	Simon Cannaneus
IOhannes	Matheus	Madianus *et* Paulus
		⟨.i. *in loco Iudae*⟩

---

62. R P Lb* OB] 1 Is fon indus sin didiu it .ui. fers .lxx. for .c. filet isin mbiait *Lb*, *and add.:* .i. it .u. uide .lx. for .ccc. don biait oc tabert anma a hiffurn ⁊ se paissi .lxx. for .c. in cech uide. Ocus in lín uide sin don biait ise sin doímne iffuirn 2 .i. clxxui. *R P* Ocus] ⁊ *abbrev.* *R* Et *P* 3 isin biait] biat *R corr.*⟩ biait *OB* 4 a pein *P* 7 trina *P*.

63. R P C] 1 INcipit in .ui.edh aes *C* etate *R P* 2 haec est *om. C* Is i ind aes *C* aés *om. P* 3 iṁ *add. before* numir *C* fuire *C* fa daínibh *C* 4 iar ndíriuchscríbunn *and* isin scribtúir *reversed C* 5 assa inaberta *C* 6 F.I.N.I.T dona haesaibh *add. after* na aéssi-si *C* 7 Ab initio – .dcclii. *om. C*.

64. R P] 3 ⁊ *om. P* 5 Hi .xu. b. flathiusa *R P* 7 Et isin bliadain hi sin *P* ⁊ a desc. *P* 8 deec *P*.

65. R P IT] 2 Philippus *P* 3 Thadeus *P* 4 Thomas *P* 5 Mattheus *P* Madian *P* 6 .i. in loco Iudae *add. after* Paulus *P*.

66. It hé immorro anmann na dá descipul sechtmogat bátar ic Íhesu Críst.,

.i. IAcobus	Amplias	IGnatius
IUstus	Urbanus	Simon Quirinensis
Mathathias	Cleopas	Alaxender . Ruphus
IOseph	Erodiones	Nathanel . Necodimus
IOseph	Assimmerges	IUdas . Iacobus
Marcus	IAson	Simon . Simon ⟨.i. Coriarius⟩ .l.
Barnabas	Sephanus	Lucas . Barnabas
Lucas	Pilippus	Stephanus Corissius
Cleopas	Procurus	Milichius . Gaias
.x. Serica	.xxx. Nicanor	Flegonta . Ermen
Semeon	Parmina	Appellen . Probabilis
Lucias	Aquila	Dionisius Ariopagita .lx.
INáran	IUdas	Appenitus . Iessus
Stortenes	Siluanus	IUstus . Stachue
Caphas	Simon	Pomplius . Arizobulus
Tatrieus	Cleopa	Stefanus Corinthensis
Erenet	Silas	Herodius . Ruphus
Pastor	Nasson	Olimphias .lxx.
Andromachas	Agabas	Titus .i.
.xx. IOhamas	.xl. Annanias	Filimon .ii.,

67. *Prima persecutio sub Nerone. Secunda sub Domitiano. Tertia sub Traiano. Quarta sub Marco Antoni*[*n*]*o. Quinta sub Seuero. Sexta sub Maximiano. Septima sub Decio. Octaua sub Ualiriano. Nona sub Auriliano. Decima sub Deocletiano.*

Hi flathius in deichnebuir seo trá do-chuatar bás martra apstail ⁊ deiscipuil ⁊ martírig Íhesu Críst ar Dia fo tríb rannaib in talman.,

⟨Sarofanes, is é toísech do-rigne delb n-ídail .i. ro-cumtaig delb a meic di ór ⁊ argat iarna éc. *Et* ro-ling demun inti co mbíd ic accallaim na ndoíne, conid hé-sin in cétarracht ro-buí ar thús riam.,⟩

---

66. R P IT] 1 descipul] -l *add. supralin. R* 2 Íhesu] Ihū *R P* Ísu *IT* 3 .i. *om. P* 5 Cleophas *P* Alaxander *P* 6 Necodemus *P* 7 Assimerges *P* 8 Simon *(2°) gl.* .i. Coriarius *R P* 10 Philippus *P* Stephanus *gl.* .i. Corissius *P* *Grosjean reads as 2 names*, S. *and* C. 11 Cleophas *P* 12 .xxx. *supralin. R* 14 .lx. *supralin. R* 15 Appenitus – Filimon .ii. *in long line P* Iesus *P* 16 Stortens *P* 17 Caiphas *P* Arizobul *P* 18 *Order of names after Corinthensis:* R., O., T., H., F., P. *in P* 19 Herodius *gl. .i̊. P* 21 Agabus *IT* 22 .xl. *supralin. R* Filimon *gl. .i̊i.*, *with* it iet ind sin na da descipul .lxx.at *add. P.*

67. R P IT*] *This section follows* §68 *in P; some words shorn off by binder R* 5 dei[cnebuir?] *IT (MS. shorn)* re bas *IT (MS. shorn)* 6 mart[ire. . .?] Isu *IT (MS. shorn)* [. . .] trib rannaib *IT (MS. shorn)* in talman] *sic P*, *illegible in R (MS. shorn)* 7 Sarofanes, *etc. om. IT* Sarophanes *C* delb *om. C* delb n-ídail *om. Ld (sic)* doroíne .i. *(sic)* fuath doroinig dia mac, *with* d'ór ⁊ argat *om. Ld C* 8 inti] issin arracht *Ld C* (n-) co roibi *Ld* co raibhi *C* 9 na *om. Ld C* in *om. Ld* cétarracht *om. C* ar thús *om. Ld* ⁊ is ara furis dochuaid cach iar sin *add. after* riam *Ld.*

68. ISsind aés-[s]e trá ro-génair Críst, amal at-chua[da]mmar. Is inti dano ro-chéssair .i. iar trícha trí co leith bliadna amal it-beir Iosep, ⁊ i n-ochtmaid bliadain déc flathiusa Tibir Cessair., Ocus ro-airg iarum iffern im dligthechu na cóic n-amser.

ISs inti ro-fodlait apstail ⁊ descipuil Críst fo chet[h]araird in domuin, iarna tinfiud ó rath na n-ilbérla. Isind aés-[s]a dano ro-chrochad Petar ⁊ ro-tescad Pól la Neir Cessair. Isind aés-si dano do-chuatar bás martra apstail ⁊ descipuil ⁊ martírig ⁊ foésmidaig Íhesu ar Dia, iarna marbad do rígaib ⁊ do choradaib ⁊ do maéraib ⁊ do chonsolaib ⁊ do herrígaib écr̥áibdechaib in domuin, fo tríb rannaib in talman .i. Eoraip, Affraic, Assia.

69. Do anmannaib trí rann in domuin in so sís.
Assia dano, ingen Neir ⁊ na bandia, dianid ainm Doridis, is uaidi-sin ro-ainmniged inn Assia .i. Neptúin mac Ióib, dia mara, tuc grád di corbo hé tinscra ro-gellad di .i. tress rann in domuin do ainmnigud huaidi ara hógi do lot ⁊ ar inbuth fri Neptúin.,

Affrica .i. ó Affer mac Madian meic Abráim ro-ainmniged .i. forsluagad do-cumlai Affer i nAffraic, coro-bris cath for lucht na Affrice, co tarrasair féin tess *post* ⁊ conid de-sin ro-anmniged ind Affraic huad.,

Eorops, rí na Sicomarda, ro-chuir chath im Eoraip, conid dia anmaim do-garar Eoraip ó Eorops., Nó Europa, ingen Agenóir, ríg *Sidorum,* co tuc Ióib grád di ⁊ coros-fuc leis co hinis Crét ⁊ co nderna dá mac fria .i. Minosic ⁊ Adamaint, co tuc Ióib di a ainm forsin tres raind in domuin., ⟨Cicrops, is é toísech ro-idpair dam do Ióib, conid ass-sain anmnigther Iób.,⟩

70. Duan Dublittrech in so forsin Panechte.,

(1) Rédig dam, a Dé, do nim,
co hémid, ní hindeithbir,

---

68. R P] 1 -cuammar *P* 2 iar .xxxiii. co leith .b. *R P* Ioseb *P* 3 i n-ochtmaid bliadain déc] in .xuiii. b. *R* Ocus] ⁊ *abbrev. R* Et *P* 6 -crochad Petur *P* 10 Affraic] Affurc, *with* -ur *abbrev. R* Affraic *P.*

69. R P C Ld G*] 1 Do anmannaib – sís *om. C Ld G* sís *om. P* *Order of sections in P is:* Europe, Asia, Africa 2 dano *om. C Ld G* na bandea *C G* danadh a. *C* dianad *G* sin *om. C Ld G* 3 Is amlaidh seo focaemhnacair sain *add. after* inn Ássia *C* Nemhtuin *C* mac Ióib, dia mara *om. C Ld G* 4 conidh *C G* conid *Ld* tinscra *om. Ld* logh *C* log *G* -geall *C G Ld* in tress *C Ld G* 5 a hógi] -o- *supralin. R* do millead *G* milliud *Ld* i llóg a hoige *Ld* ⁊ ar inbuth – N. *om. C Ld G* 6 Affrica ab Affer *Ld C* mac Madian – ro-ainmniged *om. Ld C* ⁊ do clandaibh Abraimh do sein *add. after* Affer *C* ⁊ do clannaib Abraam doside *Ld* 7 sluaighedh *C* sluaged *Ld* ro tinoiled la *Ld* ro tineoladh la *C* 8 tarrassar *Ld* tarasair *C* feine tres *(sic) C* iar sin tes *Ld* post *om. C* 9 huad *om. Ld* 10 Sichimda *Ld C* conid dia a. – in domuin *om. Ld C* 10–11 is uadha ainmnigter Eoraip *C* is uaid ainmnigter E. *Ld* 13 a ainm do bith *P* 14 *Gloss add. in marg. at* §51 *R.*

70. R P L] 1 Dublitir hua Uathgaile cc. *L* Duan dublitrech .h. huathgaile

éirniud mo chesta, is gním glan,
corop espa olloman.

(2) Coíca mac ic Ádam án,
coíca ingen ardd imslán.
Ro-faémsat bith cness fri cness
ciaro-chlaínsat in cardes.

(3) Tres ros-hétla in bith buide,
ro-bréctha tria banguide;
ciaro-rígsat ríg na reb
nír' sílsat díb acht sesfer.

(4) Triar fer, triar ingen co ngail
di chlaind airegdai Ádaim;
uadib ro-sílad in sluag
diar' línad domun dimmbuan.

(5) Caín, Séth ocus Sile
na trí meicc cen mórmire;
Pibb, Olla, Pithibb cen brath
in triar ingen imuallach.

(6) Pibb ainm do mnaí Chaín chain,
Olla sétig Séth sírglain;
ben Sile, solasta a níam,
Pithibb forasta fírfíal.

(7) Sessiur sain ra seircc snáma,
uallcha áille imslána;
ro-línsat na treba thair
do chlaind Eua ocus Ádaim.

(8) Ro-mallach Dia Chaín cruaid
is cach oén no-geinfed uaid;
hé féin ro-thimgair co trén
triana fingail for Abél.,

---

inso forsin Panechte *P* 5 *1 st. add. here L P (manu altera) :* Adam is Eua aṅgbaid. / cétdias ro thecht corpanmain. / ro chetaig Dia dóib malle / tusmiud co cóir a clainde. 7 is .l. *L* ard *L* 8 -faemsat *L* cnes ri cnes *L* 9 ciar chloensat in carddes *L* 10 Trén ros étlá *L (sic leg.* ?) 11 banchuire *L* 13 sesfer] *sic R* (-fer *in ras.* ?) 14 cen ail *L* 15 airegda *L* 16 uathib *L* 17 dimbuan *L* 18 Sili *L* 19 -miri *L* 22 Píb *L* 23 setig Séith *L* setaig, *with* a *expuncted R* 24 solustusa a nniab *(sic) L* 25 Pithib forusta firfíal *L* 26 ri seir *L* 31 uad *L* 32 -thimmairg *L* 34 Fuacair *L* Ro fuacair *P*

(9) "Fúcair," ar in Coimdiu cáid
do chlannaib Séth, co soérbáig,
"náro-ḟaéma duine díb
ingena claíne Cäín."

(10) Huair táncatar dar thimna
na fir uallcha eissidna,
cure ro-chráid díliu dron,
ros-báid huili acht oénochtor.

(11) Noé 'sa trí meic cen mebail,
cona séitchib soérgelaib;
ochtor do síl Séth cen sál
náro-emsat Chaín cennmár.

(12) Sém, Chám, Iaféth na n-iäth,
trí meicc Noé meic Lamiäch;
a trí mná gríbda glanna:
Olla, Oliua, Oliuana.

(13) Copha sétig Noé noémglain,
Olla ben Sém sírsaéglaig;
ben Cháim Oliua indlaga,
ben Iaféth Oliuana.

(14) IS siat-sain lucht na háircce
co sult is co saérḟaélte;
gabsat cen aithbe, cen fell,
in domun aithle dílenn.

(15) Bliadain dóib isind áirc úair
ós diamair mara moṅgruaid,
céin baé in díliu, adbar áig,
for dreich in talman tonnbáin.

(16) Sechtmad fichet, dia festa,
for Oéne, iar cor bissexa,
hi teirt kalaind Mai miadaig
luid esse iar certbliadain.

---

35 Séith *L* 36 nir faema *L* 37 cloína *L* 38 thancatar dar timna *L* darm *R* 39 essidna *L* 40 cuire *L* 42 meibail *R* mebail *L* 43 co séitchib saergelaib *L* 44 ochtur do ṡíl Séith *L* 45 naro emsat *R* nar ḟaemsat *L* cnedmar *L* 51 b. Ṡéim ṡírṡaeglaig *L* sirsaeglaib *R* 52 in loga *L* 54 na hairce *L* 55 co saerṡlánte *L* 58 issind á. ḟuair *L* 60 buí *L* adbar n-áig *L* 61 os dreich *L* 62 *One st. add. here in* P *(manu alt.) from Rec. III (B Lc)* 63 ar aíne ar *L*

(17) Ó ro-fég Noé ar cach leth
in tír luchair lántoirtech,
di cach thoíb, cid bad dattu?
ro-fáid a trí mórmaccu.

(18) Tuc d'Iafféth in nEoraip n-áin,
tuc do Sém Assia im[ṡ]láin;
isind Affraic cen tám thess
ro-lín Cám a c[h]aladchness.

(19) Ro-mallach a athair án
in mac dianid comainm Cám;
conid hé—ar chlaéne ro-chind—
Caín na ndoéne iar ndílinn.

(20) Huad ro-génatar co ṅgail
goborchinn is fomoraig,
líne luchorpán lerda
is cach díne dodelbda.

(21) Doíne na dá cenn, ba col,
is na dá corp hi comchengol,
is na hoénchossaig odra
is na guilbnig grenngorma.

(22) Cech duine atá thair cen chenn
ic imthecht a glind i ṅglenn,
is a bél bán asa bruinne,
do chlaind Chám co corluinne.

(23) Cethri meic maithi ic Cám chass,
fri hág ocus fri hernm[b]as:
Chus, fo bruth na n-esgal n-án,
Mesrom is Futh is Channán.

(24) Na hEtheopacdai huili,
nom-geib gráin fria ṅgormduibe,
do chlainnd Chus meic Cáim na cles,
ónt sruth cosin sál sairdes.

---

64 hi .iii. kl. *R P* i t-t kl. *L* 65 eiste *L* re c. *L* 66 Or ḟég *L* for cech *L* 67 -torthech *L* 68 do cech thaíb *L* 69 -ḟóid *L* 70 in nEuraip *L* 71 Asia *L* 72 issin *L* cen tar tes *L* 74 *Four stt. add. here in* P *(manu alt.) from Rec. III* (B)[1],[4] (B Lc)[2],[3] 75 dian c. *L* 76 ar chloíne *L* 80 luchrapan *L* 81 cech duine dodelba *L* duine dedelbda, *with* o *add. above* e *(1°) of* dodelbda *R* 82 co col *L* 83 na *om. L* 85 gulbnig gergorma *L* 89 co roluinde *L* 90 mathe oc C. *L* 91 ri hág ⁊ ri hernmas *L* fri hernbass *P* (hernmas *R*) 92 Caus *(sic) L* 93 Mesram *L* 95 na ṅgormduibe *L* 96 do chl. Chauis *L* 100 lucht na

(25) Clanna Futh meic Cáim do chéin,
ro-línsat in clár comréid
is hucht Affraice as cech aird
co Sliab n-athslaiti nAthlaint.

(26) Égeptacdai im sruth Níl náir,
do chlannaib Mesrom meic Cáim;
óthá sruth Nuchuil andes
co Muir Torrén na tromthress.

(27) Secht mórthuatha Cannáin c[h]ruaid,
etir aness is atuaid;
'siat clann Channáin at-chluine,
ind fir falláin foltbuidi.

(28) Oénmac déc Cannán c[h]liaraig,
meblaig meirgig mórmiadaig,
ro-línsat tír 'nar garb grian,
ó Muir Marb co Muir Toirrian.

(29) Tuc Dia díth do cach thaéb thair
for claind ind fir chlaén chuilig;
ó ro-thairṅgir a tír trén
do chlaind ainglig Israhél.

(30) Go munchenn ṅGaitiden ṅgluair
ó sruth Eofrait anairthuaid,
ro-sílsat ó Chám na cnet
deich prímchenéla fichet.

(31) Ro-iadus gabáil Cáim cain
isin chamáir Chétamain,
i tír na Laignech co léir,
cencop ainmech ní hamréid. Rédig.,

(32) Ro-línsat in nEoraip n-aird
clanna Iaféth maith mórgairg;
fuaratar d'uaslecht ó Dia
conid leo tuaiscert nAssia.

---

hAffraice *L* 103 Mesraim *L* 104 anes *L* 106 Sech *(sic) L* 108 itchluine *L* 111 mórmiadaig] or *written above 1st* m *R* 113 *Two stt. add. here in* P *(manu alt.) from Rec. III* (B Lc), *with ref. mk* 114 do cech thaíb thair *L* 115 chloín *L* 117 aṅglig *L* 118 Go] *sic R P* Co *L* ṅGaditan *L* 119 Eufráit *L* 123 issin ch. chetṡamain *L* 124 na llaignech co lléir *L* 125 anmech *L* 129 tuascertleth

(33) Ó Sléib Imai 'sin Túr thind
siarthuaid co sruth Danaim,
ocus in Scithia cen cháin,
la claind Iaféth enechnáir.

(34) INn uair náros-talla thair
clanna Iäféth inmain,
ro-threbsat Eoraip cen raind,
siar ro-seolait a seolcraind.

(35) Óthá Slébe Riphi ruaid
risna Gaéthlaigib atuaid
cosin tráig lescbáin lechtaig
hisind Espáin immechtraig.

(36) Ocht meic ic Iaféth na n-áth,
ní himthigtis etarthráth:
Gomér, Magoch, Madue mass,
Iaban, Tubal is Tiaras.

(37) Massoch, Maseca na sreth,
ic dul séta ba sétrech;
uaidib ro-seolta na sluaig
dochum nEorpa anairthuaid.

(38) Galatacdai, mar at-chén,
do c[h]lainn glégaistai Gomér;
isat bladaig a frecrai,
do c[h]laind Magaig Scithecdai.

(39) Síl Madue Meda míne,
ro-hailte fri ardríge;
Ionnai na ṅgrianán ṅglan,
ó Iabán ro-chinsetar.

(40) Celtiberdai, nít callai,
Hiberdai ocus Espandai
is ó Thubal ro-thaitne
bunad na trí n-ardaiccme.

---

na hAsia *L* 130 sin tuir *L* 131 siartuaith *L* 133 ri claind *L* 134 ind uair niras talla *L* 136 ra- *L* 137 ra ṡeolsat *L* 138 sleibte Rifi *L* sl- *R* 140 lectaig *L* 141 issin nEspain n-imechtraig *L* 142 Ocht] *sic R L P; see note in LL Vol. 3,* p. 567 n. 4, *where suggested emendation is wrong.* ic *om. L* 144 Madai mas *L* 145 Tiras *L* 146 Masséca *L* 147 saetrach *L* 148 uadib ra seolta *L* 150 mar atgén *L* 153 Magoich *L* na S. *L* 155 re hardríge *L* 156 Iondai na ṅgrian *L* 157 ro gensetar *L* 158 nít ciallai *L* 164 Traiecdai *L* 165 cen chnetecla *L*

(41) Capadocdai ó Massoch mín,
imda torud 'na tromthír!
Síl Tiras Traicecdai thair,
cen chnaiteclae for conair.

(42) Íbad is Baad co becht
dá mac do Magoch mórchert;
do-ruacht a sírblad dar sál,
ó Íbad rígrad Rómán.

(43) Foénius mac Baaid, ní bréc,
meic Magoch mín na mórchét,
nocorb' athair cen ecna,
hé athair na Scithecda.

(44) IS dia síl Gaédil glana,
ro[p]sat aégid ágmara;
gabsat dar sluag féigseṅg Fáil
rígi nÉrenn a hEspáin.,

(45) IN mac aili Magoch maith,
Íbath airegda, int ardflaith,
mac dó-side Alanius án
ótát Fraiṅc ocu[s] Rómán.

(46) IS uad Saxain cen suire
ocus Bretain barrbuide,
ocus Albánnai arin maig
cosin nAssia n-airtheraig.

(47) Trí meic ic Alán cen brón,
Arbon, Negua, Hissiccón;
ro-sílsat mór ciniud caém
thair in n-iniud na n-ardnoém.

(48) Ro-gon mór ṅgelhua do gáib
oénmac Negua meic Aláin;
no-chathed caslus calaid
Saxus, ótát Saxanaig.

---

166 Baath *L* 169 Iabad *L* 170 Baaith *L* 171 na morthet *R* na tromthét *L* 172 nocor *L* 173 senathair *L* 175 rosat *R* ropsat *L P* aígid *L* 176 ar slúag *L* 178 Magoich *L* 179 Ibath *L* 180 ain *R* án *L* 181 athair Frañc ⁊ Román *L* ocu romain *(sic) R* 185 issin *L* 186 al án *R*, *with connecting mark manu rec.* 187 Isicon *L* 190 Ro gon mór gelua da gáib *L* 191 mac meic

(49) Nocon déntais gleic im glór
cethri meic hic Issicón;
Romanus, Fraṅcus hi fus,
Albanus ocus Brittus.

(50) Fuair ó chách cádus is cháin
Romanus, ótát Rómáin;
Francus, ótát Fraiṅc co fír,
ní dénad saint im saébgním.

(51) Albanus, ba mac málla,
senathair na nAlbánna;
mór do gliccus ro-chertaig
Brittus, ótát fírBretnaig.

(52) ISat airegda ar cach thráig
clanna ilerda Iouáin,
is leo cach treb thana thiar
i n-insib Mara Torrian.

(53) Sluind cóic prímchenéla déc
ó Iaféth, ní immarbréc;
do-gnítis tétnais co trén
i n-écmais a fochenél.

(54) Co[m]lín clainne Iaféth aitt,
etir Assia ocus Eoraip,
ní faigbet Goídil co glé
do síl oénfir i n-oénré. Rédig.

(55) Clanna Sém is iat is lia
i n-airechas na hAssia;
ó sruth Gaind a ṅgleo fri grian,
leo cen raind co Muir Torrian.

(56) Ó Muir Romuir cosind rúin,
co Sliab Cucais, co Sliab Túir,
is re clainn Sém cach slige,
slaind—ní chél—a cardine.

(mc̄ mc̄) A. *R* 192 ni chated *L* 194 Nocho *L* na glor *L* 195 Isicon *L* 202 Albanius *L* 204 ra chertaig *L* 206 Is *L* cech *L* 207 clanna airegda Iobain *L* 208 cech, *with* thana *om. L* 210 sloind *L* 212 donítis *L* 214 Colin *R P* Comlín *L* 216 ni fagbat *L* 219 na Scithia *L* 220 a ṅgle ra grian *L* 222 *This st. follows lines 230–3 in L* cosin *L* 223 cu sliab *L* 224 ra claind

(57) Cóic meic ic Sém, sachla in síl,
riu ní gabtha fo chomlín;
Elam na dá ṅglas[s]úl ṅglan,
Lude, Assúr is Iaram.

(58) Arifaxad, ard a feb,
ciarbo garg nirbu glémer;
fuair eladain is acra
senathair na Callacda.

(59) Elam, ba cruaid gním a gaé,
huaid atát Elamitae;
Lidetai ó Luide, ní liach,
lucht ónád buidi badbfiach.

(60) Robo chassúr crann a gaé
Assúr, ótát Asardae;
Sirecdai ó Ṡáram na sluag,
airecht na n-álad n-induar.

(61) Cethri meic Sáraim na sreth,
ros-horddaig Ísu aṅglech.
sluinn hi fus scur na scél:
Hus ocus Ul is Gethér.

(62) Mess in cethramad mac mín
áirmidir icond ardríg;
nocorbo clann ḟir ónnai,
uad atát na hEönnai.

(63) Hus mac Sáraim, sochla in rí,
ótát Traconitidi;
Armiannai, airdairc in dám,
ó hUl inraic enechnár.

(64) Arcani, is émech a ferg,
aicmi na curad crobderg;
ro-siacht co Bethil a mblad,
ó Gethéir ro-génsitar.

Séim *L* is ro *R* 225 ni chél ar cach ardḟine *L* ní chél *gl.* nó ni scer *R* ni cer *P* 226 *This and the next st. follow lines 221–4 L* 228 da ṅglassúl *L* na nglassul *P* 229 Luide Asur is Aram *L* 231 nirbo *L* 232 elathain *L* 234 crand a gae *L*, *with next 4 lines om. by homoioteleuton* (gaé : gaé) 239 Assardai *L* 241 na n-ilad innuair *L* 244 sloind *L* 245 Us et Ul *P* 247 armither acon a. *L* 248 ciarbo chland *L*, *with* ar caí *add. after* ónnai 253 o Ur erdairc *L* 254 Arcannai *L* 255 croibderg *L* 257 o Gethil ro genatar *L* 258 Sarain

(65) Clanna Sáraim meic Sém sain,
do chéin rodas-cualabair;
ro-gabsat, ní hiṅglind, i ṅgait,
ó sruth nInd co sruth nEofrait.

(66) Sala, no-bíd ór ria hatt,
mac álaind Arafaxat;
mac do Sala Éber ard,
toísech na trénḟer tréngarg.

(67) Fallec is Iachtan cen ail,
dá mac Ébeir ingenglain;
Éber mac Sala na slat,
Sala mac Arafaxat.

(68) Ó Éber mac Sala ille
anmnigter na hÉbraide;
is glélerda ruc ón Tur
bérla nÉberda a oénur.

(69) Trí meic déc ic Iachtan án,
ic fiur na n-airer n-imslán;
is leo cach rind is cach rian
ó sruth Ind cosin [n]Acian.

(70) Elmodad is Saleph slán,
Asarmoth, Iaire imnár,
Adumar, Adustal ard,
Decla, Ebal féig fírgarg.

(71) Abimel, Sabaä sút—
mairg risa mbíd a ṅgarbgrúc!
Offir, robo garg a gal,
Ebila ardd, Iöbab.

(72) Clanna Iactain tairbig thair,
i[n]d ḟir chardig crechloṅgig
níros-lamsat lucht ba lia,
ro-gabsat na dá India.

---

meic Ṡéim *L* 259 O chéin rodos cualabair *L* 260 niṅglind *(sic) L* 261 co s. Eufrait *L* 262 re att *L* 263 Arfaxat *L* 264 airbert ard *(sic) L* 271 ainmnigter *L* 272 lerda *om. L* 275 ic fir *L* 276 cech *(bis) L* 277 co sruth nAcian *(sic) L* 278 Elimúdad, *with* is *om. L* 279 Isarmath Iare *L* 280 Adumar *gl.* nó Aduram *R* Aduram Adustal ard *P* Adumar A. a. *L* 281 Ebla *gl.* nó Ebal *L* 282 Sala *(sic) L* 283 risa mbia a saérgrúc *L* 284 Ofir ropo *L* 286 tarbig *L* 287 id fir *R* ind ḟir *L P* (f-) 289 ucht na

(73) Atát im sruth nEofrait n-ard
int airecht rígda rogarg;
in ca[ch] thír thenn im Thigir,
is díb cenn cech ardinaid.

(74) For cuit clanni Cannáin cóir,
ind ḟir airegdai ardmóir,
atát, ní sét cen slaide,
dá threib déc na nÉbraide.

(75) Secht cenéla fichet fég!
i n-écmais a fochenél,
atát do chlannaib Sém sain,
noco-chél ar Gaídelaib.

(76) Trícha cenél Cáim c[h]olaig,
a cóic déc Iaféth foraib,
trí noí chenél Séim na slat,
is a dó sain sechtmogat.

(77) Dóib ro-mesctha na bérlai
d'imdugud a mórhérgnai;
a dó sechtmogat, ní suail,
ic tarmesc in Tuir Nemruaid.

(78) Oénbérla ro-baí co sain
i[c] clainn uaibrechtaig Ádaim,
cech airm i mbaí sídmag selb,
diarb' ainm gríbglan Gairthigern.

(79) Ó ro-fuc Éber ón Tur
nír' glémer in gnáthugud;
ar ro-thidnaic ro-len de
bérla n-indraic nÉbraide.

(80) I cinn deich ṁbliadan iar sin
ar-rícht la Foénius Forsaid
in bérla bélblasta bind,
Goédelg glégasta gniïm.

---

da I. *L* 290 nEufrait *L* 292 /in/ cech thir *L* 293 ardenig *L* 294 For *supralin. L* 300 sein *L* 303 oraib *L* 305 sin *L* 309 tairmesc *L* Nebruaid *L* Nembruaith *P* 310 Ba hoenbérla, *with* ro-baí *om. L* 312 cia cairm *(sic) L* 314 Oros fuc *L* 315 ni glemer *L* 316 ora thidnaic *L* 317 b. n-airdairc *L* n-indraic *gl.* nó nirdaircc *R* nirdairc *P* 319 Fenius Farsaid *L* 323 ro ḟigius *L*

(81) Níro-rigius réim dar recht,
ros-figius féin co fírchert
craéb chaibniusa clanni Noé
cen aéb duilgiusa ar oénchoé.

(82) Missi don chuachmaig ón chill,
hUa hUathgail a hUsenglind;
rom-ruca sech saébi snéid
torud Aéne ind Ríg roréid!
Rédig dam, a Dé, do nim.,

---

325 con aeb *R* cen aíb ndoilgiusa *L* 327 Uathgail *L* ó Uissenglind *L*
328 rom fuca *L* 329 aíni in R. *L*.

TRANSLATION

1. (Here) begins the Pandicept, i.e. Dublittir Ua hUathgaile's translation into Irish of Jerome's Pandicept [=Vulgate] (follows) below: concerning the chief branches of the world and the conquests of the world, concerning its many peoples and the number of their languages, concerning the ages of their princes and their names, concerning also the Ages of the World and the duration of each Age.

2. According to the Septuagint here:

(1) The first Age of the pleasant world (was) from the beginning of the world to the deluge—240 years together, with 2002 years.

(2) The second Age—no shame—was from the deluge to Abraham; 900 years, it is granted from of old, and 42 years.

(3) (There were) 80 years with fame, and 20 years, 300, no more, from the creation to Abraham.

(4) From Abraham to the Temple of God, 900 years, a lasting time; it is a sufficient length, according to rule, (and) 84 years.

(5) There are 505 years from Abraham till the parting of the Red Sea before Moses and his great host, it is no falsehood.

(6) From Moses to the strong Temple, I will say it was 400 years; 79 years (added) to that—thereby is the enumeration more correct.

(7) (There are) 75 and 300 years after Troy of the hosts was destroyed to the thirty-fifth year after Moses's Age, it is sought by you.

(8) (There are) 34 years and 800, by a fair rule, from Abraham to the siege of Troy, without error or great lie.

(9) From the time when Troy of the towers was sacked until the Temple was built (there were) 151 years, it is no crooked path. The first Age.

3. The variation in the Hebrew Verity from the Septuagint, here:

(1) The first Age of the pleasant world, from Adam to the deluge, (was of) 56 years, a clear utterance, and 1600 years.

(2) The second Age then, from the deluge to Abraham, (was of) 92 years, a clear and lovely utterance, and 200 smooth-sounding years.

(3) The third age—look truly!—from Abraham to David, (was of) 42 years, without reproach, and 900 years.

(4) The fourth Age, correct and fitting, (was) from then to the Babylonian captivity: that is 73 years and 400 fine years.

(5) The fifth Age (was) from the fine, smooth captivity to the birth of the Son of God in Bethlehem: there are 89 years in it, and 500 fair, narrow years.

(6) The sixth Age (was) from the birth of the true Christ to the Judgement day of great conflict: no one but beloved God knows what will be in that Age.

(7) The seventh Age, it is a pure, bright creation, (will be) of equal duration with all the others, from Abel—truly generous his hue—to the last just man.

(8) The eighth Age (will be) from that on: that is the everlasting Age. I relate, and it is no great lie I tell, there will be no end to its hundredth (Age).

(9) Christ of tribulations our very dear friend; Christ, may he come to my great relief! Christ, who has sought us in the distant past; Christ our protector after centuries. The first Age of the pleasant world.

4a. The Ages of Man are six in number: the first Age of Man is infancy, which is completed in seven years. The second Age is youth, which extends to the fourteenth year. The third is adolescence, up to age twenty-eight. The fourth is young manhood, up to the fiftieth year. The fifth is middle-age, from age fifty to age seventy. The sixth is old age, which has no set length. Senility, indeed, is the final stage of old age.

4. There are six Ages of the world, i.e. from Adam to the deluge (is) the first Age; from the deluge to Abraham (is) the second Age; from Abraham to David (is) the third Age; from David to the Babylonian captivity (is) the fourth Age; from the captivity to Christ (is) the fifth Age; from Christ to the Judgement (is) the sixth Age; from Abel, son of Adam, to the martyrdom of Enoch and Elias at the verge of doom (is) the seventh Age; from the Judgement onwards, including the day of Judgement itself, is the eighth Age, as we have related above.

5. It is to be enquired, how many years each Age contains, except the last Age, for it has no end in the first place as far as we are concerned. And who are the princes of every Age and what are the reigns of those princes? And in which of those Ages was the world divided into three parts, and what are the names of those divisions? And whence did they derive their names?

6. How did the family of Noe divide, and in how many distinct races did they remain? How many languages do they possess and why were the languages multiplied? For it is only one language that we find for them in the beginning: Gairthigern was the name of that language, i.e. the language that is today called the language of the Jews, as the poet says:

7. (1) Gairthigern was the name of the language that the proud and noble son of God [gl. i. e. Adam] had, and the race of stately Adam, before the building of Nemrod's Tower.

(2) Though the Hebrew language has remained to the people of the beautiful world, the name of the common language after the Judgement day of abysses will be Gairthigern. Gairthigern.

8. And in what Age were the languages multiplied, and are the races more numerous than the languages? How many races are there, and what are the peoples that do not complete the enumeration of the races, but which are included in the races that are related to them? How many races are there, and which are the races that changed their names compared with their original state?

9. This is the number of years in the first Age to begin with, i.e. 1656 years. Adam, moreover, was the first leader of that Age. It is to be enquired here, how many children did Adam beget? Not difficult! Fifty sons and fifty daughters, as the historians of the Romans adduce. But Jerome recounts (the names of) only three of Adam's sons, i.e. Cain, Abel, and Seth. According to other historians, however, Adam's children are more numerous than the number which we gave for his sons in the first place, for these are their names:

10. Cain, Abel, Seth, Cham, Camur, Cumul, Iudas, Iudas, Leui, Ubull, Aboll, Abilon, Sarath, Saliath, Silith, Seig, Gismus, Gessmus, Lagor, Ligor, Liuiath, Lon, Orth, Eth, Horam, Gad, Tigri, Teo, Thul, Pin, Pille, Fomor, For, Feth, Gusmus, Nemath, Pan, Peor, Pennan, Alluriath, Mediath, Ham, Balad, Borad, Naath, Narchon, Heth, Ceth, Silath, Sile, concerning whom the poet says:

11. (1) Adam and famous Eve, who had fine and perfect sons; fifty, here, is the number of their sons, and fifty-two daughters.

(2) Cain, Abel, Seth—not perverse—Cham, Camur, and Cumul the fair-skinned; Iudas, Iudas, Leui the wealthy (?), Ubal, Abol, and Abilon.

(3) Sarath, Saliath, Silith and Seig, Gismus, Gesmus, with clear meaning; Lagor, Ligor, Liuiath, and Lon, Orth, Heth, Oram, (and) Gad of great size.

(4) Fomor, For, Feth, and the bright Gusmus; Tigri, Teo, Thul and Pille; Alluriath, Mediath, and Ham; Nemath, Pan, Peor, and Pennan.

(5) Heth, Ceth, Silath, and Sile of the hosts; Balad, Borad, Naath, and Nachor. Though we recount them, east and west, those are the names of Adam's sons. Of Adam. ⟨Hieronimus: There were as many sons of Adam as there are Sundays in the year, i.e. fifty-two. There were as many daughters as there are languages, i.e. seventy-two⟩.

12. And only three of those sons had families: Cain, Seth, and Sile, i.e. the youngest of Adam's sons, howsoever it be. These here are their three wives, and they were three daughters of Adam, i.e. Pip, Cain's wife; Olla, Seth's wife; and Pithib, Sile's wife.

13. Adam was the first father, and Eve the first mother. Cain, moreover, was their first-born, and it was by him that a city was first constructed, i.e. the city of Henoch; and he gave that name to it from the name of his own first-born son, i.e. Henoch was his name. And it was by him [=Cain] was made the first ploughing and the first reaping.

Abel, the second son of Adam, he was the first just man and the first martyr of Adam's race. Lamech ⟨i.e. bigamist⟩, son of Mathusala, son of Maviael, son of Irad, son of Henoch, son of Cain, son of Adam: he was the first man to take two wives, i.e. Ada and Sella, as Jerome says, commenting on Genesis.

Ada, then, bore Lamech two sons; Jabel was the first son's name, and it was he that first practised herding and being with herds in the wilderness. Jubal, the second son, was the first man to practise the lyre and the organ.

Moreover Sella bore another son to the said Lamech, i.e. Tubalcain was his name. He was the first smith and the first craftsman and the first mason. And Sella bore a daughter afterwards, i.e. Noema, Tubalcain's sister. Henoch, son of Jared, of the race of Seth, he was the first ever man of letters.

14. These are the principal men of the first Age, with the duration of their lives, starting with Seth:
Adam's life, 930 (years); Seth's life, 612 (years); Cainan's life, 910 (years); Jared's life, 965 (years); Mathusala's life, 969 (years); Enos's life, 905 (years); Malaleel's life, 900 (years); Henoch's life, 865 (years); Lamech's life, 777 (years), i.e. Noe's father.

15. Many inquire here concerning the contemporaneity of Mathusala with Adam, and after Adam to the flood; and of the coeval life of Sem, son of Noe, with Mathusala. Mathusala was two-hundred and forty-three years living contemporaneously with Adam. He lived for seven-hundred and twenty-six years after Adam until the flood. His life lasted in all nine-hundred and sixty-nine years. Sem, son of Noe, however, was alive for ninety-eight years contemporaneously with Mathusala, and for five-hundred and two years after the flood.

16. This song concerns Mathusala and Sem.

(1) Three years, with their fame, and two-hundred and forty years, was the wise and intelligent Mathusala coeval with Adam.

(2) Twenty-six years, that is a fact, and seven-hundred fair years,

he was alive until the flood, after Adam of the true judgements.

(3) Sixty-nine years after that, and nine-hundred years, all that was, without doubt, the good life of Mathusala.

(4) Ninety-eight years—it were not weak—was Sem, son of Noe of the brilliant families, coeval, without any deceit, with the venerable Mathusala.

(5) Two and five-hundred fair years was Sem, son of the pure-strengthened Noe, under the course of stars without interruption in this life after the flood.

(6) Christ who formed the solid earth without fear or envy, may I reach the beautiful heaven in which he is, after bearing witness to the three.

17. God commanded, moreover, of the offspring of Seth that they consort not with the families of Cain, and that they should not beget children by them, and that they should not take wives from among them. The family of Seth, however, transgressed that instruction and they took to themselves the daughters of the family of Cain—for they were very beautiful—and they bore children by them in defiance of God. So that it was through that that the monstrous creatures of the world were born, i.e. Fomoraig and Luchorpáin and every horrible, misshapen species of man.

After God had seen them contravene his commandment, however, he determined to destroy completely the human race; so that it was for that reason the flood was sent over the earth, to drown the family of Cain.

18. After the flood had been sent, then, it drowned all the human race and all the animals, save Noe and his three sons, and their four wives. For he was the only faithful man to be found of the offspring of Seth who had not consorted with the race of Cain. And that is the close of that Age, for there was a dawning and a setting of every Age.

The deluge was pouring down for forty days and forty nights. It was one hundred and fifty days without diminishing, and it was then that God sent the winds to draw up the waters.

19. It is enquired of here concerning the dimensions of the Ark, and of its shape and symbolical meaning. It is interpreted as 'arca' in Greek and 'secreta' in Latin, i.e. hidden. The length of the Ark, however, signifies the lasting nature of perfection, i.e. its length signifies the perseverance of perfection. Its width signifies the breadth of charity, i.e. its breadth signifies the extent of charity. Its height signifies the loftiness of hope, i.e. the height signifies the rarity and sharpness of the anticipation that man has of God, i.e. its height, i.e. one cubit, i.e. the unity and universality (at once) of the Catholic faith throughout the whole world is signified by that.

20. Here is a question: At what age of the moon, and on what day of the week, and on what day of the solar month was the Ark entered and left? And what kind of year (was it), 'common' or 'embolismic'? Not difficult! It was entered and departed from on the 27th of May, when the Ark happened upon Mount Armenia. It was entered on the 13th Kalends of June, and it was left on the 7th Ides of May, as regards the day of the solar month. Whence is that derived? Not difficult! For there are eleven days between the 7th Ides and the 13th, and that, moreover, is the amount by which a solar year surpasses a lunar year. For there are three hundred and fifty-four days in that [=the lunar year], and that is what separates the 13th and the 7th Ides at the end of a year.

It was entered, then, on a Friday. Whence is that derived? Not difficult! For Adam's transgression was on a Friday. It is fitting, therefore, that it should be on that day that retribution should come upon the world.

It is asked, on what day of the week was the Ark left? Not difficult! i.e. on a Tuesday. Whence is that derived? Not difficult! For it was entered on the 13th Kalends of June. Hence Noe was in the Ark for a year and seventeen days. Moreover, on the 17th of May the deluge began to pour. Noe, then, was six hundred years old when the deluge came.

There are four people of whom Scripture speaks here as being the oldest; it is to be sought.

21. This poem instructs about Adam and Jared, Mathusala and Noe.

(1) Mathusala and Noe, without sorrow, Adam and Jared, these are the four oldest, without sorrowful fault, of whom the Canon speaks.

(2) Adam was nine hundred and thirty years old—that is what it says, fittingly. Noe spent nine hundred and fifty years in this life—fair the obligation!

(3) Nine hundred and sixty (and) two years—if any should be seeking it I will not conceal it from every exposition—that was the sum of Jared's time.

(4) Nine hundred and sixty-nine years—it is not false for anyone who tells it—there is no danger in saying it firmly, that was the life of old Mathusala. Mathusala.

22. The beginning of the second Age. The second Age of the world, moreover, two hundred and ninety-two years there are in it. Noe, moreover, was the first leader of that Age. ⟨Noe was the first to construct an altar after the deluge⟩. Noe was four hundred and fifty years alive after the deluge, so that nine hundred and fifty years was his age in all.

23. God greeted Noe and his sons and said to them: 'Increase and multiply and fill the whole earth, and I will strike my friendship with you, and I will send the flood no more over the world until the common end comes. Moreover, I will give a sign of my friendship to you in the heavens, and for as long as that sign shall be seen no end or destruction will come upon the family of Noe. This, then, is the sign, i.e. I will set my staff in the heavens', i.e. the rainbow; and that is the history of the rainbow, i.e. its being given as a sign to the family of Noe after the deluge, as a sign of their compact with God for as long as the rainbow will be seen. And it is clear, then, the rainbow did not exist before the deluge.

24. Concerning the family of Noe hereafter.

Noe begot three sons before the deluge, and it is from them that the seventy-two races derived after the deluge. This, then, is how those races gave issue: twenty-seven of them from Sem; thirty from Cham, and fifteen from Japheth. So that they are seventy-two races in all, and they were given seventy-two languages afterwards, at the stopping of (the building of) Nemrod's Tower. And at the end of ten years following that Foénius Forsaid fashioned the Irish language from the seventy-two languages, and gave it to his foster-son, to the son of Agnoman [=Goédel Glas].

This, however, is what multiplied the number of the races beyond the number of the languages, for there are in Africa many races with the same language and the cause of that was that there were only seventy-two races there when the languages were multiplied, and though the races multiplied subsequently they are not listed in the enumeration of distinct races, but are subordinated to the other races that are related to them. Whence there are more races, in effect, than there are languages, though they are no more numerous according to enumeration. For though Japheth had eight sons the enumeration of the races gives the peoples of only three of them. And though six sons are mentioned as being of Sem, the enumeration gives the peoples of only two of them. And though four sons are named as of Cham, the peoples of only three of them are reckoned. And it is not that all the other sons had no issue, but that nothing was born of them to which it were proper to give the name of a race; and that much will be clear if every son of Noe is named in turn, with their families, all in one line.

25. Concerning the family of Japheth, son of Noe, hereafter.

Gomer, Magoch, Madai, Javan, Thubal, Mosoch, Thiras, Masseca. Japheth, then, and Olibana his wife, they had eight sons. Gomer, from him are the Galatae, and they are the same as the Galli; Gallogreci is another name for them. Magoch, from him are the Scythians. Madai, from whom are the Medes. Javan, from whom the Ionians come and from whom the Ionian Sea is named; and from them sprang the Aeolians, from whom the Iolici are named; and it is from them that the fifth language of the Greeks gets its name, i.e. the Aeolian language. Thubal, from whom are the Hiberi and Hispani and Celtiberi.

Mosoch, from him are Cappadocians. Thiras, from whom are the Thracians, and he had seven sons. The family of Gomer, son of Japheth, i.e. Ascenez, son of Gomer, from whom are the Regini. Riphath, son of Gomer, from whom are the Paplagoni, a race of people who dwell in the Rifi mountains and who are also known as the Colchi. Thogorma, son of Gomer, from whom are the Phrygians. Those are the three sons of Gomer, son of Japheth.

The two sons of Magoch, son of Japheth, son of Noe, i.e. Baath, and Ibath. A son of Baath was Foénius Forsaid, from whom are the Scythians and the Goths. Foénius Forsaid, moreover, was the son of Baath, son of Magoch, son of Japheth, son of Noe, and so on.

Ibath, moreover, the other son of Magoch, Elonius or Alanius was a son of his. He had three sons, i.e. Armon, Negua, and Hissicon. Armon had five sons, i.e. Gothus, Uolegothus, Cebidus, Bargandus, and Longobardus. Negua, moreover, had three sons, i.e. Uandalus, Saxus, and Bogardus. Hissicon, moreover, had four sons, i.e. Francus, Romanus, Albanus, i.e. from whom is named the eastern Albania in great Asia, and Brittus, from whom is named the island of Britain.

26. It was then that the world was divided into three parts, i.e. Europe, Africa, and Asia. Sem was in Asia, Cham was in Africa, and Japheth in Europe. And the first man of the line of Japheth to come to Europe was Alanius, the son of Ibath, son of Magoch, son of Japheth, son of Noe. And Alanius came with his three sons, i.e. Armon, Negua, and Hissicon, and it was here the sons of whom we have spoken have established themselves. Saxus, son of Negua, son of Alanius, son of Ibath, son of Magoch, son of Japheth, son of Noe: from him are the Saxons. Then Javan, son of Japheth, son of Noe: he had four sons, i.e. Elisa, Tharsis, Cethim, and Dodanim. Tharsis, from whom are the Cethi; and from them is derived the name of the chief city of Cyprus, i.e. Citheum. Dodanim, moreover, from him are the Rodii, and by them were divided the islands of the Tyrrhenean Sea, which is called the Mediterranean, with its various races and their languages.

27. Those are the fifteen chief races of the family of Japheth, with their subordinate races. They occupied many lands in Asia, from Mount Imai and from Mount Tur to the river Danube and as far as Scythia; and they occupied the whole of Europe as far as the shore of the western ocean of the island of Britain, and the angled Spain, with an angle of territory.

Concerning the family of Japheth, son of Noe, with their chief races and minor races, and concerning their branches and lands, both in Asia and in Europe. The end.

28. Concerning the race of Cham son of Noe now, this below:
Cham, then, and Oliua his wife, they had four sons, i.e. Chus, Phuth, Mesraim, and Chanaan. Chus, from whom are the Chussi; they are called the Ethiopians today. Mesraim, from whom is named Egypt. ⟨The first altar after the flood in Africa was made by Mesraim⟩. Phuth, from him are the Africans or Libyans; they were also called Phuthei at another time and it is from them the river Phuth is named.

Chanaan, from him are the Chanaanites. It was their land the Israelites seized after the destruction and expulsion of the Chanaanites. Chus son of Cham had seven sons, i.e. Saba, from whom are the Sabei; Hevila, from whom are the Getuli who dwell in the wilderness of Africa; Sabatha, from whom are the Sabatheni, i.e. their old name; today, however, they are called Astabari. Regma, Sabata, Acha, and Nemrod. It was by him [sc. Nemrod] that Babylon was first built, for although it was built afterwards by Ninus son of Bel, when he obtained the kingship of the Assyrians, it was by Nemrod that the walls of Babylon were first raised.

29. Babilonia, i.e. 'confusio', i.e. confusion, because of the fact that it was in that spot that languages were confounded. However, Sessach is its honoured name. And by Nemrod too was built the city of Arach; another name for it is Edissa. It was by him also that the city of Achad and the city of Chalanne were built. The name of the latter now, however, is Seleucia; from Seleuco the king it was named. All those are in the Plain of Sennaar. Doram, moreover, is another name for the Plain of Sennaar.

It is from the line of Nemrod that the Assyrians descend, according to some. Or, alternatively, Assur comes from the line of Sem son of Noe, i.e. Assur son of Sem son of Noe. And Assur was born in the Plain of Sennaar, and by him were built the cities of Nineve, Chale, and Resen. The latter is a large city that stands between Nineve and Chale.

Regma, the son of Chus son of Cham son of Noe, had two sons, i.e. Saba and Dadan, from whom are the people of Ethiopia in the eastern land. The name of Saba son of Regma is spelt with (the letter) 'SIN', while that of Saba son of Chus is spelt with (the letter) 'SAMECH'.

The offspring of Mesraim son of Cham son of Noe, i.e. Ludim, Anamin, Laabim, Nephthuim, Phetrusim, and Chasluim. It is from them that the Philistines sprang, and the Capturini, and countless other races; and they are neither certain nor definite today, for they have altered their abodes and their names.

30. Concerning the race of Chanaan son of Cham son of Noe hereafter, in sequence.

Chanaan, the son of Cham son of Noe, had eleven sons; Sidon, 〈i.e. the first-born〉, Hethites, Jebusites, Amorrhites, Gergesites, Hevites, Aracites, Sinites, Aradius, Samarius, Amatheus, who was the youngest. Sidon, from him is named the chief city of Phoenicia, 〈i.e. Sidon〉. Aracheus, by him was built Arachas, i.e. a city that faces Tripoli, near Mount Libanus. Aradius, from whom are the Aradii, and it is they who occupied the island that is called Aradum; there is a narrow strait between them and the shore of Phoenicia. Samarius, from whom are the Samarians, and it was by him that the city of Samaria was built.

The end, concerning Cham.

31. Concerning the family of Sem son of Noe hereafter this time. Sem son of Noe, Olla was his wife. It is of his line that all the Hebrews come. He had five sons, i.e. Aelam 〈i.e. the first-born〉, Assur, Arphaxad, Lud, and Aram. Aelam, from whom are the Elamitae; they are the princes of Persia and Syria. Assur, from whom are the Assyrians, in fact; and by him was built Nineve, Chale, and Resen, as we have said above. 〈The Assyrians are from Assur son of Sem son of Noe. Syria, however, is from Assirim son of Daddan son of Iaxan son of Abraham〉. Arphaxad, from him are the Chaldaeans, and by him the royal city was built, i.e. Igbathanis; and he built the walls of square stones. Each wall was seventy cubits in height and thirty cubits in width. Its towers were a hundred cubits high. That is the chief city of the Medes today.

Lud, from whom is named Lydia 〈i.e. the Lydians, and those races occupied a large portion in Asia from the river Eufrates to the Gulf of India of the great ocean in the eastern Orient〉. Aram, from him is named Syria. The main city of Syria is Damascus. Arphaxad son of Sem son of Noe, Sale was a son of his and Heber was a son of Sale. From him are named the Hebrews, i.e. from Heber son of Sale son of Arphaxad son of Sem son of Noe. Heber had two sons, i.e. Phaleg and Jectan. Phaleg, i.e. 'division', for it was in his time that the languages were divided.

32. Jectan son of Heber son of Sale had thirteen sons, as they are enumerated: Elmodad, Saleph, Asarmoth, Jare, Aduram, Uzal, Decla, Ebal, Abimael, Saba, Ophir, Hevila, Jobab. There are sixty-four races of his line in India, and it is they who have occupied the whole of India and a large portion of Asia, i.e. from the river Euphrates eastwards to the eastern ocean. The family of Aram son of Sem son of Noe, i.e. Us, from him are the Traconiti and by him was built Damascus; that territory stands between Palestine and Coelensyria.

Hul, from him are the Armenians. Gether, from him are the Arcani. Mes, who is also called Mosoch, from him are the Meones. Those are all the line of Aram son of Sem son of Noe, and they dwell in India.

33. Concerning the history of the Fomoraig, and of the Luchorpáin, and of the monstrous creatures, this below.

Once, as Noe was in his tabernacle sleeping, having drunk intoxicating wine, and he naked, his son came towards him, i.e. Cham, and he saw how he was and laughed at him and told his brothers, i.e. Japheth and Sem. They then came with their backs turned away, that they might not see their father's nakedness and the member whereby their very own bodies were begotten; and they put his mantle over him.

34. Noe arose from his sleep thereafter and it was revealed to him that Cham had mocked him; and he cursed him afterwards [=Cham], but he blessed the other two. Thus it was Cham who was the first to be cursed after the Flood, whence he is the successor to Cain after the Flood. And from him sprang the Luchorpáin and the Fomoraig, and the goat-heads, and every kind of ill-shapen species of humanity; and it is for that reason the Chanaanites were destroyed and their land given to the Israelites, as a sign of the self-same curse, for the Chanaanites were of the race of Cham.

That, then, is the origin of the monsters, and they are *not* of the race of Cain, as the Irish say, for none of his line survived the deluge, because the very purpose of the deluge was to drown the race of Cain; and even the whole race of Seth were drowned along with them, except Noe and his three sons and their four wives, as Moses, son of Amra, relates that in the Book of Genesis. And it was God himself who gave that Law to Moses on Mount Sinai, and it was he himself [=God] wrote it with his own hand.

35. These are the leaders of the second Age, according to the genealogical line of Sem, son of Noe. Noe, 950 (years); Sem, 600 (years); Arphaxad, 439 (years); Sale, 833 (years); Heber, 464 (years); Phaleg, 239 (years); Ragau, 239 (years); Serug, 230 (years); Nachor, 167 (years); Thare, 70 (years).

Thare had three sons, i.e. Abraham, Nachor ⟨who first made a wall of stones⟩, and Aran. Lot was a son of that Aran. Aran, moreover, had two daughters, i.e. Jescha and Melcha, the two daughters of Aran, son of Thare. They were sisters of Lot, and Jescha and Sarai are one and the same. And Aran died before his father, i.e. before Thare, and he was the first son after the Flood to precede his father in death; and he died in Ur of the Chaldees.

35a. As the Irish poet tells that,

(1) Who the first son was to die before his father, I will relate in

fine verse: it was Aran, son of Thare, son of Nachor, after he had been made an outlaw.

36. Lot, son of Aran, moreover, had two daughters, i.e. Iachether and Iachereth were their Hebrew names, Achiros and Miros were their Greek names, Sadibilis and Adherens were their Latin names. It was they who gave an excess of wine to their father, because of their being separated, so that he made them pregnant in his drunkenness and begot two sons by them, i.e. Moab and Ammon, concerning whom is this poem:

37. (1) The daughters of Lot—let it be read by you of the stories!—a wearisome and wicked tale: the demons begot a pure and shameful offspring by the son of Aran.

(2) Iachether, the woman without portion, was the elder of the little family. She gave wine to her father in the afternoon whereby he perpetrated [?] an unjust deed.

(3) Iachereth was the other woman—let the historians learn it from you!—She committed a deed in her house, a rough deed, the outraging of her God and of the cleric.

(4) Achiros with hatefulness, and Miros with shame, were their Greek names; as goodly verse has distinguished them, memorise the names of the daughters. Daughters.

(5) Sadibilis of insidious evil, she was the eldest of the family; 'Clinging to evil', it is a truth I tell, she was the youngest of the daughters. Daughters.

(6) The sons that were made then through a foolish deed with their father, were Moab and Ammon, it is a truth I tell; that was the family of the daughters. Daughters.

38. Abraham and Nachor, then, the two sons of Thare, took two wives, i.e. Sarai and Melcha, the two daughters of their own brother, i.e. the two daughters of Aran, son of Thare. Abraham, then, took to himself Sarai, who was also called Jescha. Nachor, however, took Melcha, and Melcha bore him eight sons. These are their names: Hus, Buz, Camuel, Cased, Azau, Pheldas, Jedlaph, Bathuel.

From Bathuel, son of Nachor, were born Laban, the son, and Rebecca, the daughter. Hus, son of Nachor, from him was Jacob, and of his line was Balaam the magician. Camuel, moreover, was the father of the Syrians. Nachor's concubine, i.e. Roma, she was mother to Tabee and Gaham, to Tahas and Maacha.

Those are the divisions and the numerous branches of the sons of Noe and the end of the second Age, up to now.

39. Concerning the third Age of the world and its leaders here below. There are nine hundred and forty-two years in the third Age of the world, i.e. from the birth of Abraham in the land of the Chaldees to the obtaining of the kingship by David ⟨The Chasdeians are now called Chaldaeans⟩. The birth of Abraham, then, is the opening of this Age, according to correct reckoning. Abraham was eighty-six years old when he begot Ismael by Agar the Egyptian ⟨The Agareni are from Agar⟩. He was, moreover, one hundred years old when he begot Isaac by Sarai.

He fathered other sons indeed by Cetura, i.e. by the wife he took after Sarai had died ⟨The Saracens are from Sarai⟩. These are their names: Zamran, Jecsan, Madan, Madian, Jesboc, and Suë. Jecsan, son of Abraham, son of Thare, he had two sons, i.e. Saba and Dadan. The family of Dadan, i.e. Assurim and Latusim and Loömim. The family of Madian, son of Abraham, i.e. Epha and Opher, Henoch, Abida, and Eldaa.

That above is the family of Abraham and Cetura. This below, however, is the family of Ismael, son of Abraham, and of Agar the Egyptian, Sarai's handmaid; Ismael was the first-born of Abraham. ⟨The Ismohelites are from Ismael⟩. This is Ismael's first-born, i.e. Nabaioth ⟨from whom are the Nabatheni⟩. He occupied the territory from the river Euphrates to the Red Sea, and to him belongs Nabathena; that is a province in the land of Arabia, towards the east.

40. Nabaioth, Dehin, Cedar, Abdeel, Mabsan, Masma, Duma, Maasaadad, Thema, Jethur, Naphis, Cedma. Those are the offspring of Ismael, son of Abraham, and they are the twelve leaders of the Twelve Tribes of Israel; and their names survive today on their citadels and their cities. The territory they occupied was from Mount Euilath to Sur, which is opposite Egypt, the path that leads to Assyria. Ismael died, then, after one hundred and thirty-seven years.

41. Concerning the family of Isaac, son of Abraham, this below. Isaac, son of Abraham, son of Thare, son of Nachor took a wife, i.e. Rebecca, the daughter of Bathuel, son of Nachor, son of Thare, i.e. Laban's sister. Rebecca bore Isaac two sons at one birth, i.e. Jacob and Esau.

Jacob went to the land of Mesopotamia, to his mother's brother, namely to Laban, the son of Bathuel, son of Nachor. And he took to himself the two daughters of Laban, i.e. Lia and Rachel, and he had children by them, and by their handmaids also, i.e. by Bala, Rachel's handmaid, and by Zelpha, Lia's handmaid. And the two women and their slaves bore twelve sons and one daughter to Jacob; Dina was her name.

42. These are the names, firstly of Lia's sons:
The sons of Lia: Ruben, Simeon, Levi, Juda, Issachar, Zabulon.

The sons of Bala, however, Rachel's slave: Dan, Nephthali. The sons of Zelfa, i.e. Lia's slave: Gad, Aser. The sons of Rachel, i.e. Joseph, Benjamin.

43. Oéngus mac Suibni sang this poem on the subject of the twelve sons of Jacob.

(1) The twelve sons of Jacob, practise, let you remember! The eight sons of the two noble-women, and the four sons of the two slaves.

(2) The six sons of truly-pure Lia, you have heard of them: Ruben, Simeon, Levi, Juda, Issachar, Zabulon, brightest amongst hosts.

(3) The two sons of Zelfa, abounding in pure treasures, the slave of perfect Lia, were two lusty (?) brothers, Gad, Aser of abundant splendour.

(4) The two sons of the handmaid Bala, I reckon them; she was the eldest, noble and cheerful: Dan and Nephthalim, no forgetting.

(5) The two great warrior sons of Rachel, they were most renowned amongst heroes; the youngest, the white-haired one, was Benjamin; Joseph was the greatest among sons. Two.

(6) The two famous and desirable daughters of Laban, son of the many-mantled Bathuel, they were two white sisters with yellow hair, Lia and Rachel, and the eight sons. Two.

44. The sons of Ruben: Henoch, Phallu, Hesron, Charmi. The sons of Simeon: Namuel, Ahod, Jamin, Jachin, Zare, Saul. The sons of Levi: Gerson, Merari, Caath, who bore Amram ⟨i.e. the father of Moses and Aaron⟩. The sons of Joseph: Ephraim, Manasses. The sons of Ephraim: Suthala, Becher, Thenen. The son of Manasses: Machir, the father ⟨i.e. of Galaad⟩. Galaad had many sons, these are their names: Jezer, Helec, Asriel, Sechem, Semida, Hepher, the father of Salphaad; and he had no sons but only five daughters. The sons of Juda: Her, Onan ⟨who both died in the land of Chanaan⟩, Sela, Phares, Zara. The sons of Phares: Hesron, Hamul. The sons of Issachar: Thola, Jasub. The sons of Dan: Phua, Semran, Suchaim. The sons of Nephthalim: Jasiel, Jeser. The sons of Zabulon: Sared, Jahelel. The sons of Benjamin: Bela, Asabel, Ahiram, Supham. The sons of Gad: Sephon Aggi, Suni, Ozni, Arod, Ariel. The sons of Aser: Jemna, Jessui, Brie.

45. This below is the family of Esau, i.e. Eliphaz, his first-born. It is he that is referred to in the Book of Job, saying: 'These are the three friends of Job, i.e. Eliphaz the Themanite, Baalad the Suhite, and Sophar the Naamathite', and Thamna was the name of his concubine. These are the names of the rest of his sons: Rahuel, Jehus, Ihelon, Core. The sons of Eliphaz, i.e. Theman, Omar, Sepho, Gatham, Cenez, and Amalec. The sons of Rahuel: Nahath, Zara, Samma, and

Meza. Horreus was a son of Seir, and that is recalled here because the concubine of Eliphaz, son of Esau, was of the family of the Horrei. These above are the family of Abraham, with their peoples.

Abraham left all his patrimony, both of land and stock, to Isaac. However, he did give gifts to the sons of the concubines, i.e. to Ismael, son of Agar the Egyptian, and to the sons of Cetura. And he set them apart from Isaac and put them in the eastern region of Asia, facing India.

46. Abraham died after the hundred and seventy-fifth year of his age; and he was buried in the place that is known as 'The double-cave' (Spelonca Duplex). That is in the land of Ephron, son of Seor the Hethite, directly opposite the valley of Mambre. It was Abraham himself, moreover, who purchased the site from the sons of Heth in preparation for his burial, so that it was in that spot that Abraham was buried, and Sara, his wife.

And the glory and prosperity that were Abraham's settled on Isaac, and from him are descended all the Israelites. And as for Christ, he is traced back to Isaac in his human genealogy.

47. These are the noble patriarchs of the third Age, with the lengths of their lives: Abraham's life, one hundred and seventy-five; Isaac's life, one hundred and eighty; Jacob's life, one hundred and forty-six.

48. These, moreover, are the Judges of the same Age, and it is not their full number of years that is recorded here but only the number of years in their reigns.

Jesus	reigned for	26	Thola	reigned for	26
Gothoniel	,, ,,	40	Jair	,, ,,	22
Aod	,, ,,	80	Jephthe	,, ,,	6
Deborra	,, ,,	40	Hesebon	,, ,,	7
Godeon	,, ,,	40	Samson	,, ,,	20
Abimelech	,, ,,	3	Heli, the priest reigned for		40
			Samuel	reigned for	40

49. Saul was the first king who ruled in Israel. He reigned for forty years. And Saul was killed afterwards with his son, i.e. Jonathan, on Mount Gelboe, by the Philistines; and that is the close of that Age.

After that David obtained the kingship of the Two Tribes, and a grandson of Saul, i.e. Isboseth son of Jonathan son of Saul, acceded to the kingship of the Ten Tribes. That is the third Age.

⟨Rechab and Baana, the two sons of Remmon the Berothite, killed Isboseth son of Jonathan son of Saul son of Cis son of Abiel son of Seror son of Bechorath son of Aphia son of a man of Jemini.

Samuel son of Elcanna son of Jeroham son of Eliu son of Thohu son of Suph, the Ephraimite from Mount Ephraim, son of Elcana son of Mahath son of Amasai son of Elcanna son of Johel son of Azarias.

Saphaneth or Somnofaneth was Joseph's name in Egyptian. If the name is in Hebrew it is interpreted as 'saviour of the world'. If the name is in Egyptian it is said to be 'keeper of dreams'. Moses was called Ammoebar by his parents; it is interpreted as 'son of a son'⟩.

50. An account of the fourth Age this below.
Three hundred and seventy-three years, that is the number of years in the fourth Age. This, moreover, is the event from which it proceeds, the accession of David to the kingship. He ruled over Israel for forty years, i.e. seven years and six months in Hebron and thirty-two years in Jerusalem.

It is to be enquired of here concerning the number of David's family, and of the order in which they were born, whether in Hebron or in Jerusalem. These, firstly, are David's sons in Hebron: Amnon, moreover, was his first-born; Achinoam, of Jezrahel, was his mother. Cheleab was the second son; Abigail, the wife of Nabal from Mount Carmel, was his mother. Absolom was the third son; Maacha, daughter of Tholmai king of Gessur, was his mother. Adonias was the fourth son; Haggith, the Egyptian, was his mother. Saphathia was the fifth son; Abital was his mother. Jethraam, by Egla, David's wife, was the sixth son, i.e. the son of a queen. Those are the sons of David in Hebron.

These, moreover, are his sons in Jerusalem, i.e. Samua, Sobab, Nathan, Solomon. These, moreover, are the names of his daughters: Ibar, Elisua, Nepheg, Japhia, Elisama, Elioda, and Eliphaleth. So that the total number of David's offspring was thus seventeen. Solomon then, his son, was the one who succeeded him.

In this Age was begun the kingship of the Macedonians, and Caranus was the name of the first king of them who ruled. There were twenty-seven years between that year when the Macedonians began to reign until the first Olympiad was held by the Athenians. That was done, moreover, four hundred and five years after the siege of Troy. Twenty-six years from the first Olympic Festival until Rome was founded.

51. 'Rome was founded', i.e. Rome was founded on Mount Palantinus, i.e. Mount Palantinus was the name of the mountain on which it was built. It was begun on the eleventh Kalends of May by Romulus and Remus, i.e. the two sons of Rea Siluea, the daughter of Minitor, son of Prochus.

That Rea was a vestal virgin, i.e. a virgin who was reared in the temple of Mars. But she was violated by a priest of the temple so that she became pregnant by him and bore two sons. But what she said was, that the offspring belonged to Mars, and it was for that reason that the two sons were cast upon the Tiber, i.e. upon the river, in a small cradle; for one dare not kill them for dread of Mars, for he was their god.

The mother, however, was buried alive because her virginity had been defiled. Amullius, her father's brother, was the one who buried her. Fustulus, however, the king's herdsman, was the one who discovered the two sons on the bank of the river Tiber, and he brought them home to his wife, i.e. Luppa, indeed, was her name. She reared the two sons until they were grown up.

The two sons were told afterwards that Amullius had killed their mother, and had cast them upon the river. And they assembled their foster-father's household, i.e. the host of the herdsmen, and they captured the king's house, i.e. Amullius, and killed him in retribution for (the death of) their mother. And they gave the kingship to their grandfather, i.e. to Minitor, son of Prochus, i.e. to their mother's father; and he died, so that Romulus acceded to the kingship. And Rome was built by him in the sixth year of his reign, according to some.

52. These are the kings of the Israelites during the period of this Age, and their reigns.
David, forty; Solomon, forty; Roboam, seventeen; Abia ⟨or Abiasa⟩, three years; Asa, forty years; Josafath, twenty-five; Joram, eight years; Ochosias and Gotholia ⟨i.e. his mother. Ochosia, the daughter of Achab, son of Ambre, was the mother of Ochosias⟩, one year; Joas, forty years; Amasias, twenty-nine; Ozias, who is also called Ozarias, fifty-two; Joathan, sixteen; Achaz, sixteen; Ezechias, twenty-eight; Manasses, fifty-five years; Josias, thirty-one years ⟨or Hammon, twelve⟩; Jotha, three months ⟨or Joachaz, i.e. the son of Josias, three months⟩; Joachim, eleven years; Jochin, who was also called Jochonias, three months and ten days; Sedechias, eleven years.

53. In the eleventh year of the reign of Sedechias the Jewish people were taken into the Babilonian captivity, and Jerusalem was totally razed and the great temple of Solomon burnt down. There were four hundred and thirty years, or four hundred and thirty-four as some say, between its construction and its burning.

Nabuzardan, the military commander of Nabuchodonosor, was the man who destroyed Jerusalem, and he took with him the whole Jewish nation and their king, i.e. Sedechias, into captivity in Babylon. And they were seventy years in that captivity until Cyrus and the great Darius, son of Astiages, released them; Darius, the son of Arbeus, moreover, was the last Persian king before the rule of the Greeks; and until Jerusalem and the great temple were built again by Esdras and Nehemias.

And that is the close of the fourth Age and the beginning of the fifth Age.

54. Hence the fourth Age is from the accession of David to the kingship to the return from the captivity. In this Age the three youths were thrown into the furnace by Nabuchodonosor, i.e. Sidrach, Misach, and Abdenago. And God brought them safely from that fire, and it consumed many thousands of Nabuchodonosor's household.

And it was then that Daniel was thrown into the lions' den, after he had been accused by the stewards of the king and by the priests of the idols. And Daniel survived the lions, so that the host of the stewards and priests was cast into the den thereafter, and the lions of the den devoured them.

55. The historians of the Hebrews relate that Sedechias, son of Josia, was blinded by the household of Nabuchodonosor in Reblatha, and that he was never brought to Babylon at all—which is evident from the fact of the alliance that existed between Joachin, king of Judea, and Euil-Merodach, son of Nabuchodonosor, after they had been imprisoned in the one dungeon. That is to say, when Nabuchodonosor had been for seven years eating grass and dwelling stooped and naked among the wild oxen and domestic flocks, his followers gave his kingship to his son. When, however, Nabuchodonosor recovered his senses and recovered his kingship, he imprisoned his son for seizing the kingship in his stead; and he cast him into the same dungeon as the king of Judea until Nabuchodonosor himself was dead.

Then the household of Nabuchodonosor brought Euil-Merodach out of the dungeon in order that he might succeed to his father's kingship. But he did not accept it until there had been raised up to him the corpse and remains of his father, to ensure that he was really dead, and that his own kingship, moreover, might not be fleeting. And his remains were drawn up for him with ropes and hooks from out of its grave, and after that Euil-Merodach accepted the kingship and he was benevolent to Joachin.

That above, however, is a digression, and the close of the fourth Age. The end. Amen.

56. This below is the fifth Age with its number of years.
This is the number of years in the fifth Age, and the fifth Age itself, i.e. five hundred and seventy-nine. All this Age is from the end of the Babylonian captivity to the birth of Christ. In the beginning of this Age, moreover, Babylon was destroyed by Cyrus and Darius, son

of Astiages, against Ballusar, son of Nabuzardan, son of Neocusser, son of Euil-Merodach, son of Nabuchodonosor, son of Merodach Baladan, son of Baladan, and so on.

It was in opposition to Ballusar, king of Chaldaea that Babylon was destroyed, and Cyrus took the kingship. And he was of the Medes and it was then that the kingship passed to the Medes. And it was that Cyrus who released the people of Israel whom he found before him in Babylon in captivity with Ballusar. They were thirty thousand in number.

57. It was, indeed, a matter for wonder to the men of the world that Babylon should be destroyed, because of its strength and because of the size of its construction. For it was first built by Nemrod, son of Chus, son of Cham, son of Noe; and it was rebuilt by Ninus, son of Bel, son of Plosc, son of Philiris Agamul, son of Feronnesis, son of Omulus, son of Githlis, son of Therris, son of Assur, son of Sem, son of Noe, and by Ninus's wife thereafter, i.e. Semiramis indeed was her name. She was the daughter of Zambri, son of Suul, son of Buz, king of India.

The wall of Babylon was constructed thus, i.e. the wall was compact with baked lime and bitumen in the form of a square with symmetrical walls. Its wall was fifty cubits thick, two hundred cubits high, and four hundred and eighty stadia ⟨or sixty miles⟩ in its circumference. There were a hundred bronze doors set into it.

It says in the Books of Antiquities that such was the thickness of its wall that twenty four-wheeled chariots could course between the rows of houses on the top of its wall. The river Euphrates passed through it under stone archways. Cyrus, therefore, came, each man having a spade in his hand so that they divided the river into little streams without the inhabitants knowing. So Cyrus's host came by way of the river-course until they were in the centre of the city, without being heard by the inhabitants of the city, and thus was Babylon destroyed.

58. This poem is on the subject of Babylon.

(1) Babylon, it has been heard far away, was the citadel that Ninus, son of Bel, built because of constant dread of the plundering of hosts; a city unparalleled and vast.

(2) The fair city was square in shape, a sacred sod to the chiefs. It was pleasant and bright, a sparkling jewel, with a hundred doors of bronze.

(3) It was a full sixty miles in circumference, that was its measurement, it was not grim; in close sequence of paces and in very strong courses.

(4) Its wall was fifty cubits in girth—it were very difficult for any

mortal to destroy it! It was two hundred cubits in height, a clear construction, reaching up to the sky.

(5) Twenty four-horsed chariots, it is fine for you, used to fit on the summit of its wall between two rows of houses; it is a feat without narrow concealment for you.

(6) There was never built, in the east or the west, among all the dwelling-places of the descendants of Adam a stronghold to compare with Babylon; I assert this for it is a perfect and fitting claim.

(7) The river Euphrates passes through its centre, whereof arose clamorous conflict and clashing. So that it was by reason of that fact that its garrison was destroyed and Babylon was overcome. Babylon.

(8) Cyrus came with all his host to the swift-flowing, ruddy river. He divided and dispersed it in turn until it was a smooth and suitable pathway.

(9) They went with fiery strength along the same course as the river up to the door of the palace wherein was the king in Babylon. Babylon.

(10) After that he destroyed Ninus's city with its king-folk and its king, Ballusar—great was his fame—who was a son of Negussar.

(11) Negussar, with the speed of his horses, he was a son of Nabuzardan. Nabuzardan, hard in battle, was a son of Euil-Merodach.

(12) Euil-Merodach himself was a son of the famous and generous Nabuchodonosor; for it was by Nabuchodonosor, no deceit, that Jerusalem was first destroyed.

(13) He took a great plunder from God's city and he destroyed its buildings. They came with him to his house, warriors and clerics, women and children.

(14) They were seventy years in captivity in Babylon until Cyrus came, a clear compact, and released them from their bondage.

(15) Then Cyrus said to them: 'Rise up and go to your own country and travel vigorously until you reach Jerusalem'.

(16) After that they journeyed southwards towards their own land, without debility; and there they built the city of God, both its buildings and its houses.

(17) Then the fair Cyrus sought the kingship of the people of the world. His glory lasted for thirty years, in the high-kingship in Babylon. Babylon.

(18) Then Cyrus went with all his host to the proud and cold land of Scythia, seeking tribute in more distant lands, but the queen of Scythia killed him.

(19) There were four empires without fault that were fair and prosperous because of the extent of their power and which governed the difficult world, as the Canon relates.

(20) The empire of the famed Assyrians until Cyrus came, greater than any prince! The empire of the Medes and Persians, it was skilled, until there came to them the son of Philip [=Alexander the Great].

(21) The empire of the Greeks, fierce was their battle-cry, until there came to them the Romans. The Romans were then in power up to the end of the world.

(22) The location of the famous tower of Nemrod is on the plain of Senaar—name (it)! Around the river Euphrates with glory Babylon was constructed. Babylon.

59. Here is considered the matter of the deaths of the chief prophets and the people by whom they were killed, and the places in which they were buried.

Manasses, son of Ezechias, killed Isaias, son of Amos, then, in this manner: he strung him up and cut him lengthwise with a serrated saw, so that he died and was buried under the oak tree of Ragel. Jeremias, however, was stoned to death by the populace in Egypt, at Tamna; and he was buried in the self-same Tamna, the place where the pharoahs, the kings of Egypt, used to be buried. And that is the death of Jeremias, son of Helcias from Anathoth.

The prophet Ezechiel, moreover, him the leaders of the people of Israel killed because of the rigorousness of his admonition and because of the extent to which he used rebuke them for the crime of their impiety. The populace buried him in the land of Hauram, beside the grave of Araphaxad. The prophet Daniel, then ⟨i.e. the son of Abda⟩, after the completion of his days in every perfection, died in the Babylonian captivity. And he was buried with honour alone in the royal mausoleum where no other person was ever buried before him and in which no one will be buried after him.

60. It is asked here, moreover, how many days' journey there was for the children of Israel from Babylon to Jerusalem. Not difficult! Three hundred and sixty-five days' journey, for that is the distance between the mystical Babylon, i.e. from hell, wherein is all confusion and tribulation, to the heavenly Jerusalem, wherein is all peace and happiness. Now, there are one hundred and seventy-six paces in every day's journey, and twenty-two stadia in every pace, as is said.

61. (1) (There are) seven times fifty journeys ⟨i.e. three hundred and sixty-five journeys in all⟩, with significance, (and) fifteen without miscalculation, from Babylon ⟨i.e. from hell⟩ of the stirring up of strifes ⟨i.e. that causes teeth to chatter⟩ to the city of Jerusalem ⟨i.e. to heaven in that case⟩.

(2) (There are) a hundred and seventy-six paces ⟨i.e. the number of verses in the *Beati* in that case⟩ in every journey ⟨i.e. in every step of the *Beati*⟩—a vast amount! Sages ⟨i.e. learned people⟩ reckon ⟨i.e. calculate⟩, it is clear, but the nature of each pace is different ⟨i.e. a literal pace and a mystical pace⟩.

(3) (There are) twenty-two stadia ⟨i.e. the twenty-two books of the Old Testament⟩ without concealment in each particular pace; (each) with mysteries of Scripture, not base, (according to) the shape of the Old Testament ⟨i.e. the twenty-two books⟩.

(4) (There are) a hundred and twenty-five paces ⟨i.e. the eighth part of a mile⟩ in every stadium ⟨i.e. in every single book⟩ of the signification of paths; philosophers testify thereto, it is not feeble, according to the geometrical shape of the world.

(5) This is the exposition that precedes the 118th psalm: let every sage who hears it examine it diligently at every time.

(6) David (who was) by the will of heaven's king the king-prophet and the king-poet has looked upon this mystery with grace, through the septiform spirit. Three hundred and fifty.

62. This then is the journey that the soul makes while the *Beati* is being recited, i.e. one step to every verse, i.e. one hundred and twenty-six (steps); and the import of the twenty-two books (of the Old Testament) is in every verse of the *Beati,* and that is why the *Beati* brings a soul out of hell after a year, for more than any other prayer it is in harmony with the twenty-two books of the Old Testament, i.e. the fullness of the whole is in each separate verse, and there are twenty-two chapters in it according to the number (of letters) of the Hebrew alphabet.

So it was God, then, that fulfilled David's prophecy through their journeys, and not they themselves that arranged them. Thus was the fifth Age brought to a close.

63. The sixth Age begins.
This is the sixth Age: the sixth Age is from the birth of Christ to the Judgement. There is no definite number of years set down for this Age that is known to mortals in the first place, though it might be known to God. For there is no place in Scripture, according to the literal text, whence such a number might derive, though it might be possible to infer it from something which would provide a definite number of years for this Age.

From the beginning of the world according to the Septuagint is five thousand, one hundred and ninety years. According to the Hebrew Verity it is three thousand, nine hundred and fifty-two years. From the foundation of the city (of Rome) is seven hundred and fifty-two (years).

64. It is through Christ, who was born of the pure Virgin Mary at the beginning of the sixth Age, in the forty-second year of the reign of Caesar Augustus, that the souls of the five preceding Ages who had fallen through Adam were delivered from every transgression.

In the fifteenth year of the reign of Tiberius Caesar, moreover, Christ was baptised by John the Baptist in Ennon, near Jerusalem, in the thirtieth year of his own age. And that was the year in which he chose the Apostles and Disciples, i.e. twelve Apostles and seventy-two Disciples.

65. These are the names of the Apostles:
Petrus Simon, Andreas, Iacobus Zebedei, Iohannes, Pilippus, Bartholomeus, Tomas, Matheus, Iacobus Alphei, Tatheus, Simon Cannaneus, Madianus, and Paulus ⟨i.e. in the place of Iudas⟩.

66. The names, moreover, of the seventy-two Disciples whom Jesus Christ had are: 1. Iacobus, Iustus, Mathathias, Ioseph, Ioseph, Marcus, Barnabas, Lucas, Cleopas—10. Serica, Semeon, Lucias, Inaran, Stortenes, Caphas, Tatrieus, Erenet, Pastor, Andromachas—20. Iohamas, Amplias, Urbanus, Cleopas, Erodiones, Assimmerges, Iason, Sephanus, Pilippus, Procurus—30. Nicanor, Parmina, Aquila, Iudas, Siluanus, Simon, Cleopa, Silas, Nasson, Agabas—40. Annanias, Ignatius, Simon Quirinensis, Alexander, Ruphus, Nathanel, Necodimus, Iudas, Iacobus, Simon—50. Simon ⟨i.e. Coriarius⟩, Lucas, Barnabas, Stephanus, Corissius, Milichius, Gaias, Flegonta, Ermen, Appellen, Probabilis, Dionisius Ariopagita, Appenitus, Iessus, Iustus, Stachue, Pomplius, Arizobulus, Stefanus Corinthensis, Herodius, Ruphus—70. Olimphias—1. Titus—2. Filimon.

67. The first persecution was under Nero. The second was under Domitian. The third was under Trajan. The fourth was under Marcus Antoninus. The fifth was under Seuerus. The sixth was under Maximian. The seventh was under Dacian. The eighth was under Ualirian. The ninth was under Aurilian. The tenth was under Diocletian.

In the reigns of these ten, then, the Apostles and Disciples and Martyrs of Jesus Christ suffered martyrdom for God in the three parts of the world.

⟨Sarofanes, he was the first who fashioned the image of an idol, i.e. he made an image of his son in gold and silver after his death, and a demon leapt into it and used to talk to people (from it), so that that is the first idol that there ever was⟩.

68. In this Age then, Christ was born, as we related. It was in this Age also that he was crucified, i.e. when he was thirty-three and a half years of age, as Josephus says, and in the eighteenth year of the reign of Tiberius Caesar. And he harrowed hell thereafter to redeem the righteous of the five (preceding) Ages.

It was in this Age, then, that the Apostles and Disciples were dispersed to the four corners of the earth after they had been inspired by the gift of many languages. In this Age, moreover, Peter was crucified and Paul was cut down by Nero Caesar. In this Age too the Apostles and Disciples of Jesus, the Martyrs and the confessors of Jesus suffered martyrdom for God when they were killed by the kings and potentates, stewards and consuls, and the impious governors of the world, in the three continents of the world, i.e, Europe, Africa, and Asia.

69. Concerning the names of the three continents this below. Asia, then, the daughter of Ner and the goddess, who was called Doridis, from her has been named Asia. That is, Neptune, son of Jupiter and god of the sea, fell in love with her, and the dowry that was promised her was, that a third part of the world be named after her for the destroying of her virginity and that she be with Neptune.

Africa, i.e. from Apher, son of Madian, son of Abraham, it was named. That is, Apher moved a great host into Africa and he defeated the Africans in battle, so that he himself remained in the south thereafter, and hence Africa was named after him.

Europs, king of the Sicomari, went to war for Europe, whence it is from his name that Europe is called from Europs. Alternatively, Europa was the daughter of Agenor, king of the Sidori, and Jupiter fell in love with her and carried her off with him to the island of Crete, and begot two sons by her, i.e. Minosic and Adamaint; so that Jupiter granted to her that her own name should be upon part of the world. ⟨Cicrops was the first who offered an ox to Jupiter, whence Jupiter is named⟩.

70. This is Dublittir Ua hUathaile's poem on the Pandicept.

(1) Make easy for me, O God from heaven, it is not uncertain, it is a pure deed; the answer to my question for the poets.

(2) Famous Adam had fifty sons and fifty famous and perfect daughters. Though they were violating (God's) covenant thereby, they agreed to mate with one another.

(3) For a time the pleasant world escaped, they were deceived by the soliciting of womenfolk. Though they had accepted (?) the king of the heavens only six of them gave issue.

(4) Three men and three women with power, of Adam's pre-eminent family; from them was born the host that filled this transitory world.

(5) Cain, Seth, and Sile were the three sons without great strangeness; Pibb, Olla, and Pithibb without treachery were the three haughty daughters.

(6) Pibb was the name of Cain's fair wife; Olla was the ever-pure Seth's wife; Sile's wife, brilliant her lustre, was the perfect and truly modest Pithibb.

(7) Those were the six, before the floods ebbed away (?), proud, beautiful, and perfect, who filled the dwellings in the east with the family of Adam and Eve.

(8) God cursed Cain, the hard of heart, and everyone who should come of his seed; Cain himself he punished severely for his kin-slaying of Abel.

(9) 'I announce', said the fair Creator, 'to the races of Seth with noble threat that no one of them accept the daughters of the race of Cain (as wives).'

(10) Since they transgressed the command, those proud and impure men, the band whom a strong flood scourged; it drowned all but eight of them.

(11) Noe and his three sons without shame, with their bright and noble wives, were the eight people of Seth's race without stain who did not accept Cain of the large head.

(12) Sem, Cham, and Japheth of the territories were the three sons of Noe, son of Lamech. Their three griffin-like and pure wives were Olla, Oliua, and Oliuana.

(13) Copha was Noe's wife of holy purity, Olla was wife of the long-lived Sem. Cham's wife was the famous Oliua, Japheth's wife was Oliuana.

(14) Those were the occupants of the ark with cheerfulness and noble joy; they inhabited without decay or treachery the whole world after the flood.

(15) They were a year in the cold ark above the solitude of the russet-hued waves, while the flood—a source of strife—covered the face of the white-earthed land.

(16) (It was) on the 27th, if it should be known, on a Friday, after the passage of a leap-year, that Noe came out of it on the 3rd Kalends of noble May after a whole year.

(17) After Noe had gazed out on all sides at the bright and fruitful land he sent out his fine sons in all directions, what would be more pleasant?

(18) To Japheth he gave bright Europe; to Sem he gave the perfect Asia; while in Africa without stain, in the south, Cham with his hard skin settled.

(19) I have closed the occupation of the branches of fair Cham clearly at the dawn of May Day, in the land of the Leinstermen clearly; though it be not faulty it is not unclear.

(20) The races of the good and fierce Japheth occupied famous Europe; they received such nobility from God that to them belongs the north of Asia.

(21) From Mount Imai in the arable land northwestward to the river Danube, and Scythia without tribute, all belongs to the honourable family of Japheth.

(22) When they could be accommodated no more in the east the races of beloved Japheth occupied Europe without any partition; their sails were set westward.

(23) From the red Riphi mountains northwards towards the Marshes as far as the tranquil, grave-strewn shore in remote Spain.

(24) Japheth of the fords had eight sons, they used not to go about at evening time: Gomer, Magoch, Madai the handsome, Javan, Thubal, and Thiras.

(25) His famous father cursed the son whose name was Cham, so that it is he—he excelled in perversity—is the Cain of the people after the Flood.

(26) From him sprang the goat-heads and the Fomoraig with power, and a line of numerous Luchorpáin, and every misshapen generation.

(27) The people with the two heads, it was a crime and the two bodies attached together, and the dark, one-legged creatures, and the dark-hosted, sharp-beaked creatures.

(28) Everyone in the east without a head roaming from valley to valley, his white mouth gaping from his chest, he is of Cham's race with fierceness.

(29) Cham the curly-haired had four fine sons for battle and iron palms (?): Chus, under the crushing (cascade) of the steaming falls (?), Mesraim, Phuth, and Chanaan.

(30) All the Ethiopians—I am horrified at their blue blackness—are of the line of Chus, son of Cham the devious, from the river (Nile) to the south-eastern coast.

(31) The race of Phuth, son of Cham, from afar, they occupied the level plain in the heart of Africa from all sides up to Mount Atlas of the many staves (?).

(32) The Egyptians around the noble river Nile are of the races of Mesraim, son of Cham. (They extend) from the Niger river from the south to the Mediterranean of the heavy waves.

(33) (There are) seven great peoples of hard Chanaan both from the south and from the north; those are the races of Chanaan that you hear, the healthy, fair-haired men.

(34) The eleven sons of Chanaan of the hosts, (they were) shameful (?), standard-bearing (?), of great honour; they occupied the territory where the sun was harsh, from the Dead Sea to the Mediterranean.

(35) God sent a great privation over all the eastern land, upon the race of the wicked and sinful man, after he had promised their strong land to the angelic people of Israel.

(36) From the river Euphrates to the peninsula of the clear Gatiden, from the northeast, (there) thirty great tribes gave issue of Cham of the groans.

(37) Mosoch, Masseca of the ranks, was swift (?); over paths from them were despatched the hosts towards Europe from the northeast.

(38) The Galati, as I recognise, (were) of the brilliant race of Gomer; their answers are famous. From the race of Magog are the Scythians.

(39) The fair Medes are the race of Madai; they were nurtured for great kingship. The Ionians of the clear bowers sprang from Javan.

(40) The Celtiberi, they are not criminal; the Hiberi and the Hispani, it is from Thubal that the origin of those three famous groups has shone brightly.

(41) The Cappadocians are from the fair Mosoch—many are the fruits in their luxuriant land! The Thracians in the east are the race of Thiras, without a groan of fear on any path.

(42) Ibad and Baad precisely were two sons of the righteous Magoch; their enduring fame has reached over the seas; from Ibad is the royal line of the Romans.

(43) Foénius son of Baad, it is no lie, son of Magoch the fair of the great hosts. He was no foolish ancestor; he was ancestor to the Scythians.

(44) It is of his line that the fair Gaels are; they were warlike guests. They seized sovereignty from Spain over the keen and graceful host of Ireland (Fál).

(45) The other son of the good Magoch was Ibad the pre-eminent, the great prince. The famous Alanius was a son of his, from whom are the Franks and the Romans.

(46) From him (also) are the Saxons without . . ., and the yellow-haired Britons; Albanians too on the plain as far as the east of Asia.

(47) Alanius had three sons without sorrow: Arbon, Negua and Hissicon. They gave issue to a great number of fine tribes in the east in the place of the great saints.

(48) The pre-eminent son of Negua wounded many a related grandson with spears. Saxus, from whom are the Saxons used to eat the twisty herb of the shore.

(49) The four sons of Hissicon used never quarrel over glory; Romanus, Francus here, Albanus, and Brittus.

(50) Romanus, from whom are the Romans, received honour and tribute from everyone. Francus, from whom are the Franks truly, was not wont to be over-eager in doing wicked deeds.

(51) Albanus, a pleasant son, was ancestor to the Albanians. Brittus, from whom are the true Britons, set right many a problem ingeniously.

(52) The innumerable races of Jovan are pre-eminent on every shore; to them belongs every compact holding in the west on the islands of the Mediterranean.

(53) Name the fifteen great races of Japheth, not including their lesser tribes, it is no deceit; they used to perpetrate great violence (?).

(54) All the number of pleasant Japheth's race (that are) both in Asia and Europe trace their descent from one man in one period, the

Gaels do not find it clearly (?).

(55) The races of Sem are the most numerous in the kingships of Asia; their battle against the sun extends from the river Ganges—they possess without division as far as the Mediterranean.

(56) From the Red Sea, in which lies mystery, from the Caucasus to Mount Tur, every route belongs to the race of Sem; mention their relationship. I shall not hide it.

(57) Sem had five sons, renowned the offspring! No one dared engage them with equal numbers: Aelam of the two clear, blue eyes; Lud, Assur, and Aram.

(58) Arphaxad, famed his wealth, though he was rough he was not completely reckless. The ancestor of the Chaldaeans received good education and lands (?).

(59) Twisted and sharp (?) was the head of his spear, Assur's, from whom are the Assyrians. The Syrians are from Aram of the hosts, the lordship that dealt out bitterly cold wounds.

(60) Aelam—hard was the action of his spear! From him are the Elamitae. The Lydians are from Lud, not wretched; a host from whom the scaldcrow received little (?).

(61) The angelic Jesus arranged the four sons of Aram of the ranks. Name them here, before the account ends: Us and Hul and Gether.

(62) Mes was the fourth gentle son who is reckoned as belonging to the high-king; he was not the offspring of a foolish man, from him are the Eonni.

(63) Us son of Aram—famous the king—from whom are the Traconiti. The Armenians—renowned the group—are from the honourable, just Hul.

(64) The Arcani, quick is their temper, the group of the red-handed warriors. Their fame has reached as far as Bethlehem; they sprang from Gether.

(65) Thos are the races of Aram son of Sem; you have heard them from of yore. They seized—not in theft—from the river Indus to the Euphrates, it was not insecure (?).

(66) Sale—his helmet used to be adorned with gold—was the beautiful son of Arphaxad. The famous Heber was a son of Sale's, the leader of the fierce and powerful men.

(67) Phaleg and Jectan, without disgrace, were the two sons of the clean finger-nailed Heber. Heber was the son of Sale of the assaults; Sale was son of Arphaxad.

(68) From Heber son of Sale are named the Hebrews up to this time. Clearly he alone brought the Hebrew language from the Tower of Nemrod.

(69) The famous Jectan had thirteen sons—the man of the perfect lands. To them belongs every headland and path from the river Indus to the ocean.

(70) Elmodad and the healthy Saleph, Asarmoth and very noble Jare, Aduram and famous Huzal, Decla, Ebal the conspicuous and truly fierce.

(71) Abimael and Saba there—woe to him against whom they used to hold a grudge! Ophir—fierce was his valour—Hevila the famous, and Jobab.

(72) The families of fruitful Jectan in the east, the allied and pirating man, no host dared face them that was not greater in number; they seized the two Indias.

(73) Near the famous river Euphrates is (situated) the royal and very fierce principality; in every firm country about the Tigris the head of every high place comes from them.

(74) In the portion of the righteous family of Chanaan, the pre-eminent and great men, are the Twelve Tribes of Israel—it is no path without slaughter!

(75) See! twenty-seven peoples, not counting their lesser ones; they are of the race of excellent Sem; I will not conceal it from Irishmen.

(76) Thirty races of sinful Cham, fifteen of Japheth's rule over them. Twenty-seven races of Sem of the assaults—that makes seventy-two.

(77) For them the languages were confused in order to multiply their great understanding. (There were) seventy-two, it is no little matter, at the dispersal of Nemrod's Tower.

(78) There was one language up till then for the proud family of Adam; in every place where there was possession of peaceful plains studded with elf-mounds (?)—a language whose splendid name was Gairthigern.

(79) After Heber had brought it from the Tower—not clearly mad was the common use—since he bestowed it it remained after him: the honourable language of Hebrew.

(80) At the end of ten years thereafter there was found by Foénius Forsaid the sweet-sounding and melodious language: the skillful and dexterous Irish that I use.

(81) I have not extended one course beyond what is right. I myself have woven together with great exactitude the genealogy of the family of Noe, without a semblance of difficulty in any way.

(82) I am from the cookoo's plain (?), from the monastery; Ua hUathgaile from Killeshin. May the results of the Friday of the very-good king bear me swiftly past evils. Make easy for me, O God, from heaven!

NOTES AND COMMENTARY

1. This prologue is possibly an original item, not dependent on a Latin model. For a hypothetical reconstruction of the process that may have gone into its composition see Hans P. A. Oskamp 'On the author of *Sex Aetates Mundi*' *Studia Celtica* 3 (1968) pp. 127–40, at pp. 130–1. However, a possible source for this section may be the *Exordium libri* to the Eusebio-Hieronimian Chronicle; see Rudolf Helm (ed) *Die Chronik des Hieronymus (Hieronymi Chronicon)*, Eusebius Werke 7 = *Die griechischen-christlichen Schriftsteller der ersten drei Jahrhunderte* (Leipzig 1913/Berlin 1956), and the edition in Migne, *Patrologia Latina* [*MPL*] 27, cols. 34–702, at col. 61 B: 'Incipiunt tempora totius saeculi, regesque gentium omnium, quibus locis, quibusque temporibus in suis provinciis, et quantum regnaverint, vel si quid memoriae dignum generationes, nativitates, et regna, et ducatus, per omnem actum judicum, et omnium regem Juda', etc.

The editors of the *MPL* edition, col. 61 n. a, remark that this section occurs in many MSS and in all the older editions save Scaliger's; the section is wanting however in Helm's edition, but he does not remark on the fact; see his Vorwort, p. 7. I do not know if this section is an addition of the later MSS of the Chronicle.

1.1. *Panechte*] This seems to be an alternative form of *Pandecht* (Lat. *Pandecta).*

2. There were so many doctrines current in the Middle Ages on the subject of the six Ages, and the date of Advent in particular, that it is difficult now to be sure of the precise source for any one chronology. Some put the date of Advent at Anno Mundi 5000, others 5008, 5228, 5500, or 5530; see Charles W. Jones (ed) *Bedae opera de temporibus*, Medieval Academy of America Publications No. 41 (Cambridge, Mass. 1943) p. 134. According to the Eusebio-Hieronimian Chronicle, the Creation occurred in B.C. 5199; but the Septuagint reckoning – differently computed by different authors – is most often considered to be B.C. 5190. It was this Septuagint reckoning that became popular in Ireland as the 'school reckoning'; see Bartholomew Mac Carthy, *The codex Palatino-Vaticanus, No. 830*, RIA Todd Lecture Series Vol. 3 (Dublin 1892) p. 240.

But there was no certainty about the figure: Eusebius-Jerome said 5199, though both expressed open doubt about its accuracy. But their continuators – in particular Isidore – did not transcribe the critical queries and the notion became a set one. In Isidore's own reckoning the Creation was in B.C. 5196, and this is also the figure in *Saltair na Rann.*

When, therefore, Bede wrote in his *De temporibus* (A.D. 705): 'Dominus nascitur, completus ab Adam annis mmmdccccclii' his novelty lay "not so much in differing from other chronologies, as in differing so much". (Jones, ed. cit., p. 134). For a discussion of the whole question see Anna-Dorothee von den Brinken, *Studien zur lateinischen Weltchronistik, bis in das Zeitalter Ottos von Freising* (Düsseldorf 1957).

2.2–5. Cf. Eusebius (ed. Helm, p. 15 = *MPL* 27, col. 57 A): 'A diluuio usque ad Adam annos .mmccxlii., in quibus nulla penitus nec Graeca nec barbara et, ut loquar in commune, gentilis inuenitur historia.'

2.6–9. Cf. Eusebius, loc. cit.: 'A natiuiate Abraham usque ad totius orbis diluuium inuenies retrorsum annos .dcccclii.'

2.10–13. This is merely the sum of the two preceding figures.

2.14–17. This is the sum of two figures in Eusebius (ed. Helm, p. 17 = *MPL*, cols. 58 B/59 A): 'A natiuitate quippe Abraham usque ad Moysea et egressum Israhelis ex Aegypto computantur anni .dv., a Moyseo autem usque ad Solomonem et primam aedificationem templi anni .cccclxxviiii. secundum minorem tamen numerum, quem tertius regnorum liber continet. Nam iuxta uolumen iudicum supputantur anni .dc.'

2.18–21. See the first sentence in the note above.

2.22–5. See the second sentence in the note above.

2.26–9. Cf. Eusebius (ed. Helm, pp. 17–18 = *MPL*, col. 59 A): 'A Cecrope usque ad captiuitatem Troiae anni .cccxxviiii.' Eusebius had already remarked that Cecrops and Moses were contemporaries.

2.29. *in chúiced bliadain tríchat*] I have not identified the source of this figure.

2.30–3. Cf. Eusebius, loc. cit., 'Si enim diligenter enumeres, ab ultima aetate Nini usque ad Troiae captiuitatem inuenies annos .dcccxxxiiii.' Eusebius had earlier remarked that Abraham and Ninus were contemporaries.

2.34–7. This figure is computed by subtracting the 834 of the previous stanza from the 984 of lines 14–17; but the figure should be 150, not 151 as here.

3.1. *Debi na Fírinni Ébraide*] The 'Hebrew Verity' or Jerome's Vulgate. The figures assigned to the Ages of the world in this section owed their wide dissemination ultimately to the computistical writings of Bede. Though he was aware that the Vulgate gave figures that differed greatly from those of the Septuagint bible, Eusebius did not work out the full implications of the fact in his Chronicle. Nor, for that matter, did Jerome in his continuation of Eusebius, a fact which perhaps more than any other provoked the anger of conservative churchmen against the new, 'revolutionary' dating of Bede.

But Bede knew what most of his antagonists did not: that Jerome's continuation of the Eusebian Chronicle *antedated* his revision of the bible according to the Hebrew version. The exact figures were set out by Bede in the Chronicle which he appended to his great *De temporum ratione*, ed. Theodor Mommsen, *Monumenta Germaniae Historica*, *Auctores Antiquissimi* Vol. 13 [Chronica Minora 3] (Berlin $1898^1/1961^2$) pp. 247–327, at pp. 247–8; but since SAM is not immediately dependent on Bede I will not give the figures here.

3.27–30. This concept of the seventh Age, of equal duration with the sixth, is in Bede; the idea may, however, have become a commonplace of medieval thought by the time SAM was composed. For the notion of Abel as the first just man *(fírén)* and martyr, see §13.5.

3.30–3. This idea is also in Bede, though our text does not appear to have drawn directly on that source. The doctrine of the seventh Age leading into an eighth Age of *paraousia* finds expression also in the (8th c., Irish?) *Catechesis Celtica*, ed. André Wilmart, *Analecta Reginensia. Studi e Testi* 59 (1933) pp. 29–112, at p. 56: 'Item isti VIII dies paschae significant VIII tempora vitae praesentis a principio mundi usque ad iudicium, quia sub forma ebdomadis constituit Deus hunc mundum. Ipsa est VII aetas dies iudicii, in quo fiunt mille anni, dum iudicentur vivi et mortui secundum merita uniuscuiusque.'

3.34–7. Invocatory verses such as this are not uncommon in Mid. Ir. synchronistic poetry; for an example of such identificatory patterns in later Irish verse see Tomás Ó Concheanainn 'A feature of the poetry of Fearghal Óg Mac an Bhaird' *Éigse* 15 (1974) pp. 235–51.

4a. Though from a strictly palaeographical point of view this section occurs as an extended gloss in *R*, fol. 41^r marg. supra, it is clearly intended to be included in the body of the text, along with a number of other details which are written into the margin of that MS. The inspiration is clearly from Isidore, *Isidori Hispalensis episcopi Etymologiarum sive Originum libri XX*, ed. Wallace M. Lindsay (Oxford 1911[1]), at *Etym.* XI 2. 1–8:
'Gradus aetatis sex sunt: infantia, pueritia, adolescentia, iuventus, gravitas atque senectus. Prima aetas infantia est pueri nascentis ad lucem, quae porrigitur in septem annis. Secunda aetas pueritia, id est pura et necdum ad generandum apta, tendens usque ad quartumdecimum annum. Tertia adolescentia ad gignendum adulta, quae porrigitur usque ad viginti octo annos. Quarta iuventus firmissima aetatum omnium, finiens in quinquagesimo anno. Quinta aetas senioris, id est gravitas, quae est declinatio a iuventute in senectutum..Quae aetas a quinquagesimo anno incipiens septuagesimo terminatur. Sexta aetas senectus, quae nullo annorum tempore finitur..Senium autem pars est ultima senectutis,' etc.
Note the omission of *est* in the last sentence of the SAM text, a characteristic feature of Hiberno-Latin usage; see Bengt Löfstedt (ed) *Der hibernolateinische Grammatiker Malsachanus*, Studia Latina Upsaliensia 3 (Uppsala 1965) pp. 121–2. Other Hiberno-latinisms occur in §§11, 29, 36, 46.

4. This section serves as a prose summary of §§2 and 3, the introductory poems on the chronology of the six Ages. It must be pointed out that the prose, while bearing on the substance of §3 more than of §2, is more detailed on the subject of the seventh Age than is §3 and cannot therefore derive directly from that poem. The sections that follow have reference exclusively to the Vulgate chronology.

4.5. *martra hEle ⁊ Enóc*] The theme of Enoch and Elias, destined to battle to the death with Antichrist on the eve of Doomsday, was a popular one in medieval literature; see *MPL Suppl.* 3, col. 150 ff., *De Enoc et Elia.* The theme found particular expression in Mid. Ir. literature: *Dá Brón flatha nime*, ed. Georges Dottin 'Les deux chagrins du royaume du ciel' *Revue Celtique* 21 (1900) pp. 349–87, treats in especial of the second Advent, and the story of the 'Two Sorrows' recurs in *Fís Adomnáin*, ed. Ernst Windisch 'Fís Adamnáin, Die Vision des Adamnán' *Irische Texte* 1 (1880) pp. 165–96. The Mid. Ir. *Duan in choícat cest*, ed. Kuno Meyer 'Mitteilungen aus irischen Handschriften' *Zeitschrift für celtische Philologie* 4 (1903) pp. 234–7, has a curious detail on this theme, §9: *cía brón fil i nim glan gurm*? to which is given the answer: *.i. Helí ⁊ Énóc ná cumgat etigal la hénu a parrthus*, 'Enoch and Elias who are unable to fly with the birds in Paradise.'

For a discussion of the literature on this subject see Martin McNamara, M.S.C., *The apocrypha in the Irish Church* (Dublin 1975) No. 9, pp. 24–7.

5. The data from §5–§8 comprise, in effect, an index to the material discussed in the subsequent sections of SAM. They serve to enlarge the scope of the material whose basic framework has been laid out in §4, a short *definitio temporum.* As such, then, it seems unlikely to have derived from any extraneous source; note also that §1, in all likelihood, derives from these sections, if not from Eusebius.

5.2. *ní fil crích furri*] An echo of §3.30–3.

5.2–3. *airig cecha aíssi*] See notes to §1 above.

5.4–5. Though the division of the continents is discussed first in §26, in the first Age of the world, the discussion of their names comes only in §69. Thus the homogeneity of the text, and the probability that these brief sections here under discussion are intended to preface the 'body' of SAM to follow, are clearly borne out.

6.1. *cia lín cenél*] The MS. contraction in *R* for this word is *gñ*, i.e. Lat. *genus;* the word is nowhere written out in our text but does occur among the *R* genealogies; see Michael A. O'Brien (ed) *Corpus genealogiarum Hiberniae* I (Dublin $1962^1/1976^2$) pp. 142–3, 156, etc.

The problem here posed is answered by the text in §24, as is the question of the number of languages in the world. See the notes to §24 for a full discussion of the topic.

6.3. *oénbérla*] The subject of the first language was a favourite one with medieval exegetes; the level of sophistry which resulted from such investigations was such that Bede was driven to protest at the nonsense put forth in alleged answer to the query. A good example of such enquiry, representative both of patristic and early medieval thinking, is Hrabanus Maurus, *Commentariorum in Genesim libri IV* (*MPL* 107, cols. 439–670, at col. 484 A): 'Primam autem linguam fuisse generi humano Hebraeam videtur, ex eo quod nomina cuncta nominum quousque ad divisionem linguarum in Genesi legimus, illius constat esse loquelae.'

6.3. *Gairthigern*] The origin of this name has never been satisfactorily explained. I can see no better solution than that of Robert A. S. Macalister (ed) *Lebor Gabála Érenn* I (Dublin 1938) p. 248, who writes: 'we might guess that it is a corruption of some sort of rendering of the *Vox Domini* of the Psalter, the language being assumed to be the speech of Heaven' [i.e. *gair*+*tigern* 'Lords' call or voice']. Though Macalister's edition of these verses leaves something to be desired he may be right in regard to this problem.

The occurrence of *Gairthigern* in the *Lebor Bretnach*, the Irish version of the *Historia Brittonum*, as the Irish form of the name Vortigern can be no more than a curious coincidence.

7.5. *Ca ro-llen*] I take this to be the conj. *cia* (for vocalism see *OIG* §§48, 115)+3 p. sg. pret./perf. <*lenaid*, i.e. 'though it has remained'; note that *bérla* still shows a neut., *io*-stem declension, though *bérla nÉbra* may have been a petrified phrase like *Sliab n* – etc. in placenames.

For a similar notion of the primal language see Hrabanus Maurus, op. cit. (*MPL* 107, col. 530 CD): 'Si quis quaerit in qua familia illa permansit lingua quae primitus Adam data fuit, sciat credibile esse quod in familia Heber, ex quo Hebraei dicti sunt, in ea parte hominum qua Dei portio permansit, in qua et Christus nasciturus erat. Oportuit enim ut in ea lingua salus mundo praedicatur primo, per quam primum intraverat mors in mundum. Ostendit quoque titulus in cruce Salvatoris scriptus, hanc esse omnium linguarum primam.'

8.2–3 *numir cenél*] Cf. §24, to which this present section is merely an index. For a discussion of what *numir cenél* may mean see the notes to §24.

§9. The sources for this section are not all known to me. The initial chronology is, of course, derived from §3.2–5; note that the figures in this section and in §§22, 39, 50 and 56 all derive from the Vulgate reckoning, without reference to the Septuagint chronology of §2.

§9.3–4. *coíca mac ⁊ coíca ingen*] I have no precise source for these numbers, despite the reference to *stairscríbnidi na Rómán* in the text. However, a parallel passage occurs in the Irish, Ps. Bede's *Excerptiones patrum Collectanea* (*MPL* 94, cols. 539–60, at col. 544 B): 'Quot filios habuit Adam? Triginta filios, et triginta filias. Aliter. Filiorum Adam computatio, ut alii dicunt, sexaginta duo; et filiarum computatio, quinquaginta tres sunt.'

The figures are clearly corrupt, due no doubt to the misreading of Roman numerals; unfortunately, there is no surviving MS. of the *Collectanea* with which we might compare the printed text. The details given at the end of §11 have no parallel, to my knowledge, in the large corpus of Hiberno-Latin literature on the subject of the *Dies Dominica;* see Robert Priebsch, *The Letter from Heaven on the observance of the Lord's Day* (Oxford 1936); McNamara, *Apocrypha*, Nos. 52 A, B, C; pp. 60–4; and Robert E. McNally, *Scriptores Hiberniae Minores* 1, *Corpus Christianorum Series Latina* 108 B, p. 175 ff.

One medieval Irish text, almost exactly contemporary with SAM, provides a similar set of figures for the number of Adam's offspring: the Chronicon of Marianus Scottus of Mainz († 1082). The full text of the poem in question is given by MacCarthy, *The codex Palatino-Vaticanus*, p. 26 and by Bruno Güterbock 'Aus irischen Handschriften in Turin und Rom' *Zeitschrift für vergleichende Sprachforschung* 33 [N.F. 13] (1895) pp. 86–105, at p. 95. I give the relevant verses here (in a reconstructed text):

Dá mac déc ar fichit ann,
oénben cech fir nos-digbann;
is fichi mac, mór in ler,
is dá mnaí im cech oénfer.

Coíca mac, dá mac co mblad,
dá ingen ar sechtmogat;
is ed ruc Eua do chlainn
d'Ádaim céin baé i colainn.

In *Saltair na Rann* the number of sons and daughters is given as 72:

Bretha do Ádaum, ro-clos,
cen gábud íar [n]-immarbus
sechtmoga mac la dís dein;
a chertchumma d'ingenaib.

See David Greene & Fergus Kelly (ed) *The Irish Adam and Eve story from Saltair na Rann* 1 (Dublin 1976) pp. 90–1.

9.4. *Cirini*] The reference is to Jerome's commentary on Genesis, ed. Paul de Lagarde, *S. Hieronymi presbyteri Hebraicae Quaestiones in libro Geneseos*, *CCSL* 72, pp. 1–56; see *Hier* 4. 1, 2 and 25.

9.5–6. *iar n-araili senchaidib*] Note the uncertainty, which was evident also in the Ps. Bedan *Collectanea* (note to §9.3–4); in fact, the number of sons listed in §10 is the same as that given *chétus* in §9.3.

10. I know of no other independent text that contains these names. The list in the Book of Uí Maine, fol. 95ʳa [39] 1–10 [= the *Bansenchas*] is taken directly from this text and has no independent value. The poem in Marianus Scottus's Chronicle has the following verse:

Sili sósar na mac mín
ruc in rígan don roríg;
Sechna solus, grian ba gel,
ba sí sósar na n-ingen.

The *Duan in choícat cest*, *ZCP* 4 (1903) p. 236, touches on the topic but names only Caín and Pennán.

11.4. *dias ar choícait*] This number conflicts with that cited in the prose at the end of this section (72); there may have been some confusion with Roman numerals here. The names in the verses are identical with those listed in §10, except that *Narchon* of §10.2 = *Nachor* in §11.18.

12.1. *níro-clannaigset acht triur*] An obvious inference from Genesis.

12.2. *sóssar mac nÁdaim*] Cf. the verse cited in note §10 above, and the notes to §9.3–4.

12.2. *a trí mná*] These names are derived from apocryphal sources. The *Duan in choícat cest* gives the name of Pihib, Cain's wife (sic), who is further described as *ingen Ádhaim, ben Chaín;* there is some confusion in the *Duan* concerning these names. I believe the names that occur in *Lebor Gabála* are derived from this text (SAM); the names in the *Bansenchas*, as noted above, are certainly taken from SAM.

13.2. Based on *Gn* 4. 1 ff.: 'Adam vero cognovit Havam uxorem suam quae concepit et peperit Cain. . (2) rursusque peperit fratrem eius Abel. Fuit autem Abel pastor ovium et Cain agricola. . (7) Cognovit autem Cain uxorem suam quae concepit et peperit Enoch et aedificavit civitatem vocavitque nomen eius ex nomine filii sui Enoch.'

The *Duan in choícat cest* reads for this: *.i. Caín dorigni in cé*[*t*]- *chathrig ⁊ tuc ainm a meic prímgenni fuirri .i. Enoch .i. Enoch ainm na cathrach.*

13.4. *is leis do-rigned cétar*] Based on *Gn* 4.2: 'fuit autem Abel pastor ovium et Cain agricola.' This sentence was misunderstood by Martin McNamara 'A plea for Hiberno-Latin biblical studies' *Irish Theological Quarterly* 34 (1972) pp. 337–53, at p. 351, where he reads: *cét ár* 'first slaughter'.

13.5. *Abél*] For Abel as the first just man see Robert Atkinson (ed) *The passions and the homilies from Leabhar Breac*, RIA Todd Lecture Series Vol. 2 (Dublin 1887), lines 6097–8: *Abél cétus, in cétfhírén ⁊ in cétmartír.*

13.6. *Laméch*] Based on *Gn* 4. 18–19: 'Porro Enoch genuit Irad et Irad genuit Maviahel et Maviahel genuit Matusahel et Matusahel genuit Lamech (19) qui accepit uxores duas nomen uni Ada et nomen alteri Sella.'

13.8. *ut Hironimus dicit*] I have been unable to find any such reference in *Hier*.

14.3. *Malalel acccc.*] *Gn* 5.17 gives Malalahel a life-span of 895 years; note that *Lc* reads .dccc.cxu. (*rectius* .dccc.xcu.?). Though I have amended numerals in other sections of the text, the reading in this case does not allow any reasonable alteration that would produce the required 895 years.

15. The *famosa quaestio* of Methuselah's age, and especially the question of whether or not he survived the Deluge, was one that vexed every medieval exegete from Jerome on. The basic source for the text is *Gn* 5.25–7; Jerome, characteristically, resolved the apparent crux by recourse to the Hebrew version of Scripture, a solution enthusiastically taken up by Bede in his *Epistola ad Pleguinam*, ed. Jones, op. cit., p. 310.
It should, perhaps, be pointed out that for this section (but more particularly for §21) there are close textual parallels in *Saltair na Rann*, line 2249 ff.

16. This section is a versification of §15, with no additional details.

17. This section is based on *Gn* 6.1 ff.: 'Cumque coepissent homines multiplicari super terram et filias procreassent (2) videntes filii Dei filias eorum quod essent pulchrae acceperunt uxores sibi ex omnibus quas elegerant.'

17.5. *torothuir*] See §§33, 34: *Senchus na fomorach ⁊ na luchorpán ⁊ na torothur*, and the notes. The idea derives from *Gn* 6.4: 'Gigantes autem erant super terram in diebus illis,' which was variously explained, e.g., by Irish Ps. Isidore, *Questiones Sancti Hysidori tam de Nouo quam de Veteri Testamentum*, ed. Robert E. McNally, *CCSL* 108 B, pp. 187–205 [= *MPL* 83, cols. 201–8]: 'Dic mihi. Quare fuit diluuium super terra? Respondit. Filii Dei acceperunt filias hominum ex omnibus quas sibi elegerant, natique sunt ex eis filii. Illi fuerunt gigantes, et multa mala fecerunt in terra, et non placuit Deo. Propterea deliuit eos Dominus per aquas diluuii.'

17.8. *do huili-dilgenn*] Cf. *OIP* Note 137, Gl. 229.

17.8. *conid dó*] Though not entirely satisfactory, this is the best emendation I can suggest for the *RP* MS. reading *conid o*, which is surely unacceptable as it stands. There are, however, some peculiar usages of the prepositional construction with *ó* in *U;* see Richard I. Best & Osborn Bergin (ed) *Lebor na Huidre, the Book of the Dun Cow* (Dublin 1929) lines 8939–40, and 9131.

18.1–2. Translated from *Gn* 7.11: 'et cataractae caeli apertae sunt (12) et facta est pluvia super terram quadraginta diebus et quadraginta noctibus. (13) In articulo diei illius ingressus est Noe et Sem et Ham et Iafeth filii eius uxor illius et tres uxores filiorum eius cum eis in arcam.'

18.2. *int oénḟírén*] Based on *Gn* 6.9: 'Noe vir iustus atque perfectus fuit in generationibus suis cum Deo ambulavit.'

18.4. *ro-baé matan*] I have no precise source for this phrase, though the idea of a 'dawning' and an 'evening' to every Age must have been a commonplace of medieval exegesis; cf. (Irish?) Ps. Bede's *Commentarii in Pentateuchum*,

MPL 91, cols. 189–394, at col. 203 C: 'Pergamus ergo per has mundi aetates.. secundo saeculo factum est..Hujus vespera fit confusio linguarum.'

18.5–7. Based on *Gn* 7.12 ff.: 'Et facta est pluvia super terram quadraginta diebus et quadraginta noctibus. (24) Obtinueruntque aquae terras centum quinquaginta diebus. (8.1) adduxit spiritum super terram et inminutae sunt aquae.'

19. This is an important section in the text, for it vividly marks the continuity of the Irish (Hiberno-Latin) exegetical tradition from the 7th to the 11th century. The symbolism of the Ark was, of course, an important theme in medieval exegesis generally, following on the examples of commentaries such as Ambrose's *De Noe et Arca*. Our section, however, has close parallels in a 7th century Hiberno-Latin commentary, the *Tractatus Hilarii in septem epistolas catholicas*, ed. R. E. McNally, *CCSL* 108 B, pp. 51–124.

McNally remarks of this text (Introd., p. xvi ff.): 'Since the Reichenau commentary of the anonymous Scottus is basic to Ps. Hilary's work and reflects an older exegetical tradition, while Bede's *expositio*, later in origin, depends at least partially on Ps. Hilary, the date of the composition of this latter work must be placed between the years 690 and 708. The determination of this date results from the relation of Ps. Hilary both to the anonymous Scottus and to Bede, while its Irish character results from literary parallels which exist between it and works of known Irish provenance.' The following passage from the *Tractatus* shows the similarity to the SAM text; (*CCSL* 108 B, p. 91): 'Trecenta in longitudine habebat [arca] cubita, id est perseuerantiam in fide Trinitatis; quinquaginta in latitudine, id est caritatis longitudo (*sic*, *rectius* latitudo?); triginta in altitudine, id est tres leges ad caelum ascendentes; id est tristige.'
perseuerantiam perfectionis significat = perseuerantiam in fide Trinitatis
latitudinem caritatis significat = id est caritatis longitudo (latitudo?)
altitudinem spei significat = id est tres leges ad caelum ascendentes

McNally cites no source for the Ps. Hilary passage, though it has clear echoes in Origen as well as in other Hiberno-Latin commentaries. It should also be noted, perhaps, that there is a close parallel between the SAM text and Hugo of St. Victor's *De Arca Noe morali Liber I*, *MPL* 176, cols. 617–704, at col. 634 D: 'longitudo in fide Trinitatis trecentos cubitos habeat, in latitudine charitatis quinquaginta, in altitudine spei quae in Christo est triginta.'

For remarks on the possible use of Hugo's works in Ireland, and on the theme of Hiberno-Latin biblical exegesis in general, see Bernard Bischoff's seminal paper 'Wendepunkte in der Geschichte der lateinischen Exegese im Frühmittelalter' *Sacris Erudiri* 6 (1954) pp. 189–279, rev. ed. in the same author's *Mittelalterliche Studien: Ausgewählte Aufsätze zur Schriftkunde und Literaturgeschichte*, 3 vols (Stuttgart 1966–7, 1981) Vol. 1, pp. 205–73. A reference from the Gospels of Maél Brigte *secundum Ug* is cited in *SE*, p. 275 = *Mitt. Stud.*, p. 270, n. 143.

19.6. *a hailt .i. a hairddi*] I have no precise source for the Latin allegorical interpretation that follows.

20. The material in this section is set in a question-and-answer format that is common in medieval exegetical texts generally. As a didactic technique the question-and-answer scheme can be traced back to the Fathers of the Church, but the scheme found particular favour with the Irish, e.g., the title of the Irish biblical work found in Lyons, Bibl. mun., MS. 447 (376) fol. 106^{r} (saec. IX) reads: *Interrogationes uel responsiones tam de ueteri quam de nouo testamento;* on the Irish character of the work see Bischoff 'Wendepunkte', *SE*, p. 224 ff. =

Mitt. Stud., p. 231 ff. Another example is the Irish academic dialogue preserved in Paris, Bibl. nat., MS. lat. 10616 (saec. VIII–IX), fols. 94r–131r, which opens: *Incipit interrogatio de singulas questiones quem discipulus postolauit magistrum* (cited by McNally, *CCSL* 108 B, p. 192 n. 23). Nor was the format exclusive to Hiberno-Latin texts, for it is used also in the Old-Irish treatise on the Psalter, ed. Kuno Meyer, *Hibernica Minora*, Anecdota Oxoniensia (Oxford 1894), which is discussed by Martin McNamara 'Psalter text and Psalter study in the early Irish Church (A.D. 600–1200)' *Proceedings of the Royal Irish Academy* 73 C 7 (1973) pp. 201–98, at pp. 229–30; see also the discussion by Pádraig Ó Néill 'Airbertach mac Cosse's poem on the Psalter' *Éigse* 17 (1977) pp. 19–46, where the continuity of the Irish exegetical tradition is again well illustrated.

20.1–3. The problem discussed in this section has its origin in the ambiguities of the Genesis account of the flood, especially *Gn* 7.11 and 8.3–4. According to *Gn* 8.3–4, the flood began exactly with the beginning of the calendar year 600 in the life of Noah and ceased exactly with the end of this same year, which was understood to have been a *bliadain éscae*, a lunar year of 354 days. According to the other version, however, the flood commenced 47 days after the first day of the calendar year, i.e. on the 17th day of the second month (as in *Gn* 7.11), and ended on the 27th day of the second month in the following year (as in *Gn* 8.14). This second theory, therefore, has added 11 days (reckoning inclusively) to the lunar year of 354 days, thereby advancing the theory that the year of the flood should be reckoned as a solar year of 365 days, *bliadain gréne*. The SAM text, however, implies that the flood occurred in a leap-year, as the following table shows:

(Macalister, *Lebor Gabála* 1, p. 244)	*Year*	*Month*	*Day*
Noah enters Ark	600	2	10
Flood begins	600	2	17
Flood last 150 days [= 5 months], therefore Ark settles	600	7	17
Mountain-tops appear	600	10	1
Raven sent out after 40 days	600	11	11
Noah opens Ark	601	1	1
Noah leaves Ark	601	2	27
	— 600	2	10
Period spent in Ark	1		17

If the flood occurred in a leap-year then that year had 366 days; 366 + 17 = 383 = 7 × 54, 5 remaining. If the first of these extra days was a Friday *(Oéndiden do-chuas inti)*, then the fifth would have been a Tuesday.

20.2–3. *hi commun nó i n-emblesim*] Common years contain 12 lunar months; embolismic years contain one additional month 'thrown in' (μῆν ἐμβόλιμος). Though not in the *DIL*, *emblesim* is attested already in the Karlsruhe Bede; cf. Stokes & Strachan, *Thesaurus Palaeohibernicus* 2, p. 10.

20.2. ⁊ *ticht essi*] Note that *P* omits these words, but they do not adversely affect the sense so far as I can see; the parallelism with §20.4 seems clear.

20.7. *treticim*] Another example of Irish latinity; cf. §§4a, 11, and 29.

21. Note the close resemblance between these verses and lines 2249–52 of *Saltair na Rann:*

Cethrur gelda, gnímraid gúir,
febdai adfét in scriptúir
sinium saégul ós cach maig
bátar 'sind aimsir toísig.

SR has the Old Ir. superl. ending in *-um*, for which the later construction with *is* has been substituted in SAM; the similarity may be due merely to identity of subject-matter.

21.7. *trícha, noí cét*] Cf. *Gn* 5.5: 'Et factum est omne tempus quod vixit Adam anni nongenti triginta.'

21.9. *coíca, noí cét*] Cf. *Gn* 9.29: 'Et impleti sunt omnes dies eius (*sc.* Noe) nongentorum quinquaginta annorum.'

21.11. *sesca, noí cét*] Cf. *Gn* 5.20: 'Et facti sunt omnes dies Iared nongenti sexaginta duo anni.' Note that I have amended the figures in accordance with this and the reading in *P;* cf. the years allotted to Iareth in §14.

21.15. *noí mbliadna sescat, noí cét*] Cf. *Gn* 5.27: 'Et facti sunt omnes dies Mathusalae nongenti sexaginta novem anni.'

22. This section is based solely on *Gn.*

22.3 *Noe primum altare fecit*] Based on *Gn* 8.20: 'Aedificavit autem Noe altare Domino.'

22.3. *Coíca ar tríb cétaib*] Cf. *Gn* 9.28: 'Vixit autem Noe post diluvium trecentis quinquaginta annis (29) et impleti sunt omnes dies eius nongentorum quinquaginta annorum.' Note that I have corrected the *R* reading in accordance with this and the evidence of *PCLc.*

23.1–6. Translated from *Gn* 9.1, 11–13, and 15–16: 'Benedixitque Deus Noe et filiis eius et dixit ad eos "Crescite et multiplicamini et implete terram (11) Statuam pactum meum vobiscum..neque erit deinceps diluvium dissipans terram (15) Et recordabor foederis mei vobiscum..(12) Hoc signum foederis.. (16) Eritque arcus in nubibus".'

23.4. *in céin*] Note that this older form of the conj. (with the art.) occurs here alongside *i céin* §23.8 and *hi céin* §62.1.

23.6 *mo fidbocc*] Lit. 'my staff, billhook', which has no precedent in *Gn.*

24.1–2. Based on *Gn* 9.19: 'Tres isti sunt filii Noe et ab his disseminatum est omne hominum genus super universam terram.'

24.3. *Is amlaid so*] Taken from Isidore, *Etym* IX 2.2: 'Gentes autem a quibus divisa est terra, quindecim sunt de Iaphet, triginta et una de Cham, viginti et septem de Sem, quae fiunt septuaginta tres, vel potius, ut ratio declarat, septuaginta duae.'
There is no such passage either in *Gn* or in *Hier.*

24.4. *trícha immorro ó Chám*] Note that the author of SAM adopts the more usual figure for the number of Ham's offspring.

24.5–9. The notion of 72 languages corresponding to the 72 descendants of Noah is based ultimately on *Gn* 10, where the Septuagint text of the bible lists the 72. At the time of the Tower of Babel they are supposed to have separated into 72 linguistic groups, which are mystically related to the 72 books of Scripture. See, e.g., the Irish Ps. Bede's *Collectanea, MPL* 94, col. 542 A: 'Veteris Testamenti sunt libri quinquaginta *(rectius* quadraginta) quinque, Novi autem viginti septem; (544 C) Quot linguae? Septuaginta duae'; a combination of the two themes occurs in Irish Ps. Isidore's *Questiones tam de Novo quam de Veteri Testamentum, CCSL* 108 B, p. 192: [Quaestio 3] 'Dic mihi. Quanti libri intellecuntur in Nouum testamentum? Respondit. Viginti VII. Et in uetus testamentum lex Moysi XLV libri sunt. Iuxta septuagenta duae linguas, septuagenta duo libri intellecuntur.'

The theme recurs in Hrabanus Maurus, *Commentarium in Paralipomena,* II. 23, *MPL* 109, cols. 279–540, at col. 388 B: 'Unde Salvator in Evangelio 72 discipulos ad praedicandum misit (*Lc* X) quia sanctae Trinitatis fidem cum lucis operibus cuique ad justitiam sufficere demonstrare voluit; ter vicies enim et quater terni 72 faciunt. Quo numero et linguarum diversitas ac librorum Veteris Novique Testamenti series comprehenditur.'

The whole subject is discussed in Arno Borst, *Der Turmbau von Babel. Geschichte der Meinungen über Ursprung und Vielfalt der Sprachen und Völker,* 4 vols (Stuttgart 1957–63), in six parts.

24.10–23. It is not quite clear what the precise meaning is of the *numir (árim) cenél* in this and the following passage. It seems reasonably certain, however, that the author of SAM had at his disposal both *Hier* and *Etym* to augment the underlying details of *Gn.* Cf. *Etym* IX 2.39: 'Et si omnia considerentur, plura tamen gentium mutata quam manentia vocabula apparent; quibus postea nomina diversa dedit ratio.' The word *ratio* here seems to provide the equivalent of the Irish *árim (numir).*

24.17. *ocht meic ic Iaféth*] *Gn* 10.2 gives only 7 sons for Japhet: 'Filii Iafeth Gomer Magog et Madai, Iavan et Thubal et Mosoch et Thiras.' Both *Hier* and *Etym* follow this reckoning. The Masseca of SAM is probably the result of a misunderstanding or confusion of *Etym* IX 2.30: 'Mosoch, ex quo Cappadoces. Vnde et urbs apud eos usque hodie Mazaca dicitur.' Note that Masseca alone of the 'eight' is unmentioned in the subsequent prose elaboration of the list.

24.20. *ní áirimthir*] Note the constant juxtaposition of active and passive forms in this section: *ní tharta i n-áirim; ní thabair in numir; ní thabair in árim; ní áirimthir;* it might be possible to read *ní thabair i n-árim,* with *thabair* as a late passive form, but I have preferred to see it as a doublet form of *ní thabair in numir.*

24.20. Note that in §25 the four sons of Ham and their descendants are, in fact, named. The reference here seems to be to *Etym*, where indeed only Chus, Mesraim, and Chanaan are given sons. This seems to confirm the surmise above that the SAM author is referring to the *ratio* of *Etym* IX 2.39. Worth noting is the precise meaning attached to the words *sluind ceníuil* in this passage.

25.2. *Olibana*] This woman is nowhere mentioned in the bible; see the notes to §§28, 36 and 70. Cf. also Macalister, *Lebor Gabála* 1, pp. 211–13.

25.2. *ocht maccu*] See the note to §24.17 above, and §70.

25.3–10. This is taken from *Hier* 10.2: 'Sunt autem Gomer Galatae, Magog Scythae, Madai Medi, Iauan Iones, qui et Graeci (unde et mare Ionium). Thubal Iberi, qui et Hispani, a quibus Celtiberi. . Mosoch Cappadoces. . Thiras Thraces.'

The additional section on the Aeolian language is from *Hier* 10.4–5: 'De Ionibus, id est de Graecis, nascuntur Elisei, qui uocantur Aeolides: unde et quinta lingua Graeciae AEOLIS appellatur.'

25.11 ⁊ *septem filios habuit*] I have no source for this detail.

25.11. *Clanna Gomér*] Cf. *Hier* 10.3: 'Filii Gomer Ascenez et Rifath et Thogorma. Ascenez Graeci Reginos uocant, Rifath Paphlagonas, Thogorma Phrygas.' For this passage *Etym* reads (IX 2.32–3): 'Filii Gomer, nepotes Iaphet. Aschanaz, a quo Sarmatae, quos Graeci Rheginos vocant. (33) Riphath, a quo Paphlagones. Gotorna, a quo sunt Phryges.'

Either or both of these sources may have been drawn upon.

25.13. *cenél doíni. . Colchi sunt*] Cf. *Etym* IX 2.82–3: 'Thraces ex filio Iaphet, qui vocatus est Thiras. . (83) Istrorum gens originem a Colchis ducit.'

25.14. The *U* reading: *mac sin Gomer mac Iafed* is due to a misunderstanding of the editors. Following the pattern set by the remainder of the *U* fragment we should perhaps read: *Mac sin Gomér meic Iaféd;* an alternative rendering would be to posit the omission of the *Trí* in the text and emending accordingly thus: *meic sin Gomér meic Iaféd.* Either way, the second *mac* of the *U* edition should be expanded as *meic.*

25.17. *a quo sunt Scithi ⁊ Gothi*] Cf. *Etym* IX 2.27: 'Magog, a quo arbitrantur Scythas et Gothos traxisse originem'; and *Etym* XIV 3.31: 'Scythia sicut et Gothia a Magog filio Iaphet cognominata.' Note that the objection raised at this point by Hans Oskamp, *Studia Celtica* 3 (1968) p. 135, has no validity; it results from his having arbitrarily equated the personages of Gothus, son of Armon, and the Gothi. The suggested dependence on the *Lebor Bretnach* for this detail is misleading.

26.1–5. This is the text translated in the *Lebor Bretnach, the Irish version of the Historia Britonum ascribed to Nennius*, ed. Anton G. van Hamel, Irish MSS Commission (Dublin 1932) p. 6, §5: 'Iar ndilinn tra rorandad in doman i tri itir maccu Noe .i. Eoraip ⁊ Affricc ⁊ Assia. Sem in n-Assia, Cam i n-Affraic, Iathfeth i n-Eoraip. Cedfear thanic in n-Eoraip ar tus do sil Iafed .i. Alanius cona tri macaib .i. Hissicon ⁊ Gothus no Armen ⁊ Negua.'

Whether this passage (§5 of the *Lebor Bretnach*) belonged to the original of that text, or whether it is a later borrowing from SAM is a problem that cannot be discussed here; see above, pp. 49–50, and David N. Dumville 'The textual history of "Lebor Bretnach": a preliminary study' *Éigse* 16 (1975–6) pp. 255–73.

26.7–8. *Saxus. . is uad atát Saxain*] Though nowhere stated in *Etym*, the deduction seems a fairly obvious one. The same deduction is made in the *Lebor Bretnach.*

26.8–13. Translated from *Gn* 10.4 and *Hier* 10.4–5; *Gn* 10.4: 'Filii autem Iavan Elisa et Tharsis Cetthim et Dodanim.' Cf. *Etym* IX 2.35: 'Tharsis, a quo Cilices, ut Iosephus arbitratur. Unde et metropolis civitas eorum Tharsus dicitur.' This is a detail which is not in *Hier*, which otherwise continues: 'Cethim Citii, a quibus hodieque urbs Cypri Citium nominatur. Dodanim Rhodii,' etc.

26.12–13. This can hardly be derived from *Hier*, whose continuation of the above passage is incorporated into §27 of SAM.

27.1. All but this sentence is derived from *Hier* 10.5: 'Et uidebimus omnes poene insulas et totius orbis litora terraque mari uicinas graecis accolis occupatas, qui..ab Amano et Tauro montibus omnia maritima loca usque ad oceanum possedere britannicum.'

Cf. A. G. van Hamel 'On Lebor Gabála' *ZCP* 10 (1915) pp. 97–197, at pp. 127–31, who says that *Lebor Gabála* (Version A: MSS Book of Leinster and Book of Fermoy) borrowed this passage from SAM.

28.2. *Oliua*] This woman is nowhere mentioned in the bible; see notes to §§25, 36, and 70, and Macalister, *Lebor Gabála* I, pp. 211–13.

28.2–6. This is based on *Gn* 10.6 and *Hier* 10.6, and possibly also on *Etym* IX 2.10 ff.; *Gn* 10.6: 'Filii autem Ham Chus et Mesraim et Fut et Chanaan.' The additional details are from *Hier:* 'Chus usque hodie ab Hebraeis Aethiopia nuncupatur, Mesraim Aegyptus, Fut Libyes, a quo et Mauritaniae fluuius usque in praesens Fut dicitur omnisque circa eum regio futensis.'

Cf. also I *Par* 1.8 on the same subject.

28.4. *La Mesrom do-rónad altóir*] I have no source for this statement; it is obviously intended to parallel the detail about Noah in §22.3.

28.5. *uad Affacdai*] Cf. *Etym* IX 2.118: 'Africam autem initio habuere Libyes, deinde Afri, post haec Getuli, postremum Mauri et Numides.' Note that *Etym* IX.2.10 has for the first sentence: 'Chus, a quo Aethiopes progeniti', which may be closer to the Irish than *Hier*.

28.7. Cf. *Hier* 10.6: 'Porro Chanaan optinuit terram, quam Iudaei deinceps possederunt, eiectis Chananaeis.' See also *Etym* IX 2.22: 'Filii Chanaam undecim, ex quo Chananaeorum decem gentes, quorum terram his expulsis Iudaei possederunt.'

28.8–11. Based on *Gn* 10.7, and *Hier* 10.7 with perhaps *Etym* IX 2.3 ff.: *Gn:* 'Filii Chus Saba et Hevila et Sabatha et Regma et Sabathaca'; *Hier:* 'Saba a quo Sabaei..Euila Gaetuli: in parte remotioris Africae, heremo cohaerentes. Sabatha, a quo Sabatheni, qui nunc Astabari nominantur. Rehema uero et Sabathaca paulatim antiqua uocabula perdidere, et quae pro ueteribus habeant, ignoratur.'

Cf. also I *Par* 1.9 on the same subject.

28.11. *Sabata, Acha*] Note that the author of SAM has made two names of the biblical Sabathaca, thus accounting for his *secht meic*.

28.11. *Nebroth*] Based on *Gn* 10.8 and 10: 'Porro Chus genuit Nemrod.. (10) fuit autem principium regni eius Babylon.' This is not in *Etym*, but see I *Par* 1.10. The subject of Babylon is taken up again at greater length in §§57 and 58; see the notes to those sections.

29.1–4. Based on *Gn* 10.10, and *Hier* 10.10; *Gn:* 'Fuit autem principium regni eius Babylon et Arach et Archad et Chalanne in terra Sennar'; *Hier:* 'Babel enim interpretatur confusio. Regnauit autem et in Arach, hoc est in Edessa, et in Achad, quae nunc dicitur Nisibis, et in Chalanne, quae postea uerso nomine a Seleuco rege est dicta Seleucia.'

29.1. *confussio*] A characteristically Irish spelling, with double-*s* in medial position; see Löfstedt, *Malsachanus*, pp. 102–3.

29.2. *Sessach*] Based apparently on *Ier* 51.41: 'Quomodo capta est Sesach et comprehensa est inclyta universae terrae! Quomodo facta est in stuporem Babylon inter gentes.'

29.4. *Doram*] Cf. *Dan* 3.1: 'Nabuchodonosor rex fecit statuam auream. . et statuit eam in campo Duram provinciae Babylonis.'

29.6. *iar fairind*] I know of no tradition that relates Assur to Nimrod, but the derivation from Sem is in *Etym* IX 2.3: 'Filii Sem quinque singulariter gentes singulas procreaverunt. Quorum primus Elam, a quo Elamitae principes Persidis: secundus Assur, a quo Assyriorum pullulavit imperium.'
The SAM author takes up this point again in §31, where he makes clear the relationship of the Syrians and Assyrians; see the notes to §31.

29.7. *is ann ro-génair Assúr*] Cf. *Gn* 10.11: 'De terra illa egressus est Assur et aedificavit Nineven et plateas civitatis et Chale. (12) Resen quoque inter Nineven et Chale haec est civitas magna.' *Hier* differs considerably at this point and was not used.

29.10–12. Based on *Gn* 10.7, but translated from either *Hier* 10.7 or *Etym* IX 2.17–18, which are identical.
Gn: 'Filii Regma Saba et Dadan; *Hier:* Hic Saba per sin litteram scribitur, supra uero per samech. . Dadan gens est Aethiopiae in occidentali plaga.' The Saba referred to as *supra* is the Saba son of Chus in *Gn* 10.7; cf. Jerome's *Liber interpretationis Hebraicorum nominum*, ed. Paul de Lagarde, *CCSL* 72, pp. 57–161, sub lit. *Gn* R–S: 'Siquidem apud Hebraeos tres S sunt litterae: una, quae dicitur samech, et simpliciter legitur quasi per S nostram litteram describatur; alia sin, in qua stridor quidam non nostri sermonis interstrepit; tertia sade, quam aures nostrae penitus reformidant. Sicubi ergo euenerit ut eadem nomina aliter atque aliter interpretentur, illud in causa est quod diuersis scripta sunt litteris.'
It is instructive to see the botch made of this passage in the *B* text of SAM, where that scribe writes: *gens moriens tali plaga*, and glosses that in Irish thus: *.i. ciniud ara tainic plaigh* 'a race on whom came a plague'! This is not uncharacteristic of some of the inanities perpetrated in the *B* and *Lc* recensions, which are the result of a near total ignorance of Latin.

29.13–16. Translated from *Gn* 10.13–14, with additions from *Hier* 10.13–14 or *Etym* IX 2.19–20, which are identical.
Gn: 'At vero Mesraim genuit Ludim et Anamim et Laabim Nepthuim (14) et Phetrusim et Gesluim de quibus egressi sunt Philistim et Capthurim.' The addition from *Hier* is: 'ceterae sex gentes ignotae nobis sunt, quia bello Aethiopico subuersae usque ad obliuionem praeteritorum nominum peruenere.' The same material is found in 1 *Par* 1.11–12.

30.1–5. Based on the list in *Gn* 10.15–18: 'Chanaan autem genuit Sidonem primogenitum suum Ettheum et Iebuseum et Amorreum Gergeslum (17) Eveum et Araceum Sineum (18) et Aradium Samariten et Amatheum' [=1 *Par* 1.13–14].
This section is illustrated in Françoise Henry & Geneviève L. Marsh-Micheli 'A century of Irish illumination (1070–1170)' *PRIA* 62 C 5 (1961–3) pp. 101–65, Pl. XVIa.

30.5. *qui fuit iunior*] Not in the bible, but an obvious deduction.

30.6–12. Translated from either *Hier* 10.15–18 or *Etym* IX 2.22–5. *Hier:* 'De Chanaan primus natus est Sidon, a quo urbs in Phoenice Sidon uocatur. Dein Aracaeus, qui Arcas condidit, oppidum contra Tripolim in radicibus Libani situm..Aradii sunt, qui Aradum insulam possederunt, angusto freto a Phoenicis litore separatam. Samaraei Emissa nobilis Syriae Coeles ciuitas.'

30.10–11. *eturru ⁊ trácht na Foénice*] This rendering of *Aradum insula ..angusto freto a Phoenicis litore separata* implies a use of the 'elliptical' construction, where 'a singular pronoun may be omitted where a plural concept, expressed in a plural verb or pronoun, consists of two elements, one already known and one about to be mentioned' *OIG* §402.

31.1–4. Based on *Gn* 10.22: 'Filii Sem Aelam et Assur et Arfaxad et Lud et Aram' [= 1 *Par* 1.17]. The additional details are from *Hier* 10.22 and *Etym* IX 2.3; *Hier:* 'Hi ab Euphrate fluuio partem Asiae usque ad Indicum oceanum tenent. Est autem Elam, a quo Elamitae principes Persidis.'
Etym: 'Filii Sem..Quorum primus Elam, a quo Elamitae principes Persidis: secundus Assur, a quo Assyriorum pullulavit imperium.'

31.2. *Olla*] Another woman whose name appears nowhere in the bible; see the notes to §§25, 28, 36, and 70.

31.2. *dia síl na hÉbraidi*] Based on *Gn* 10.24: 'At vero Arfaxad genuit Sala de quo ortus est Eber', whence *Hier* 10.24: 'Heber a quo Hebraei.' Isidore repeats the derivation in *Etym* IX 2.5: 'Heber nepos Arphaxat, a quo Hebraei'; and again in *Etym* IX 2.38: 'ex Heber Hebraei.'

31.4. *toísig Persidis ⁊ Siriae*] I know of no text that states that the Elamitae ruled in Syria as well as Persia.

31.5. *ut supra*] Referring to §29.8–9. Note that both *U* and *C* repeat the words *.i. cathir mór fil eter Ninue ⁊ Thala.*

31.5. *iar fír*] Cf. §29.0; in this section the author of SAM gives the 'standard' derivations for the Assyrians and Syrians from *Etym* IX 2.45: 'Assyrii ab Assur filio Sem vocati', and *Etym* IX 2.50: 'Syri a Surim vocati perhibentur, qui fuit nepos Abraham ex Cethura.'

31.8. *Igbathanis*] This detailed description of Igbathanis has no parallel in the other recensions; it derives from *Iud* 1.1: 'Arfaxat itaque rex Medorum subiugaverat multas imperio suo et ipse aedificavit civitatem potentissimam quam appellavit Igbathanis (2) ex lapidibus quadratis et sectis fecit muros eius in altitudine cubitorum septuaginta et in latitudine cubitorum triginta turres vero eius posuit in altitudinem cubitorum centum.'
I have emended the *R P* reading *(.xx. a láit)* in accordance with the Latin source.

31.11–14. Translated from *Gn* 10.24–5 [= 1 *Par* 1.18] and *Hier* 10.22–5; *Hier:* 'Ludim, a quo Lydia. Aram, a quo Syri: quorum metropolis est Damascus.' The additional geographical detail comes probably from *Hier* 10.22: 'Hi (*sc.* filii Sem) ab Euphrate fluuio partem Asiae usque ad Indicum oceanum tenent.'

31.16. *Fallec ⁊ Iactan*] Cf. *Gn* 10.24–5: 'At vero Arfaxad genuit Sala de quo ortus est Eber (25) natique sunt Eber filii duo nomen uni Faleg eo quod in diebus eius divisa sit terra et nomen fratris eius Iectan.'

Cf. *Hier:* 'Heber, a quo Hebraei, uaticinio quodam filio suo Phaleg nomen inposuit, qui interpretatur diuisio, ab eo, quod in diebus eius linguae in Babylone diuisae sunt.'

32. The list is derived from *Gn* 10.26–9 [= 1 *Par* 1.20–22]: 'Iectan genuit Helmodad et Saleph et Asarmoth Iare (27) et Aduram et Uzal Decla (28) et Ebal et Abimahel Saba (29) et Ophir et Evila et Iobab.'

This section too is illustrated in Henry & Marsh-Micheli, Pl. XVIb.

32.5–10. *Clanna Saram*] Translated from *Gn* 10.23 [= 1 *Par* 1.17] and *Hier* 10.23.

Gn: 'Filii Aram Us et Hul et Gether et Mes' [*Par* has Mosoch]; *Hier:* 'Hus, Trachonitidis et Damasci conditor, inter Palaestinam et Coelen Syriam tenuit principatum. .Vl, a quo Armenii. Gether, a quo Acarnanii seu Carnii. Porro Mes, pro quo LXX interpretes Mosoch dixerunt, qui nunc uocantur Maeones.'

Etym IX 2.4 differs somewhat from *Hier* and was not used.

32.6. *Traconitidi*] The author of SAM has here mistaken a city for a tribal name.

33. It should be noted that the *luchorpáin* occur in Old Irish literature as early as the saga of Fergus mac Léti, D. A. Binchy (ed) 'The saga of Fergus mac Léti', *Ériu* 16 (1952) pp. 33–48; Binchy has proposed an 8th century date for this text. He remarks, art. cit., p. 41 n. 2, 'This seems to be the earliest reference in the extant literature to the *lúchorp(án)*, later metathesized into *luchrapán*, *luppracán* (whence Anglo-Irish 'leprechaun'), *lúrapóg* (with different suffix),' etc.

Binchy queries the traditional association of the *luchorpáin* with water-sprites, but their connection here with the *fomoraig* may be said to add additional weight to the interpretation as some kind of water-sprite.

The association of *luchorpáin* and *fomoraig* recurs in §17 and again in §34; on the substance of these sections see James Carney, *Studies in Irish literature and history* (Dublin 1955/1979) pp. 102–10, and Charles Donahue 'Grendel and the *Clanna Cain*' *Journal of Celtic Studies* 1 (1950) pp. 167–75.

33.2–6. Translated from *Gn* 9.21–3: 'Bibensque vinum inebriatus est [Noe] et nudatus in tabernaculo suo (22) quod cum vidisset Ham pater Chanaan verenda scilicet patris sui esse nuda nuntiavit duobus fratribus suis foras (23) at vero Sem et Iafeth pallium inposuerunt umeris suis et incedentes retrorsum operuerunt verecunda patris sui faciesque eorum aversae erant et patris virilia non viderunt.'

Note that both *U* and *C* omit the passage concerning Noah's sexual organs, no doubt purposely.

33.3. *⁊ sé lomnocht*] U reads *⁊ is hé lomnocht.*

34.2–5. Cf. §17.4–6 and the notes to §33.1 above.

34.8–9. *amal ad-fiadat Goídil*] Confusion over the origin of the monsters was not confined to the Irish alone, as Donohue, art. cit., has pointed out. But the present passage is strictly logical in pointing out that only Noah and his family survived the flood, and that the monsters of the world could not therefore have derived from Cain.

34.12. *i nGenis rechta*] Cf. §13.9 *ic tráchtad for Geneiss rechta;* the reference is to the Pentateuch as a whole, the authorship of which was attributed traditionally to Moses.

35. There is no direct source for this list, but the idea of the ten as *airig na haísi tánaisi* probably derives from 1 *Par* 1.24–7, where they are listed consecutively (except for Noah): Sem Arfaxad Sale (25) Heber Phaleg Raau (26) Serug Nahor Thare (27) Abram.

35.2–11. Translated from *Gn* 11.27–8: 'Thare genuit Abram et Nahor et Aran. Porro Aran genuit Loth (28) Mortuusque est Aran ante Thare patrem suum in terra nativitatis suae, in Ur Chaldeorum.'

35.3. *qui primus*] I have no source for this detail.

35.5–7. The names of these two daughters are derived from the passage in *Gn* which is reproduced at greater length in §38.

35.9–11. The statement that Aran was the first man after the flood who died before his father is, of course, merely a deduction. It is another example of the passion for 'firsts' which is evident throughout the SAM text and throughout medieval Irish exegesis as a whole. The present instance has no foundation in Scripture but the idea very probably had its origin in the details of *Gn* 4.2: 'fuit autem Abel pastor ovium et Cain agricola', or *Gn* 4.20: 'Genuitque Ada Abel qui fuit pater habitantium in tentoriis atque pastorum (21) et nomen fratris eius Iubal ipse fuit pater canentium cithara et organo'; cf. §13.2–16, and §34.3. The use of *pater* in these instances no doubt prompted medieval exegetes to tease out the details of who first did various things in the bible.

35a. This verse does not occur in either *R* or *P;* its place in the SAM tradition is discussed above on pp. 15–16.

36.1–5. The details from the apocrypha included in this and the next section are unique both in Hiberno-Latin and vernacular Irish literature. The basic inspiration for the theme derives, of course, from the narrative in *Gn* 19.30–8, where the story of Lot's incest with his two daughters is told. Nowhere in the bible, however, are the names of these two daughters given, only of their offspring, Moab and Ammon.

Names for the two daughters do occur, however, in (Irish?) Ps. Bede's commentary on the Pentateuch, *MPL* 91, col. 240 BC: 'Habitavit ergo Lot in spelunca et duae filiae eius, quas propterea describit dicens: Ollam et Olibam duas sorores esse; quidam Ollam Samariam, Olibam autem quidam Iudaeam. In duas ergo partes populus diuisus, duas fecit filias legis.'

These names are curiously similar to the names given in SAM to the wives of Cain and Iafeth, §§12.3 and 25.2.

Names for Lot's daughters are also given in Irish Ps. Isidore's *Liber de Numeris*, *MPL* 83, cols. 1293–1302 (acephalous), at col. 1301 AB: 'Duas filias Lot habuit, filius fratris Abrahae, quarum una vocabatur Adach [*other MSS have* Edach], quae peperit patri filium nomine Moab, de quo Moabitae orti sunt. Altera vero, quae vocabatur Moach, quae et similiter patri suo peperit filium nomine Ammon, de quo Ammonitae exierunt. Hi duo filii non sine culpa nati sunt, quia pater filias uxores habuit, et hoc non voluntas, sed ebrietas fecit.'

In his analysis of this passage in *Der irische Liber de Numeris: eine Quellenanalyse* (Diss. Munich 1957) p. 49, Robert McNally simply notes that these names are of unknown origin ('Edach' und 'Moach', Namen unbekannten Ursprungs); cf. also his 'The imagination and early Irish biblical exegesis' *Annuale Medievale* 10 (1969) pp. 5–27, at pp. 14–15, where he cites other examples of 'names for the nameless' in Irish exegetical texts.

Fr. Martin McNamara tells me that Jewish tradition names one of Lot's daughters, the maiden *Paltit*, and he thinks there may be other examples. The *Ioca monachorum*, *MPL Suppl.* 4, at col. 915, has the following: *Duae sunt Multhae, una est filia Lot maior;* no other name is given. The names *Segor* and *Roubba* cited in Fernand Cabrol & Henri Leclercq, *Dictionnaire d'archéologie et de liturgie chrétienne* (Paris 1907–53), seem to derive from confusion of placenames.

Note the use of the *tres linguae sacrae* formula in this and the following sections. This theme was especially popular in Hiberno-Latin writings from a very early period; see, e.g., Irish Ps. Augustine, *De mirabilibus sacrae scripturae*, *MPL* 35, cols. 2149–2200, at col. 2161: 'Harum vero omnium linguarum novi Testamenti tempore, tribus linguis, hebraicae utique, graecae et latinae, principatus committitur; quia in eis crucis Christi titulus litteris hebraicis, graecis et latinis scriptus, Evangelica auctoritate perhibetur' (*Io* XIX 20).

For a general discussion of the theme see McNally 'The *tres linguae sacrae* in early Irish bible exegesis' *Theological Studies* 19 (1958) pp. 395–403.

37. This is a slight elaboration of the foregoing material, which incorporates some additional detail.

37.8. *diaro-dathaig*] Perhaps a form of *taithigid* 'practices, makes a custom of', though I am not at all sure of the form; *DIL* cite the verb under *dathaigid* 'colours, dyes, stains'. It must mean some such thing as 'by which he perpetrated a heinous deed'.

37.19. *Adherens malo*] A slight elaboration on the simple *Adherens* of §36.2, but sufficient to show that the verse is no mere rehash of the prose; it must have derived from some source more complete than any we now have.

38.1–3. Translated from *Gn* 11.29 and *Hier* 11.29; *Gn:* 'Duxerunt autem Abram et Nahor uxores nomen autem uxoris Abram Sarai et nomen uxoris Nahor Melcha filia Aran patris Melchae et patris Ieschae.' *Hier:* 'Aran filius Tharae, frater Abraham et Nachor, duas filias genuit, Melcham et Sarai, cognomento Iescam. E quibus Melcham accepit uxorem Nachor et Sarai Abraham.'

38.4–8. The list derives from *Gn* 22.20–3: 'His itaque gestis nuntiatum est Abraham quod Melcha quoque genuisset filios Nahor fratri suo (21) Hus primogenitum et Buz fratrem eius Camuhel patrem Syrorum (22) et Chased et Azau Pheldas quoque et Iedlaph (23) ac Bathuel de quo nata est Rebecca. Octo istos genuit Melcha Nahor fratri Abraham.'

38.4. *ocht maccu*] The scribe of *R* wrote *secht maccu*, having been misled by the syntax of *Gn* into thinking that *Azau* and *Pheldas* were one person (he wrote *Azaufel* on one line and *das* on the next); I have emended the reading in accordance with the *Gn* text and the readings in the other MSS.

38.6. *is uad Iób*] Cf. *Hier* 22.20–2: 'Primogenitus Nachor fratris Abraham de Melcha uxore eius filia Aran natus est Hus; de cuius stirpe Iob descendit, sicut scriptum est in exordio uoluminis eius "uir fuit in terra Hus Iob nomine".'

38.6–7. *dia síl Balam in druí*] Cf. *Hier* 22.20–2: 'Secundus natus est de Melcha Buz..Et ex huius genere est Balaam ille diuinus.' This suggests that *U* might preserve a more accurate reading: *Hus mac Nachoir is úad Iob.* ⁊ *is dia síl Buz* ⟨..⟩ *Balam in druí;* the editors of *U* thought that something was lost here in the MS., at the end of a line, but perhaps the text should read: *Is dia síl Buz Balam in druí.*

38.7–9. Translated from *Gn* 22.21 and 24: 'Camuhel patrem Syrorum; (24) Concubina vero illius (*sc.* Nahor) nomine Roma peperit Tabee et Gaom et Thaas et Maacha.'

39.2–3. Note that *U* reads *gabáil ríge do Dauid i tír Caldeorum*, which seems to be the result of a misplaced gloss; however, the words *gein Abráim* are not glossed in any of the other MSS.

39.3. *Casdei*] Cf. *Etym* IX 2.48: 'Chasdei, qui nunc Chaldei vocantur, a Chased filio Nachor fratris Abrahae cognominati sunt.'

39.5. *Ismal*] Cf. *Gn* 16.15–16, and 21.5: 'Peperitque Abrae filium qui vocavit nomen eius Ismahel (16) Octoginta et sex annorum erat quando peperit ei Agar Ismahelem (21.5) Cum centum esset annorum hac quippe aetate patris natus est Isaac.'

39.6. *Agareni a hAgar*] Cf. *Etym* IX 2.6: 'Agareni ab Agar'; cf. IX 2.57.

39.8–13. Translated from *Gn* 25.1–4: 'Abraham vero aliam duxit uxorem nomine Cetthuram (2) quae peperit ei Zamram et Iaxan et Madan et Madian et Iesboch et Sue (3) Iexan quoque genuit Saba et Dadan. Filii Dadan fuerunt Assurim et Lathusim et Loommim (4) at vero ex Madian ortus est Epha et Opher et Enoch et Abida et Eldaa. Omnes hii filii Cetthurae' [cf. 1 *Par* 1.32].

39.8. *iar n-éc Sarra*] Not specifically stated in *Gn*.

39.9. *Saraceni a Sarra*] Cf. *Etym* IX 2.6: 'Ismael filius Abraham, a quo Ismaelitae, qui nunc corrupto nomine Saraceni, quasi a Sarra'; cf. IX 2.57.

39.15. *Ismohelitae*] See the note to §39.9 above for the source.

39.16. *a quo Nabatheni*] Cf. *Etym* IX 2.7: 'Nabaioth filius Ismahel, a quo Nabathei, qui ab Euphrata in mare Rubrum inhabitant.'

39.16–18. Translated from *Gn* 25.12–13, and *Hier* 25.13–18.
Gn: 'Hae sunt generationes Ismahel filii Abraham quem peperit ei Agar Aegyptia famula Sarrae (13) Primogenitus Ismahelis Nabaioth' [cf. 1 *Par* 1.29]; *Hier:* 'Duodecim filii nascuntur Ismahelo, e quibus primogenitus fuit Nabaioth, a quo omnis regio ab Euphrate usque ad mare rubrum Nabathena usque hodie dicitur, quae pars Arabiae est.'

39.18. *i lleth fri airther*] Not in the Latin; the author of SAM may have had a map, or some other geographical text, to hand.

40.1–4. Taken from *Gn* 25.13–15: 'Primogenitus Ismahelis Nabaioth dein Cedar et Abdeel et Mabsam (14) Masma quoque et Duma et Massa (15) Adad et Thema Itur et Naphis et Cedma' [cf. 1 *Par* 1.29–31].

40.2. *Dehin*] The author of SAM mistook the *dein* of his source for a personal name, but mindful of Jerome's remark: *Duodecim filii nascuntur Ismahelo*, he reconciled the imbalance by combining *Massa* and *Adad* in line 4; for other examples of such error see §28.11 and note, and §38.4 and note.

40.5–9. Translated from *Gn* 25.16–18: 'Isti sunt filii Ismahel et haec nomina per castella et oppida eorum duodecim principes tribuum suarum (17) Anni vitae Ismahel triginta septem deficiens mortuus est et adpositus ad populum suum (18) Habitavit autem ab Evila usque Sur quae respicit Aegyptum introeuntibus Assyrios. Coram cunctus fratribus suis obiit.'

Note the slight alteration made in the sequence of his original by the author of SAM, in order to close the account with Ismael's death.

41.1–4. Translated from *Gn* 25.19–20: 'Hae quoque sunt generationes Isaac filii Abraham. Abraham genuit Isaac (20) qui cum quadraginta esset annorum duxit uxorem Rebeccam filiam Bathuel Syri de Mesopotamiam sororem Laban. . (24) et ecce gemini in utero repperti sunt.'

41.5–9. This is a highly condensed version of the narrative in *Gn* 28.2–30.21; I give the most obvious sources here: *Gn* 28.5: 'Cumque dimisset eum (*sc.* Iacob) Isaac profectus venit in Mesopotamiam Syriae ad Laban filium Bathuel Syri fratrem Rebeccae matris suae (29.16) Habebat vero (*sc.* Laban) filias duas nomen maioris Lia minor appellabatur Rahel (29.23) Et vespere filiam suam Liam introduxit ad eum (*sc.* Iacob) (24) dans ancillam filiae Zalpham nomine.'

41.9. *dá mac déc*] The numbers are made up automatically from *Gn;* they need not be cited here.

41.9. *Dina*] Cf. *Gn* 30.21: 'post quem (*sc.* the birth of Zabulon) peperit filiam nomine Dinam.'

42.1–6. The full list occurs in *Gn* 35.22–6: 'Erant autem filii Iacob duodecim (23) Filii Liae primogenitus Ruben et Symeon et Levi et Iudas et Isachar et Zabulon (24) Filii Rahel Ioseph et Beniamin (25) Filii Balae ancillae Rahelis Dan et Nepthalim (26) Filii Zelphae ancillae Liae Gad et Aser' [cf. 1 *Par* 2.1–2].

43. There is no information in these verses beyond that cited in §42.

43.12. *thétraide*] Perhaps gen. sg. of a collective from *tét* 'wanton' but the word is otherwise unattested.

43.18. *roglach*] = *rug* + *laéch* 'of great warriors'? For the prefix see Joseph Vendryes 'Irlandais *rug-* préfixe superlatif' *JCS* 1 (1950) pp. 1–3.

44.1–40. The list derives from *Gn* 46.9–11 and 20 [= *Nm* 3.19 and 26.99 ff.] *Gn:* 'Filii Ruben Enoch et Phallu et Esrom et Charmi (10) Filii Symeon Iemuhel et Iamin et Ahod et Iachin et Saher et Saul filius Chananitidis (11) Filii Levi Gerson Caath et Merari (20) Natique sunt Ioseph filii in terra Aegypti quos genuit ei Aseneth filia Putiphare sacerdotis Heliopoleos Manasses et Ephraim.' Cf. the page of biblical genealogies in TCD MS. H.3.17 (1336) col. 729, *amail adeir in Lebar Buidhe meic Murcada* (an unidentified codex). [I wish to acknowledge here the kindness of Mr. William O'Sullivan, TCD, who generously provided me with a photograph of this text]. Cf. the notes to §51.5–20.

44.4. *Filii Effraim*] Cf. *Nm* 26.35: 'Filii autem Ephraim per cognationes suas fuerunt hii Suthula a quo familia Suthulitarum Becher..Tehen (29) De Manasse ortus est Machir..Machir genuit Galaad..(30) Galaad habuit filios Hiezer..et Elec..(31) et Asrihel..et Sechem..(32) et Semida..et Epher.'

44.19. *Filii Iuda*] Cf. *Gn* 46.12: 'Filii Iuda Her et Onan et Sela et Phares et Zara.'

44.19. *ní bátar meic oca*] Cf. *Nm* 26.33: 'Fuit autem Epher pater Salphaad qui filios non habebat sed tantum filias quarum ista sunt nomina Maala et Noa et Egla et Melcha et Thersa.'

44.21. *Filii Beniemín*] The direct source is *Nm* 26.38: 'Filii Beniamin.. Bale..Azbel..Ahiram..Supham..Hupham.'

The list in *Gn* 46.21 gives seven names.

44.21–22. *.i. patrem Moisi ⁊ Aron*] Cf. 1 *Par* 23.13: 'Filii Amram Aaron et Moses.' The detail about Caath is from *Nm* 3.19: 'Filii Caath Amram et Iessaar Hebron et Ozihel.'

44.21–22. *qui ambo mortui sunt*] From *Gn* 46.12: 'Mortui sunt autem Her et Onan in terra Chanaan,' which continues: 'Natique sunt filii Phares Esrom et Amul (13) Filii Isachar Thola et Phua et Iob et Semron' [cf. *Nm* 26.23–4, and 1 *Par* 7.1].

Note that confusion has come about in the accounts of Isachar's and Dan's sons, as is clear from the reference to *Nm* 26.42: 'Filii Dan per cognationes suas Suham a quo familia Suhamitarum. Hae cognationes Dan per familias suas'; *Gn* 46.23 reads: 'Filii Dan Usim.' *Nm* 26.23: 'Filii Isachar..Thola..Phua.. Iasub..Semran.'

The immediate source seems to have been *Nm*, but the author of SAM – misled perhaps by the reference to *filii Dan* and the mention of only one – incorporated the *Phua* and *Semran* of Isachar's line into that of Dan.

44.26. *Filii Gad*] Again, *Nm* 26.15 is the direct source: 'Filii Gad..Sephon ..Aggi..Suni..(16) Ozni..(17) Heri..Arod (18) Arihel.'

The list in *Gn* 46.16 has one name more, *Esebon*.

44.33. *Filii Asser*] Here again *Nm* 26.44 is the direct source: 'Filii Aser Iemna..Iessui..Brie.'

Note then that for this whole section the author of SAM has used the details of *Nm* rather than those of *Gn*, which he had used generally up to this point.

44.35. *Filii Neptalim*] Cf. *Gn* 46.24: 'Filii Nepthalim Iasihel et Guni et Hieser et Salem.'

Nm 26.48: 'Filii Nepthalim..Iessihel..Guni..(49) Iesser..Sellem.'

I cannot explain the omission of *Guni* and *Sellem* in SAM.

45.1. *Clanna Essau*] Based on *Gn* 36.9–10: 'Hae sunt generationes Esau patris Edom in monte Seir (10) et haec nomina filiorum eius Eliphaz filius Ada uxoris Esau Rauhel quoque,' etc. More likely, perhaps, as a direct source is 1 *Par* 1.35: 'Filii Esau Eliphaz Rauhel Iaus Ialam Core.'

45.1. *is é for-athmentair*] Cf. *Hier* 36.4: 'Iste est Elifaz, cuius scriptura in Iob uolumine recordatur.' See also *Iob* 2.11: 'Igitur audientes tres amici Iob omne malum quod accidisset ei venerunt singuli de loco suo Eliphaz Themanites et Baldad Suites et Sophar Naamathites.'

45.3. *ainm a charatmná*] Cf. *Gn* 36.12: 'Erat autem Thamna concubina Eliphaz.'

45.4–5. *Filii Eliphaz*] Based probably on *Gn* 36.11–12 [cf. 1 *Par* 1.36]; 'Fueruntque filii Eliphaz Theman Omar Sephu et Gatham et Cenez.' *Par* erroniously includes *Thamna* as a son of Eliphaz.

45.5–6. *Filii Rahuel*] Probably from *Gn* 36.13 [cf. 1 *Par* 1.37]; 'Filii autem Rauhel Naath et Zara Semma et Meza.'

45.6. *Mac do Séir*] The incongruity here is only superficial; the point is clear from *Hier* 36.19: 'Esau et Edom et Seir unius nomen est hominis'; cf. *Gn* 36.19: 'Isti filii Esau. .ipse est Edom.'

45.7. *do clannaib Horreorum*] Cf. *Gn* 36.20 and 22. The relationship is made more explicit by *Hier* 36.22: 'Haec est Thamna, de qua supra dictum est "et Thamna erat concubina Elifaz filii primogeniti Esau, et ipsa natus est Amalec". Idcirco autem Chorraeorum recordatus est, quia primogenitus filiorum Esau ex filiabus eorum acceperat concubinam.'

45.9–12. From *Gn* 25.5–6: 'Deditque Abraham cuncta quae possederat Isaac. Filiis autem concubinarum largitus est munera et separavit eos ab Isaac filio suo dum adhuc ipse viveret ad plagam orientalem.'

45.9. *etir íri ⁊ indile*] I follow the *DIL* in taking this as a formulaic usage of *íriu*, f. (n), though one would expect *írinn* in the acc. An alternative would be to emend to [*t*]*íri* 'land'.

45.10. *mac Agáre*] Cf. §39.5, and 13–18.

45.11. *do macaib Cethurae*] Though the MS. contraction is clearly for *mac* I have emended in accordance with the details of §39.8–13 and the inference of the Latin text.

45.12. *i lleth fri Innecdu*] An addition characteristic of the SAM author, whose interest in topographical matters is evident throughout the text.

46.1. From *Gn* 25.7: 'Fuerunt autem dies vitae eius (*sc.* Abraham) centum septuaginta quinque anni.'

46.2. *ro-adnacht*] From *Gn* 25.9–10: 'Et sepelierunt eum Isaac et Ismahel filii sui in spelunca duplici quae sita est in agro Ephron filii Soor Hetthei e regione Mambre (10) quem emerat a filiis Heth. Ibi sepultus est ipse et Sarra uxor eius.'

46.2. *speloncа*] A spelling characteristic of Irish manuscripts, according to Elias A. Lowe, *Codices latini antiquiores* 2 (Oxford $1935^1/1972^2$) No. 272.

46.3. *agid fri agid is*] The detail is from *Gn* 25.17: 'Confirmatusque est ager quondam Ephronis in quo erat spelunca duplex respiciens Mambre'; cf. *Gn* 49.29–30, where it is described as being *contra Mambre*. I have no other example of this phrase with the prep. *is;* the more usual construction is with the preps. *fri* or *do*.

46.6. *dessid ordan*] Based on *Gn* 25.11: 'Et post obitum illius (*sc.* Abraham) benedixit Deus Isaac filio eius.'

46.7. *co Isaac berair*] Based, perhaps, on *Etym* IX 2.52: 'Israelitae vero ab Israel filio Isaac. Nam patriarcham Hebraeorum fuisse Israel, a quo duodecim Iudaeorum tribus Israelis vocabulum sortitae sunt.' Quite why Christ should be traced back only to Isaac is not clear to me. He is usually traced back to Jesse.

47. Both this and the following series seem to be derived from the Eusebio-Hieronymian Chronicle, *MPL* 27, col. 34 ff. [Note, however, that Helm's edition does not have this kind of series, but reproduces an older format].

47.1. *cona saéglaib*] Note that SAM gives the duration of their lives, not of their reigns. The figures for the first two are derived from *Gn* 25.7: 'Fuerunt autem dies vitae eius (*sc.* Abraham) centum septuaginta quinque anni', and *Gn* 35.28: 'Et conpleti sunt dies Isaac centum octoginta annorum.' I have no source for Jacob's age when he died.

The theme of Abraham, Isaac, and Jacob as *uasal-athraig* may derive from the phraseology of *Ex*, where the idea of *Deus Abraham, Deus Isaac, Deus Iacob* is constantly reiterated. All three were buried together in the *spelunca duplex* mentioned in §46.2; cf. too the narrative in *Gn* 49.29–30, where Jacob specifically refers to Abraham and Isaac as his *patres.*

48. I give here the *Regum series* of Eusebius-Jerome, from *MPL* 27, cols. 90b–91a): 'Hinc Duces: Moses, annos 40; Jesus, annos 27; Hinc Judices: Gothoniel, annos 40; Aod, annos 80; Debbora cum Barach, annos 40; Gideon, annos 40; Abimelech, annos 3; Thola, annos 22; Jair, annos 22; Jephthe, annos 6; Hesebon, annos 7; Labdon, annos 8; Samson, annos 20; Heli sacerdos, annos 40; Samuel et Saul rex, annos 40.'

It seems clear that Eusebius, and not the bible, provided the exemplar of the SAM text. The elaborate columnar arrangement of the names and figures, and the obvious confusion that has occurred with *Duces* and *Iudices* resulting in the elimination of Moses from the list, all suggest an origin in the Eusebio-Hieronymian Chronicle. Likewise, the word *Iudice* reflects the usage in Eusebius-Jerome.

48.7. *Samson*] The SAM text has here omitted Labdon; I cannot explain the omission.

48.9. *regnauit Samuel .xl.*] Uncertainty about the number of years to be accorded to Samuel and Saul individually was a recurrent feature of medieval biblical scholarship and exegesis. The bible itself gives no exact figures and later writers did their best to deduce the reigns from whatever information was available in 1 *Sm* 3 ff. The problem is discussed by Bede, *In primam partem Samuhelis*, ed. David Hurst, *CCSL* 119, pp. 1–272, at p. 68: 'Sunt qui suis Samuhelem in chronicis praetereundum penitus esse putarent, sunt qui ei septuaginta annos qui Sauli triginta adnotarent, sunt qui iuncto amborum tempore quadraginta eos annis populum rexisse perhiberent; sed unde aliquid horum adfirmari debeat inuenire requimus, unde autem cassari omnia et destrui possint facillime patet.'

49.1. *quadraginta annis*] See the above note.

49.2. *rom-marbad post Saul*] Based on 1 *Par* 10.1–2 [= 1 *Sm* 31.1–2]; the translation is not direct. The statement is not strictly accurate, since Saul took his own life.

Note the occurrence of *ra*, the Mid. Ir. prep. compounded of *la* and *re;* cf. §70.26: *ra seirrcc snáma.*

49.3. *rígi Dethrebe*] Cf. 2 *Sm* 2.10: 'Quadraginta annorum erat Hisboseth filius Saul cum regnare coepisset super Israhel et duobus annis regnavit. Sola autem domus Iuda sequebatur David.'

49.6–15. *Rechab ⁊ Banna*] The long insertion that follows occurs on fol. 43^r marg. supra of *R*, and is referred to its proper place in the text by the abbreviation *D÷ (Deest)*; the text was much damaged by the actions of the binder of *R*, but as *P* was copied from that MS. before binding it has been possible to recover the text in its entirety. The narrative derives from 2 *Sm* 4.2–7, to which some details have been added from 1 *Sm* 9.1.
2 *Sm*: 'Duo autem viri principes latronum erant filio Saul nomen uni Baana et nomen alteri Rechab filii Remmon Berothitae de filiis Beniamin . . (5) venientes igitur filii Remmon Berothitae Rechab et Baana ingressi sunt fervente die domum Hisboseth . . (6) et percusserunt eum in inguine . . (7) et percutientes interfecerunt eum.'
1 *Sm*: 'Et erat vir de Beniamin nomine Cis filius Abihel filii Seror filii Bechoreth filii Afia filii viri Iemini fortis robore.'
Clearly visible still on the upper marg. of *R* (and reproduced also in the *P* transcript) are the final words *m̄ uri m̄ emini.*, which are clearly meant to represent *meic Uri meic Emini*; but this is a misunderstanding of the Latin *filii uiri Iemini*. I have emended in accordance with the biblical text.

49.8. *Samuel mac Helcanna*] Made up from 1 *Sm* 1.1, and 1 *Par* 6.33–7;
1 *Sm*: 'Fuit vir unus de Ramathaim-sophim de monte Ephraim et nomen eius Helcana filius Hieroam filii Heliu filii Thau filii Suph Ephratheus.'
1 *Par*: 'Hii vero sunt qui adsistebant [David] cum filiis suis. De filiis Caath Heman cantor filius Iohel filii Samuhel (34) filii Helcana filii Hieroam filii Helihel filii Thou (35) filii Suph filii Helcana filii Maath filii Amasai (36) filii Helcana filii Iohel filii Azariae', etc.

49.12. *Saphaneth*] Probably from *Etym* VII 7.17–18: 'Ioseph ab eo, quod sibi alium addi mater optaverat, vocavit augmentum. Hunc Pharao Zaphanath appellavit, quod Hebraice absconditorum repertorem sonat, pro eo quod obscura somnia revelavit et sterilitatem praedixit. Tamen, quia hoc nomen ab Aegyptio ponitur, ipsius linguae debet habere rationem. Interpretatur ergo Zaphanath Aegyptio sermone salvator mundi,' etc.

50.3. *gabair*] Apparently 3 p. sg. pres. pass. ⟨*gaibid*; the Old Ir. form would have been *gaibthir*. This form may have come about by analogy with *berid/berair*.

50.4. *Cethracha bliadan*] From 1 *Par* 29.27 [= 3 *Rg* 2.11]: 'Et dies quibus regnavit super Israhel fuerunt quadraginta anni in Hebron regnavit septem annis et in Hierusalem triginta tribus.'

50.4. *⁊ sé mís*] The MSS *R* and *P* both omit the numeral, while *C*, *Lc* and *B* read *.uii. mis (misa)*. But 1 *Par* 3.4 has *in Hebron ubi regnavit septem annis et sex mensibus*, and I have followed this.

50.7–13. Probably from 1 *Par* 3.1–3 [= 2 *Sm* 3.2–5]; I give the *Sm* text, however, as being slightly closer in wording to the SAM text: 'Nati quoque sunt filii David in Hebron fuitque primogenitus eius Ammon de Ahinoem Iezrahelitide (3) et post eum Chelaab de Abigail uxore Nabal Carmeli porro tertius Absalom filius Maacha filiae Tholomai regis Gessur (4) quartus autem Adonias filius Aggith et quintus Safathia filius Abithal (5) sextus quoque Iethraam de Agla uxore David. Hii nati sunt David in Hebron.'

50.14–16. Cf. 2 *Sm* 5.13: 'Natique sunt David et alii filii et filiae (14) et haec nomina eorum qui nati sunt ei in Hierusalem Samua et Sobab et Nathan et Salomon (15) et Ibaar et Helisua et Nepheg (16) et Iafia et Helisama et Helida et Helifeleth.'

50.17–18. *Dá siar*] Made up from 2 *Sm* 17.25, and 2 *Sm* 2.18; 2 *Sm* 17: 'Amasam autem erat filius viri qui vocabatur Iethra de Hiesreli qui ingressus est ab Abigail filiam Naas sororem Sarviae quae fuit mater Ioab.'
2 *Sm* 2: 'Erant autem ibi tres filii Sarviae Ioab et Abisai et Asahel.'

50.19. *Solam*] Cf. 1 *Par* 23.1: 'Igitur David senex et plenus dierum regem constituit Salomonem filius suum super Israhel.'

50.20. *flathius na Macidónna*] Cf. Eusebius-Jerome, *MPL* 27, cols. 349–50: 'A captivitate Trojae usque ad Olimpiadem primam, anni CCCCV, Aeschyli Atheniensium judicis secundo anno prima olympias acta.'

According to Eusebius, however, this would coincide with the 37th (not the 27th) year of the Macedonian kingship. There was much confusion, however, concerning the Macedonian kingship, on which see Seán Mac Airt 'Middle-Irish poems on World Kingship' *Études Celtiques* 8 (1958–9) pp. 98–119, at p. 111.

51. The 11th of May was the traditional date for the foundation of Rome (see *MPL* 27, col. 363 n. a); cf. the poem *A rí ríchid, réidig dam*, by Gilla in Chomded ua Cormaic, printed in Best, Bergin, & O'Brien (ed) *The Book of Leinster, formerly Lebor na Núachongbála* 3 (Dublin 1957) p. 578:

In .xi. calaind Mae.
ra tuismed Róm arind roé.
Cobthach Coel sund ní gaeth gar.
rí thair Teglad Fallasar.

51.5–20. This story derives from Eusebius-Jerome (ed. Helm, pp. 84a–5a = *MPL* 27, cols. 343–4), which is reproduced in Whitley Stokes (ed) 'The Annals of Tigernach', *Revue Celtique* 16 (1895) pp. 374–419, at p. 376; the same text occurs also in a separate form in TCD MS. H. 3. 17, (1336) cols. 858–9, ed. by John Strachan 'Romulus and Remus' *Anecdota from Irish manuscripts* 3 (1910) p. 46. I give the Eusebian text here:

'Numitor, Procae superioris regis maior filius, a fratre Amulio regno pulsus in agro suo vixit. Filia eius, adimendi partus gratia uirgo Uestalis lecta. Quae cum septimo patrui anno geminos edidisset infantes, iuxta legem in terram uiua defossa est. Uerum paruulos prope ripam Tiberis expositos Faustulus regii pastor armenti ad Accam Laurentiam uxorem suam detulit, quae propter pulchritudinem et rapacitatem corporis quaestuosi Lupa a uicinis appellabatur.. Pueri cum adoleuissent, collecta pastorum et latronum manu interfecto aput Albam Amulio auum Numitorem in regnum restituunt.'

It should be noted that the 'Annals of Tigernach' (ed. Stokes, p. 376) uses the words *in uindictam matris suae* of the killing of Amulius, which corresponds exactly to the Irish phrase: *i ndígail a máthar*. There is no such phrase in Eusebius-Jerome.

51.6. *ro-helned hí*] This is one of only two examples in the text where an independent personal pr. is used as sub. or obj. of a vb.; cf. §55.14. Cf. the wording in the H. 3. 17 text: *Co ndechaid sacart in tempuill chuicci ⁊ guris-toirrchistar co rucastar da mac*, where the inf. pr. replaces the indep. pr. of SAM.

51.8. *níro-lámdas*] Kuno Meyer suggested emendation to 'ni rolámda[i]s' in 'Zur keltischen Wortkunde 8' *Sitzungsb. d. kgl. Preuss. Akad. d. Wissen.*, phil-hist Kl. 3 (Berlin 1918) pp. 618–33, at p. 629.

51.13. *Alta-si*] Apparently an ex. of 3 sg. pret. pass. with active meaning. See Johan Corthals 'Mittelirisch *berthae*' *ZCP* 37 (1979) pp. 203–6.

51.14. *combat móra*] Note the use of the fem./neut. declension in this instance of the adj., where in O.Ir. one might expect *móir*.

51.20. *iar fairind*] Eusebius-Jerome gives the following under the 21st year of Romulus's reign (ed. Helm, p. 90b = *MPL* 27, col. 349): 'Romulus primus milites sumpsit ex populo et nobilissimos centum senes ob aetatem senatores, ob similitudinem curae patres appellauit. Templa quoque et muros Romanae urbis exstruxit.'

Note that this first sentence is the source of one of the additional glosses preserved in *Ld*, fol. 24ᵛb 25–34: *Romulus is sé toíssech ro-gab amsaig riam ar tús;* this does not occur in either *R* or *P*.

52. *Ríg mac nIsrahél*] The list and regnal years derive from 1 and 2 *Par*, though the immediate source was probably Eusebius-Jerome, *MPL* 27, col. 91 BC: 'Hinc reges: David, annos 40; Salomon, annos 40; Roboam, annos 17; Abia, annos 3; Asa, annos 41; Josaphat, annos 40; Joram, annos 8; Ochosias, annus 1; Gotholia, annos 7; Joas, annos 40; Amasias, annos 29; Ozarias, annos 52; Joathan, annos 16; Achaz, annos 16; Ezechias, annos 29; Manasses, annos 55; Hammon, annos 12; Josias, annos 32; Joachaz, menses 3; Joachim, annos 11; Jochonias, menses 3; Sedechias, annos 11.'

52.2. The difficulty presented by Otholia, the usurping mother of Ochozias, in a list of 'kings' is exactly paralleled in a poem of Airbertach mac Cosse, ed. Gearóid Mac Eoin 'A poem by Airbertach mac Cosse' *Ériu* 20 (1968) pp. 112–39, where – in order to make up the twenty kings *rogabsat Hierusalem iar Saul* – it is necessary to exclude Sedechias (who reigned at the time of the destruction of the city) and Athalia [= Otholia], who – in Prof. Mac Eoin's words – 'could not be called a king'.

52.2. *Ezecheas .xxuiiii.*] Eusebius-Jerome, ed. Helm, p. 89a, gives Ezecheas a reign of 29 years *(.ann. xxviiii.)*, and I have corrected the SAM text accordingly. Note, again, that mac Cosse – as before – agrees with the *R* text of SAM by giving Ezecheas a period of 28 years.

52.5. *Ammon .xii.*] Cf. Eusebius-Jerome, ed. Helm, p. 95a: 'Amon secundum .LXX. senum interpretationum .XII. ann. regnauit, secundum Hebraeos .ann. II.' Eusebius-Jerome also assigns 32 years to Iosias, though mac Cosse (and the 'Annals of Tigernach', ed. Stokes, p. 380) give 31 years only. Mac Cosse, be it noted, gives Ammon a period of 2 years only; the Annals of Tigernach give both figures.

52.7. *Assa .xl. annis*] Eusebius-Jerome, ed. Helm, p. 73a, gives Asa a reign of 41 years; but the editors of the *MPL* ed., col. 91 C, n.d, remark that the Parmensis MS., which, in many of its peculiar readings closely resembles our text, gives Asa a reign of 40 years as here.

52.7. *Amasias .xxix.*] Eusebius-Jerome assigns a reign of 29 years to Amasias and I have emended the SAM text accordingly. Note, however, that mac Cosse, ed. Mac Eoin, p. 128 §45, gives him a reign of 19 years.

52.7–8. *filius Iossiae*] Cf. Eusebius-Jerome, ed. Helm, p. 98a: 'Ioachaz .M. III. postquem Eliacim, qui et Ioacim .ann. XI.' The Annals of Tigernach have these figures also, but mac Cosse gives two *(sic)* months to Iachaz and 11 years to Iachim. Here again, the SAM list and the figures in mac Cosse's poem are identical.

52.11. *Iochin*] The regnal years are from 2 *Par* 36.9, not from Eusebius-Jerome, though Tigernach has *Mortuo Iochim filius eius qui et Iechonias regnauit tribus mensibus ac diebus .x.* (ed. Stokes, p. 381).

The biblical sources for this table are as follows:
(a) 3 *Reg* 2.11; (b) 2 *Par* 9.30; (c) 2 *Par* 12.13; (d) 2 *Par* 12.1–2;
(e) 2 *Par* 16.13; (f) 2 *Par* 20.31; (g) 2 *Par* 21.20; (h) 2 *Par* 22.1–2, and 12;
(i) 2 *Par* 24.1; (j) 2 *Par* 25.1; (k) 2 *Par* 26.3; (l) 2 *Par* 27.1;
(m) 2 *Par* 28.1; (n) 2 *Par* 29.1; (o) 2 *Par* 33.1; (p) 2 *Par* 33.21;
(q) 2 *Par* 34.1; (r) 2 *Par* 36.2; (s) 2 *Par* 36.5; (t) 2 *Par* 36.9;
(u) 2 *Par* 36.11.

53. Based on 4 *Rg* 25.2: 'Et clausa est civitas atque vallata usque ad undecimum annum regis Sedeciae..(6) Adprehensum ergo regem duxerunt ad regem Babylonis in Reblatha..(8) Venit Nabuzardan..(9) et succendit domum Domini et domum regis et domos Hierusalem omnemque domum conbusit igni (10) et muros Hierusalem in circuitu destruxit.'

53.3. *i cind .ccccxxx.*] Eusebius-Jerome, under the 11th year of Sedechias, ed. Helm, p. 99a, reads: 'Primus annus captivitatis Hierusalem Iudaea gens capitur. Nabuchodonosor rex Chaldaeorum Hierosolymis captis templum incendit. Quod ab initio aedificationis suae permanserat annis .CCCCXLII.'

Note that, although Stokes prints the second only of these numerals, the Rawl. text of Tigernach actually has both figures: *anno ex quo fundari cepit .ccccxxx. ⟨uel ccccxxxiiii⟩*.

53.5–10. Various sources may have been drawn upon for the material in this section, e.g., 4 *Rg* 25.8, or 2 *Par* 36, or *Ier* 39.5 ff., or *Ier* 52.8 ff.

53.8. *Dair mac Arbei*] I take this to be the Darius son of Arsamus who figures also in Fland Mainistrech's poem *Rédig dam, a Dé do nim*, ed. Seán Mac Airt 'Middle-Irish poems on World Kingship' *Études Celtiques* 7 (1955–6) pp. 18–45, at pp. 42–3:

Secht mbliadna cen brón ba rí
Darius mór mac Arsabíi.

It was this Darius who led the Persians against Alexander the Great, hence the description of him here as *tigflaith Pers ar cind flathius Gréc*.

54.1. *ó gabáil ríge*] Cf. §50.3 and §3.14–17.

54.2. *Isind aés-se*] Based on *Dn* 3.20: 'Et viris fortissimis de exercitu suo (*sc.* Nabuchodonosor) iussit ut ligatis pedibus Sedrac Misac et Abdenago mitterent eos in fornacem ignis ardentem..(22) porro viros illos qui miserant Sedrac Misac et Abdenago interfecit flamma ignis.'

54.5. *Daniél*] Based on *Dn* 6.16: 'Tunc rex praecepit et adduxerunt Danihelem et miserunt eum in lacum leonum.'

54.5. *iarna chosaít*] Based on *Dn* 6.4 ff., which is not sufficiently close to the Irish text to warrant quotation.

54.6. *ro-chuirit sluag na maír*] Cf. *Dn* 6.24: 'Iubente autem rege adducti sunt viri illi qui accusaverant Danielem et in lacum leonum missi sunt ipsi et filii et uxores eorum et non pervenerunt usque ad pavimentum laci donec arriperent eos leones et omnia ossa eorum comminuerunt.'

55.1. *starigi na nÉbraidi*] The historical books of the Old Testament.

55.2. *cen a breth*] I know of no source among all the texts that narrate the events of the Captivity which does not say that Sedechias was brought to Babylon. The first part of the statement, however, has its basis in *Ier* 52.10: 'Et iugulavit rex Babylonis filios Sedeciae in oculis eius sed et omnes principes Iudae occidit in Reblatha (11) et oculos Sedeciae eruit' [cf. 4 *Rg* 25.6].

It is possible that the author of SAM read the sentence: *omnes principes Iudae occidit in Reblatha et oculos Sedeciae eruit* as implying that Sedechias too had been left in Reblatha; but the alleged corroboration of the theory which he found in the *oéntaid ro-buí eter Iochin, ríg nIuda,* ⁊ *Euilmoradach mac Nabcodóin* is not so easy to explain. This latter reference probably derives from 4 *Rg* 25.27–30: 'Sublevavit Evilmerodach rex Babylonis anno quo regnare coeperat caput Ioaichin regis Iuda de carcere', but I do not understand the reasoning of the SAM author here.

55.5. *ic geilt feoir*] The seven years of madness attributed to Nabuchodonosor is based on *Dn* 4.29.

55.14. *ba cennais hé fri Iochin*] This renders the last clause of 4 *Rg* 25.27: 'Sublevavit Evilmerodach rex Babylonis anno quo regnare coeperat caput Ioaichin regis Iuda de carcere (28) et locutus est ei benigna.' Note the indep. pers. pr. as subj.; cf. §51.6.

56.5. *for Ballasair*] Based on the details of, e.g., *Is* 39.1: 'In tempore illo misit Marodach Baladan filius Baladan rex Babylonis libros et munera ad Ezechiam.'

56.11. *trícha míli*] Cf. Eusebius-Jerome, ed. Helm, p. 102a: 'Cyrus Hebraeorum captiuitate laxata quinquaginta ferme hominum milia regredi fecit in Iudaeam.' See also Fland Mainistrech's poem, *Rédig dam, a Dé do nim*, ed. Mac Airt (1955–6) p. 30:

Caéca míle (monar nglé)
lín ríme na braiti-si

The SAM figure may possibly be an error, but I leave it stand as the source is not definite.

57. This section derives from Orosius's *Historia adversum paganos*, ed. Karl Zangemeister, *Corpus Scriptorum Ecclesiasticorum Latinorum* 5 (Vienna 1881) p. 96 (II 6.6–9): 'capitque urbem (*sc.* Babylon), quam uel humano opere exstrui potuisse uel humana uirtute destrui posse utrumque paene incredibile apud mortales erat. Namque Babylonam a Nemrot gigante fundatam, a Nino uel a Semiramide reparatam multi prodidere. Haec campi planitie undique conspicua, natura loci laetissima, castrorum facie moenibus paribus per quadrum disposita. Murorum eius uix credibilis relatu firmitas et magnitudo, id est latitudine cubitorum quinquaginta, altitudine quater tanta. Ceterum ambitus eius quadringentis et octoginta stadiis circumuenitur. Murus coctili latere atque interfuso bitumine conpactus, fossa exstrinsecus late patens uice amnis circumfluit. A fronte murorum, centum portae aereae.'

57.2. *Nebroth mac Chuis*] Cf. §28.9 for the genealogy.

57.3. *Nín mac ṁBéil*] The following is found in YBL, p. 324^{b} beside the *Description of Christ and the Apostles:* 'Ninus filius Belei filii Plosci filii Filiris filii Agamali filii Foronésis filii Omólis filii Gitilis filii Terris filii Asur filii Sém filii Noé Assirios regnare incipit.' The last three words suggest a synchronism as source; cf. also the following item from an intercalated leaf (3a) in *NLI MS. G 2:* 'Nín mac Péil meic Ploisc meic Piris meic Agamail meic Pronesis meic Gomuilis meic Pletis meic Raetis meic Ostis meic Amalís meic Fonais meic Tristís meic Asur meic Semh meic Naei meic Lamiach.'
The leaf contains a collection of detailed genealogies of such figures as Britus/Britanus, Patrick, Ninus (as above), Alexander the Great, Agamnenon, Lamiach, and Moses.

57.5. *ro-athcumtaiged*] The emendation of the SAM text is based on the details in Orosius's original, in the rendering of which, I suggest, the author of SAM omitted a crucial vb. It is clear, both from the earlier account in §28.11–13 and from Orosius's narrative, that a distinction is being made between the first foundation of Babylon by Nimrod and its reconstruction and restoration *(reparatam)* by Ninus and Semirames. The insertion of Ninus's extended pedigree clearly interrupted the train of thought, resulting in the omission of the verb.
A close comparison of the Latin and Irish texts at this point will show up the lacuna clearly:

'Babylonam a Nemrot gigante fundatam, a Nino uel Semiramide reparatam'	la Nebroth mac Chuis meic Cáim meic Noé ro-chétna-cumtacht. La Nín mac ṁBéil, etc.

There is no word in the Irish text to render *reparatam*, and the implicit contrast with the words *ro-chétna-cumtacht* has been lost. Cf. also *Etym* XV 1.4: 'Primus post diluvium Nembroth gigans Babyloniam urbem Mesopotamiae fundavit. Hanc Semiramis regina Assyriorum ampliavit, murumque urbis bitumine et cocto latere fecit.'

57.9. *Cethrochair*] = 'castrorum facie moenibus paribus per quadrum disposita.'

57.10. *Coíca cubat*] = 'latitudine cubitorum quinquaginta.'

57.10. *Dá chét cubat*] = 'altitudine quater tanta' (*sc.* 4 × 50).

57.11. *.Cccclxxx. stadi*] = 'Ceterum ambitus eius quadringentis et octoginta stadiis circumuenitur.'

57.11. *nó sesca míli*] Though not mentioned in Orosius, a circumvallation of sixty miles is mentioned in §58.10. I have no source for this figure.

57.11–12. *Cét ṅdorus n-umaide*] = 'A fronte murorum centum portae aereae.'

57.13. *i llebraib antiquitatum*] Not, as we might expect, from a Latin version of Josephus's Antiquities of the Jews, but directly borrowed from the Orosian passage cited above, which continues (II 6.10): 'Ipsa autem latitudo in consummatione pinnarum utroque latere habitaculis defensorum aeque dispositis, media in intercapedine sui citas quadrigas capit.'

57.13. *fiche cetharriad*] There is no basis in the Latin text for the number given here. It should be noted that the Irish version of Lucan's Pharsalia, ed. Whitley Stokes, *Irische Texte* 4 ii (1909) p. 4, has borrowed this description.

57.13. *for héraimm*] = 'citas.'

57.15. *Sruth nEofrait*] From Orosius, II 6.5: 'Eo opere praedictis fossoribus, etiam Euphraten longe ualidissimum et mediam Babyloniam interfluentem deriuauit.'

57.15. *fo stuagdórsib cloch*] This is not in Orosius, but the *B* version of SAM has a very elaborate description of the gateway into Babylon.

57.16–17. This is abbreviated from Orosius, II 6.4: 'Nec peragendo segnior totis copiis perpeti anno Gynden fluuium per magnas concisum deductumque fossas in quadringentos sexaginta alueos comminuit.'

57.16. ⁊ *rámann leis*] Though not explicitly stated in Orosius, the inference was obvious enough, and was made also by the compiler of the *B* recension. The account of Cyrus' capture of Babylon is reproduced in the Annals of Tigernach, ed. Stokes, p. 385.

58. The details of the first nine stanzas in this poem derive from the foregoing prose account based on Orosius.

58.6. *Cethrochair*] Cf. §57.9–10.

58.10. *Sesca mórmíli*] Cf. §57.11.

58.14. *Coíca cubat*] Cf. §57.10.

58.18. *Fichi* cetharriad] Note that the number of chariots mentioned in §57.13 is repeated here.

58.28. *ro-forbad a fóir*] *DIL* F, col. 334, 78–9 render this as 'its garrison was destroyed', suggesting a derivation from the vb. *for-ben.*

58.31. *ruitruaid*] MS. *P* glosses *ruit-* as *rioth*, and a translation 'ruddy and swift-flowing' would suit well.

58.38–49. These stanzas are derived from the genealogical details of §57.4–7, but there are differences in the details which I cannot explain. See François Glorie (ed) Sancti Hieronymi presbyteri op. I 5, *Commentariorum in Danielem CCSL* 75A, p. 820 (Bk II 1).

58.49. *ro-airggech*] This represents apparently the pronunciation of the pret.-pass. *(-ed)* which today is characteristic of the West Kerry dialect of Modern Irish; cf. Brian Ó Cuív, *Irish dialects and Irish-speaking districts* (Dublin 1967) pp. 50–1.

58.58. *At-rubairt friu*] There is no basis in the biblical account for the direct speech used here.

58.66–73. Based on the details of Orosius, II 6.12, and 7.1–6; the wording is not close enough to warrant citation here.

58.68. *trícha bliadan*] Cf. Fland Mainistrech's poem, *Rédig dam, a Dé do nim,* ed. Mac Airt (1955–6) p. 32:

Cert-trícha bliadan mbil mbalc
ro giallad in Cir comnart;
nírbu tháimnirt nírbu thrú
co ráinic co Scithecdu.

58.73. *rígan na Scithia*] The full account of Cyrus' defeat and beheading at the hands of Thamyramis is in Orosius, II 7.1–6. The *B* recension describes Thamyramis as queen of the cíchloiscthe, i.e. the Amazons; cf. Bróccán Cráibdech's poem, *Lecht Cormaic meic Culennáin,* ed. Margaret E. Dobbs 'On the graves of Leinster men' *ZCP* 24 (1954) pp. 139–53, at p. 141 §34:

Rucad cusna Cíchloscthib
iar n-argain tíri Siria;
ro-marb trí chét cethrachat
de ṡluag Pentasilia.

See also the note by Thomas Olden to Airbertach mac Cosse's 'universal geography' *Ro-fessa i curp domuin dúir, PRIA,* 2nd Ser., 2 (1884) pp. 219–52, at p. 237, and Fland Mainistrech's poem, *Rédig dam, a Dé do nim,* ed. Mac Airt (1952–4) pp. 255–80, at p. 280 §56.

58.74–85. The details of these three stanzas represent another of the common medieval divisions of World History, that based on ch. 7 of *Dn,* which describes the vision that Daniel had of four great beasts rising out of the sea, 'the first like a lion with wings of an eagle. . the second like a bear. . another beast like a leopard with four wings of a bird. . the fourth, dreadful and terrible, exceedingly strong, with great iron teeth. . and it had ten horns'.

The traditional medieval interpretation of the vision followed Jerome's *Comm. in Danielem,* ed. F. Glorie, *CCSL* 75 A, II 7.1–7, in which Jerome explained the four great beasts as allegories of the four great kingdoms of the ancient world: the Babylonian, the Persian, the Macedonian and the Roman, which, succeeding one another in the development of history, formed the four great Ages of the world. See the discussion by Robert E. McNally, *The bible in the early Middle Ages,* Woodstock Papers 4 (Westm., Maryland 1959) pp. 44–5. A similar idea was expressed by Orosius, II 1.4–6, which might equally have provided the inspiration for the SAM text; see also Mac Airt (1952–4) p. 255 ff.

58.82. *gríbda a ṅgáir*] I have emended the *R* reading, *ṅgríbda,* which seems to be a slip of the scribe's.

58.86–9. Cf. §70.290–3. The sole purpose of this stanza seems to be to provide a closing link *(dúnad)* with the opening words. The connection between Nimrod's tower and the site of Babylon is not clear.

59. The general substance of this section derives, of course, from the accumulated details of the bible. For many of the specific details, however, no precedent is to be found in the canonical books of Scripture. Close verbal analysis of the SAM text suggests that the Irish account was taken from some such text as Isidore's *Liber de ortu et obitu patrum, MPL* 83, cols. 129–56, or from the Irish Ps. Isidore's derivative text, *Liber de ortu et obitu patriarcharum, MPL* 83, cols. 1275–94, which is regarded as a product of the 8th c. from the circle of Virgil of Salzburg; see McNally 'Isidorian pseudepigrapha in the early Middle Ages' in Manuel C. Díaz y Díaz (ed) *Isidoriana* (Leon 1961) pp. 315–16, and McNamara, *The apocypha in the Irish Church,* p. 83 No. 73.

59.3–5. There is no specific source for this in the bible; the details seem to derive from one or other of the *Libri* mentioned above. The precise wording seems closest to Ps. Isidore, *MPL* 83, col. 1278 A: 'In Jerusalem praedicavit sub Manasse rege, serra sectus in duas partes occubuit, sepultus est sub quercu Ragel juxta transitum aquarum, quas olim Ezechias rex obstruxerat pulvere.'

'serra sectus in duas partes' = a rainn do thuirisc serrda iarna fot
'sepultus est sub quercu Ragel' = ro-adnaiced fo daraig Rogél
a thócbáil i n-airdde = 'Hunc autem Manasses extensum', this last sentence deriving perhaps from (genuine) Isidore.

Cf. Tigernach, ed. Stokes (1895) p. 378: 'Mannasses filius Ezechiae rexit Iudam annis .lu., apud quem Essaias profeta serra in caput adacta per longum in duas partes diuissus est.'

59.6–8. Again, there is no specific source in *Ier* for these details; the source could have been either of the above-mentioned *Libri* (or a text similar to them). I give here the Irish Ps. Isidore's text (col. 1278 C): 'Jeremias ergo ortus a vico Anathoisdes, qui viculus tribus a Jerusolymis distans millibus, captivus in Aegyptum ductus a populo apud Taphnas lapidibus obrutus obiit. Jacet vero in eodem loco sepultus, quem Pharao rex habitaverat, quia per postulationem suam defugatis ab eodem loco serpentibus, Aegyptios fecit esse securos a tactu aspidum.'
'a populo apud Taphnas lapidibus obrutus obiit' = do chlochad ón phopul, etc.
'in eodem loco vero sepultus' = ro-adnacht icon Támna cétna
'(loco) quem Pharao rex habitaverat' = airm i n-adnaictis Foroinn, etc.

59.8. *meic Chelchiae*] Cf. *Ier* 1.1: 'Verba Hieremiae filii Helciae.'

59.9–11. Either of the Isidorian texts could have served as a source; I give here the text from Isidore (col. 143 A): 'Ezechiel sacerdos, filius Buzi, genitus in terra Sarira. . Quem dux populi Israel interfecit, pro eo quod severitate et auctoritate pontificali corriperetur ab eo ob impietatem sacrilegii. Sepultus est a populo in agro Maurim, in sepulcro Sem et Arphaxat.'

'Quem dux populi Israel interfecit'	=	ro-marbsat toísig in phopuil Israélda
'pro eo quod severitate pontificali corriperetur ab eo ob impietatem sacrilegii'	=	ar díchondercligi a forcitail ⁊ a méit nadas-inchrechad im chol a n-écrábuid

For the final sentence the text of Irish Ps. Isidore seems slightly closer to the SAM wording: 'Hunc ergo sepelivit populus in Maurim, agro sepulcro Arphaxat.'

59.12–15. The source for this is again one or other of the Isidorian texts, or something very similar; Isidore reads (col. 143–4): 'Vixit autem usque ad tempus Darii regis Persarum, annis centum et decem, sepultusque est jam senex in spelunca regia, solus in captivitate cum gloria.'

Note that the gloss, *.i. mac Abda*, is derived neither from the bible nor from genuine Isidore, but from the Irish Ps. Isidore's text (col. 1279 A): 'Daniel, filius Abda.'

60. I have been unable to locate a precise source (or even an analogue) for this interesting section and its elaboration in §§61 and 62. It was pointed out by Bergin, 'A mystical interpretation of the Beati' *Ériu* 11 (1932) pp. 103–6, that the theme of the pericope was the special efficacy of the Beati (Ps. 118 = Ps. 119 Hebrews) for the relief of souls in hell. Bergin, however, noted no source for the text, but inferred rather a native origin for the prose and poem by

pointing to the many other references in Irish ecclesiastical literature to the special reverence that was accorded the Beati in the medieval Irish Church. See, e.g., the poem edited by Brian Ó Cuív 'Three Middle Irish poems' *Éigse* 16 (1975–6) pp. 1–17, at pp. 2–5, where the same division of the Psalm is made as occurs in our text: each of the twenty-two sections (corresponding to the acrostic order of the Syriac alphabet) is termed a *coibtel* 'chapter', and each verse (of which there are eight to each section) is termed a *fers*.

For further references to the subject, see the sources cited by Ó Cuív. Note that §§60 and 61 are printed also by Hans Oskamp 'On the author of *Sex Aetates Mundi*' *Studia Celtica* 3 (1968) pp. 127–40, at pp. 132–3; I have noted his readings in the apparatus where they differ from the text given here.

60.2. *ó Babilóin co Hierusálem*] The doctrine of the Two Cities – the City of God, the elect, and the City of the Devil, the reprobate – made famous by Augustine in his *De civitate Dei*, had its origins in Donatist doctrines of Two Churches: the true Church of God, visibly present in themselves, and the false Church of the false Christians (the *traditores*), which they conceived the Catholics to be. The idea was refined and developed by Tyconius, a contemporary of Augustine's, whose ideas were borrowed in large part by the latter. Tyconius's doctrine, as found *apud* Bede, *MPL* 93, col. 185 A, speaks of these Two Cities thus: 'Duae sunt enim in mundo civitates: una de abysso, altera de coelestibus oriens.'

For an interesting discussion of the Tyconian theme in Insular sources see Gerald Bonner, *St. Bede in the tradition of Western apocalyptic literature*, Jarrow Lecture (Jarrow 1966).

60.3. *ón Babilóin siansaidi*] Note that Martin McNamara 'Psalter text and Psalter study in the early Irish Church' *PRIA* 73 C 7 (1973) pp. 201–98, at p. 257, has remarked: '*Sens/sians* represents the Latin *sensus*. I have failed to find this Latin term used with the meaning of the mystical sense of Scripture in Latin texts, except perhaps in the *Eclogae* (Clm 14715, fol. 2^v) and the Reference Bible [= Bibelwerk] (Clm 14276, fol. 95^r), both Irish works, where *historia* and *sensus* are contrasted. It is used in this meaning in a homily of the *Leabhar Breac* (ed. Atkinson, line 6838), a Latin homily which may well be an Irish composition.' Cf. also *OIP*, p. 114 Gl. 133, where the three exegetical technical terms *séns*, *mórálus*, and *stoir* are used together.

The SAM text, therefore, follows clearly in the Irish exegetical tradition.

60.5. *Sechtmoga sé passe ar chét*] The word *pais* (Lat. *passus*) is used in the following poem with two senses: in the mystic sense there are twenty-two *stadia* in each *passus* (st. 3), while as a measure of distance (st. 4) there are 125 *paisse* in each *stadium;* cf. Pliny, *Historia naturalis*, ed. H. Rackham, Loeb Classical Library No. 330 (London 1958) p. 228 (II 21.85): 'Stadium centum viginti quinque nostros efficit passus, hoc est pedes sexcentos viginti quinque.'

61.1–4. Note the mystical number 365 (Gk. *tex*), the number of days in the year.

61.3. *crithnaiges détu*] This gloss may possibly derive from Jerome's *Lib. interpret. Hebr. nominum*, *CCSL* 72, p. 71: 'Sennaar excussio dentium siue feotor eorum'; Babylon was built on the Plain of Sennar.

61.16. *mundi per geometricam*] Perhaps a reference to Pliny, *Hist. nat.* II 21.85 (ed. Rackham, p. 228): 'Inconperta et haec inextricabilia, sed prodenda quia sunt prodita, in quis tamen una ratio geometricae collectionis numquam fallacis possit non repudiari.'

61.17. *Argamaint*] The *argumentum* and the *titulus* usually occurred together as the introductory comments to each Psalm; the *argumentum* gives the general meaning or guiding principle of the Psalm, the *titulus* gives the circumstances of its composition.

61.23. *ro-fég in rúin-se*] Cf. §61.11: *co rúinib screptra* in reference to each one of the 176 *paisse*.

62.1. *huidi*] Cf. *RIA MS. 23 O 48* (476), *Liber Flavus Fergusiorum* II, fol. 34[45]rb 4–7, in a collection of brief texts on the merits of the Beati; 'Is e seo trath uidi beiris an tanum as péin gin beithir a gabhail na biaiti', etc.
See Edward Gwynn 'The Liber Flavus Fergusiorum' *PRIA* 26 C 2 (1906) pp. 15–41, at p. 34 (who had not identified the text).

62.3. *do-beir in biat anmain*] A similar idea is expressed concerning the merits of saying masses for a soul, in a poem in *TCD MS. H. 3. 18*, ed. Kuno Meyer 'Neue Mitteilungen aus irischen HSS.' *Archiv für celtische Lexicographie* 3 (1907) p. 216; the last stanza reads:

In anim as truma pían
fil a n-ifurnd na n-ilrían
da breith for nem, sásad grinn,
nosfóirfitis secht n-affrinn.

62.4. *hi cind bliadna*] Referring to the 365 *uide* between the mystical Babylon and the mystical Jerusalem, with a day's journey for each *uide*.

62.7. *fáithsine ṅDauída*] I am not sure what is intended by David's prophecy here.

63.4. *iar ṅdíriuch-scríbunn*] I have no other example of this phrase.

63.7–8. These are the three great chronological systems of the Middle Ages: the *Anno Mundi* reckoning of the Septuagint, 5190; that of the Vulgate, 3952; and the *ab urbe condita* reckoning of the Romans, 752. The same information is given in Tigernach, ed. Stokes (1895) p. 406; it derives from a text of the Eusebio-Hieronymian chronicle.

64.3–4. *do-rochratar i nÁdam*] An interesting affirmation of the doctrine of original sin. Note the use of 'relative' *ocus* (7), '*who* fell'; should we perhaps read *im Ádam?* But cf. *Rm* 5.12: '*in quo omnes peccaverunt.*'

65. In the 4th c. Eusebius remarked in his *Historia Ecclesiastica*, I 12.1, that 'the names of the apostles of our Saviour are known to everyone from the Gospels. But there exists no catalogue of the seventy disciples'; cf. Eduard Schwarz & Theodor Mommsen (ed) *Die Kirchengeschichte.* Eusebius Werke 2, *Die griechischen-christlichen Schriftsteller der ersten drei Jahrhunderte*, Vol. 2 i (Leipzig 1903) pp. 81–3.
A list of the names of the twelve Apostles is given in each of the Synoptic Gospels but the lists are not identical and the problem of deciding the precise source of any particular medieval list is sometimes difficult. Ever since Edmund Bishop's pioneering study 'The litany of saints in the Stowe Missal' *Journal of Theological Studies* 7 (1905) pp. 122–36, esp. p. 135 n. A, (reprinted in his *Liturgica historica. Papers on the liturgy and religious life of the Western Church* (Oxford 1918[1]/1962[2]) pp. 137–64, at pp. 163–4 [Note C]), it has been known

that medieval liturgical MSS of Insular provenance invariably preserve a form of the list of the Apostles which is otherwise unknown outside these islands. In summary, Bishop remarked that there were 'three orders of Apostles in use in the West: (1) Irish, based on St. Matthew; (2) Mozarabic and Arles, based on the Acts of the Apostles; (3) Roman, not derived from Scripture.'

The order of names in Matthew X. 1–4 is as follows:
(1) Peter; (2) Andrew; (3) James son of Zebedee; (4) John; (5) Philip; (6) Bartholomew; (7) Thomas; (8) Matthew; (9) James son of Alpheus; (10) Thaddeus; (11) Simon the Canaanite; (12) Judas Iscariot.

It should be noted, therefore, that none of these Insular lists has Madianus; I know of no immediate source for the insertion.

66. Christian tradition was torn between the figures 70 or 72 for the numbers of the Disciples because of the divergent testimony already witnessed by *Lc* 10.1 and 17. Eusebius in the 4th c. knew the names of only five of the Seventy (Two): Barnabas, Sosthenes, Cephas, Matthias, and Thaddaeus. In subsequent centuries more than one list was circulated which included the names of these and at least sixty-five others; unfortunately, none of these lists has any foundation in historical fact.

Half a century after Eusebius, Epiphanius said that Our Lord 'sent forth also seventy-two others to preach, of whose number were the seven appointed over the widows, Stephen, Philip, Prochorus, Nichanor, Timon, Parmenas, and Nicholaus; before these also Matthias, who was numbered among the Apostles in the place of Judas [possibly = Madianus in our list?], but after these seven and Matthias before them, Mark, Luke, Justus, Barnabas, and Apelles, Rufus, Niger, and the remainder of the seventy-two.'

See Bruce M. Metzger 'Names for the nameless in the New Testament' in Patrick Granfield & Josef A. Jungmann (ed) *Kyriakon. Festschrift Johannes Quasten*. 2 vols. (Münster 1970) Vol. 1, pp. 79–99, who cites the above passage (pp. 86–7) and who adds that Epiphanius's statement is not clear and does not ring true. The earliest list of the Seventy Two known to him is in the *Chronicon Paschale* of A.D. 630, ed. George Pisida, *Patrologia Graeca* 92, cols. 519–23, and 543–6. The compilation of the names in this text draws upon a variety of New Testament sources: It begins with Matthias (whom Epiphanius also placed first among the Seventy), and continues with Sosthenes and Cephas (both of whom Eusebius mentioned), followed by Linus (2 *Tim* 4.21) and then Cleopas (*Lc* 24.18). There then follow a further twenty-six names derived from Romans 16, concluding with thirty-nine names from various Pauline epistles and from Acts.

This mechanical combination of several sources has, not surprisingly, resulted in the duplication of several names: thus, e.g., Tychicus is named twice because he is mentioned both in Ephesians and Titus. Likewise, both Demas and Erastus appear twice in the list, for the same reason.

Besides the list in the *Chronicon Paschale*, several other lists of the Seventy (Two) were in circulation in the Eastern Churches; see Theodor Schermann, *Propheten und Apostellegenden*, Texte und Untersuchungen zur Geschichte der altchristlichen Literatur 31 iii (Leipzig 1907) [but see also the criticism of this author's conclusions by Edmund Bishop, *Liturgica historica*, pp. 163–4]. For at least one of these lists there are clear points of identity in our SAM list, and an indirect dependence on some Eastern source cannot be ruled out.

Montague R. James published a list of the Seventy (Two) in 'An ancient English list of the Seventy Disciples' *JTS* 11 (1910) pp. 459–62 ('Notes and Studies') from three English MSS.:

(a) British Library, MS. Cotton Vespasian B VI (saec. IX);
(b) Corpus Christi College Cambridge, MS. 183 (ca. A.D. 931), which 'appears to have been given by King Aethelstan to the see of Cuthbert in the 10th century';
(c) Corpus Christi College Cambridge, MS. 92 (saec. XII), a MS. of Florence of Worcester.

According to James, this list is 'essentially identical with that contained in the MS. Vat. graec. 2001 (saec. XII)' designated by Schermann as *Index anonymus Graeco-Syrus* [*Propheten und Apostellegenden*, p. 300 ff.]. 'It is interesting to find', he continued, 'a list current in England so far back, whose only traceable connections are Syrian. . and a very slight study of Schermann's work will show the Graeco-Syrian list is very clearly marked off from all others.'

I give here James's list from MS. (a), with variants from the other two and with addition of capitals only:

(a) *Nomina septuaginta duorum discipulorum Christi.*

i	Iacobus Iustus	(c) Iacob	
ii	Maththias	(b c) Mathias	
iii	Ioseph		
iiii	alius Iosep	(c) Ioseph alius	
v	Marcus euuangelista	(c) Marchus	
vi	Barnabas		
vii	Lucas euuangelista		
viii	Cleopas	(c) Cleophas	
viiii	Seneca		
x	Symeon		
xi	Lucius		
xii	Manain		
xiii	Sostenes		
xiiii	Caefas	(c) Cephas	
xv	Thaddeus	(c) Taddeus	
xvi	Ermen et Pastor	(c) Ermen qui et Pastor	
xvii	Andronicus		
xviii	Iohannas	(c) Iohannes	
xviiii	Amplias		
xx	Urbanus		
xxi	Erodiones	(c) Erodion	
xxii	Asyncritis		
xxiii	Iasonem	(c) Nason	
xxiiii	Stephanus primus martir	(b) pri martir	(c) prothomartyr
xxv	Philippus		
xxvi	Prochorus		
xxvii	Nicanor		
xxviii	Timon	(c) Symon	
xxviiii	Parmena		
xxx	Aquilas	(c) Aquila	
xxxi	Iudas qui uocatur Barsabbas	(b) Barnabas	(c) Iudas *(om. cet.)*
xxxii	Silas	(c) Hilas	
xxxiii	Siluanus		
xxxiiii	Symon Cleopae	(c) Symon Cleophe	
xxxv	Nason	(c) Iason	
xxxvi	Agabas	(c) Agabus	
xxxvii	Ananias		
xxxviii	Ignatius		
xxxviiii	Symon Quirenense	(b) Symon	(c) S. Cirenensis

xl	Alexander	(b) Quirenense *(sic)*
xli	Rufus	(b) Alexander
xlii	Nathanahel	(b) Rufus
xliii	Nicodemus	(b) Nathanael
xliiii	Cleopas	(b) Nichodemus
xlv	Simon	(b) Cleophas
xlvi	Iudas	(b) Symon
xlvii	Iacobus	(b) Iudas
xlviii	Simon	(b) Iacobus
xlviiii	Simon Coriarus	(b) Symon Coriarius
l	Lucas	
li	Barnabas	
lii	Iohannes	
liii	Barnabas	
liiii	Stephanus	
lv	Chorisius	
lvi	Milichus	(c) Hilichus
lvii	Gaius	
lviii	Flegonta	
lviiii	Ermen	
	Hi sunt qui electi fuerunt ab apostolis in ordinem pro quibusdam qui recesserunt =	(b) (c) has this n. opp. Nos. 68–72, and reads 'prohis qui'
lx	Appellem Probauilis	(b) Apelles Probabilis
lxi	Dionysius Ariopagita	(b) Dyonisius
lxii	Aepenetus	
lxiii	Iesus qui dicitur Iustus	
lxiiii	Stachyn	(b) Stachin
lxv	Ponplius	
lxvi	Aristobulus	(b) Aristobolus
lxvii	Stephanus Corinthiensis	
lxviii	Erodius	
lxviiii	Rufus	
lxx	Olympus	(b) Olymphus
lxxi	Titus	
lxxii	Filimonem	

I list here the chief differences between this list and the SAM one:

(1) Iacobus Iustus is treated as two persons in our text.

(2) Ermen (=Pastor) is treated in the same way.

(3) Cleopas is repeated between Urbanus and Erodiones in the SAM list; this may be the same Cleopas who is listed as No. 44 in the English list.

(4) Timon (No. 27) is omitted from the SAM list.

(5) Silas precedes Siluanus in the English list, and is followed by Simon Cleopae.

(6) A third Simon is inserted into the English list before Iudas and Iacobus.

(7) The English list makes two persons of Stephanus Corissius.

(8) The English list reads Appellem Probauilis as one name.

(9) The English list reads Iesus qui dicitur Iustus.

These few divergences apart, it seems fairly clear that the two lists are closely related, but whether they represent two independent recensions from a common exemplar or whether the one text is immediately or intermediately dependent on the other is impossible to judge here.

67. A list of the imperial persecutions might be drawn up from the details of Orosius, VII 10 ff., or from Eusebius-Jerome, ed. Helm, p. 181 ff. [=*MPL* 27, cols. 589–90 ff.]; such a list might even be derived from a historical martyrology.

67.2. *sub Marco Antonino*] Note that both the *RP* text of SAM and the Annals of Tigernach read *M. Antonio;* this need not, however, imply any interdependence between the two.

67.5. *do-chuatar bás*] Paul Grosjean published this and the foregoing section from *R* as 'List of Apostles and Disciples (with a marginal note on the persecutions)' in *Irish Texts* 4 (1934) pp. 1–2; since this item, however, has suffered from the excessive zeal of the binder, and since he was not aware of the copy in *P*, his conjectural restorations have not always been successful.

In this instance Grosjean read *do chuatar re bás*, but overlooked the fact that this idiom requires *téit bás* (i.e. with direct acc.); I have restored the text on the evidence of §68.7: *do-chuatar bás martra*, and of the readings in the O'Clery MS. *(P)*.

67.6. *fo tríb rannaib in talman*] Grosjean read here only *trib rannaib;* the emendation is made here on the basis of comparison with §68.9–10: *fo tríb rannaib in talman*, and the readings in *P*.

67.7. *Sarofanes*] This passage was not published by Grosjean, probably because only the first few words of it in *R* have survived the binder's knife. A complete text has survived, however, in *P* and in *Ld*, fol. 14ᵛb, on the basis of which the text has been restored here.

The purpose of the passage is to recall the creation of the first pagan idol and the name of its creator; the connection with the Apostles lies in the fact that their mission was regarded as being directed against the universal spread of pagan idolatry. This connection is more clearly evident in a poem published by Kuno Meyer from *RIA MSS 23 N 10* and *B. IV. 2*, in 'Mitteilungen aus irischen HSS.' *ZCP* 13 (1921) pp. 3–30, at pp. 15–16; I give here the stanzas concerning Zerofanes:

Dorónad delb duineta
dogó tenn da cach tinde,
d'argut is d'ór Arábi,
ba mór glanáille in gille.

Docúaid díabul dobertach
isin deilb íarna dénam,
romill réimm na rígraide
ra sírluige na fégad.

The poem is also of interest as part of the large corpus of texts concerning the missions of the Apostles and the places of their deaths, on which see McNamara, *The apocrypha in the Irish Church*, pp. 83–90 Nos. 72–8.

68.1. *amal at-chuadammar*] Cf. §63.1 and §64.1–7.

68.2. *amal it-beir Iosep*] The reference is probably not, as we might be tempted to think, to the *Antiquitates Iudaeorum* of Josephus, which had a wide circulation in the Middle Ages in the Latin epitome by Hegessipus. Rather it probably derives from Eusebius-Jerome, ed. Helm, p. 175 [=*MPL* 27, cols. 571–2]: 'Argumentum autem huius rei, quod Saluator isto anno passus sit, Euangelium praebet Iohannis, in quo scribitur, post. XV. annum Tiberii Caesaris tribus annis Dominum praedicasse. Iosephus etiam uernacularus

Iudaeorum scriptor circa haec tempora die pentecostes sacerdotes primum commotionem locorum et quosdam sonitus sensisse testatur.'

The Crucifixion is traditionally believed to have taken place on March 25th in the consulate of the Gemini, C. Fufius Geminus and L. Rubellius Geminus, consuls for the year A.D. 29; this would correspond to the fifteenth year of Tiberius's reign, the date of the Crucifixion according to the oldest Christian chronology, that of *Lc* 3.1. Versions vary, however, between the 15th, 18th and 19th years of Tiberius. See E. Hennecke & W. Schneemelcher (ed) *New Testament apocrypha* 1 [English ed., ed. R. McL. Wilson (London 1962)] p. 450 n. 2; cf. also C. W. Jones, *Bedae opera de temporibus* (1943) p. 46.

68.3–4. *ro-airg iarum iffern*] A reference to the famous 'Harrowing of Hell' theme which was such a popular motif in Western apocalyptic literature throughout the Middle Ages. For a full account of the theme in Irish literature see McNamara, *Apocrypha*, pp. 68–75 Nos. 58–61. Note also that one of the *trí gáire in domuin* mentioned in the *Duan in choícat cest*, *ZCP* 4 (1903) p. 237, is *gáir iffirn oca arcain do Christ;* cf. the Book of Lismore, fol. 147^{r}b 32–9 (the idea is taken from *Dá brón flatha nime*).

The fact that the theme is not expanded upon in the SAM text may suggest a tentative chronology for the Irish version of the 'Harrowing of Hell'.

68.6–10. I have no exact source in the Latin texts for this passage.

68.10. Note that the names of the Continents are in an order different from that of §69; cf. §5.3–5 and §26.1–2.

69.1–5. Cf. *Etym* XIV 3.1: 'Asia ex nomine cuiusdam mulieris est appellata, quae apud antiquos imperium tenuit orientis.' The *Duan in choícat cest*, *ZCP* 4 (1903) p. 236 has a section about the Continents and says concerning Asia: 'Asia immorro ó Aiss ingin Neir ⁊ Neptun tuc dí ina tochra a ainm forsin tres raind.'

69.6–9. Cf. *Hier* 25.1–6: 'Dicitur autem unus ex posteris Abrahae, qui appellabatur Afer, duxisse aduersus Libyam exercitum et ibi uictus hostibus consedisse eiusque posteros ex nomine ataui Africam nuncupasse.' The *Duan in choícat cest* has '.i. Affer mac Cethura ocus Abráim, iss é rogab in Affraicc ar tús,' which follows *Etym* XIV 5.2: 'Alii dicunt Africam appellari ab uno ex posteris Abrahae de Cethura.'

It is worth noting that the account of the naming of the three Continents in Airbertach mac Cosse's 'universal geography' differs considerably from the SAM text and seems to derive from Josephus (i.e. Hegessipus) and Pomponius Mela, rather than from patristic sources; see Thomas Olden (ed) 'On the geography of Ros Ailithir' *PRIA*, 2nd Ser., 2 (1884) p. 239; cf. Kuno Meyer, *Revue Celtique* 6 (1883–5) p. 192.

69.10–14. *Eorops*] For the first etymology see Eusebius-Jerome, ed. Helm, p. 20b [=*MPL* 27, col. 76 B]: 'Sicyoniorum in Achaia regnabat rex secundus, cui nomen erat Europs'; the second etymology derives from *Etym* XIV 4.1: 'Europa quippe Agenoris regis Libyae filia fuit, quam Iovis ab Africa raptam Cretam advexit, et partem tertiam orbis ex eius nomine appellavit.' Isidore's text in turn derives from Eusebius-Jerome, ed. Helm, p. 53b: 'Europa a Cretensibus rapta est naui, cuius fuit insigne taurus.'

The *Duan in choícat cest*, *ZCP* 4 (1903) p. 236, has both versions: 'Eorops rí na Sicormada, is úad Eoraibp. Nó Eoraip ainm mná.'

69.14. *Cicrops*] See the poem *A Rí richid, réidig dam* by Gilla in Chomded hua Cormaic (Book of Leinster Vol. 3 [1957] p. 575):

Cétidpairt Ioib in dám dron
tuc Cicrops tria chomnacol.

70.1. *forsin Panechte*] Cf. §1.1–2: *tintúd Duiblitrech huí hUathgaile forsin Pandecht Cirine*. The rubric is clearly intended to suggest that the poem is a summary of the prose.

70.2. Note that MacNeill 'An Irish historical tract dated A.D. 721' *PRIA* 28 C 6 (1910) p. 137 states that Fland Mainistrech borrowed this first line for his own poem on the succession of World Kingships; but Fland died in 1056 and it is most unlikely that our poem was composed before that date, if its ascription to Dublittir hua hUathgaile can stand. There are no good reasons for denying that ascription.

70.6–9. The number of sons and daughters here allotted to Adam agrees with that of §9.3–4, but does not take account of the alternative numbers discussed in the notes to §9.3–4 and §11.3–4.

70.10. *Tres ros-hétla*] The other MSS have *Trén*, which may perhaps be a better reading.

70.18. *Sile*] Not mentioned in the bible; cf. §10.6, §11.17, §12.2.

70.20. *Pibb, Olla, Pithibb*] Not mentioned in the bible; cf. notes cited in previous comment.

70.22–5. This is a paraphrase of §12.

70.26. *ra seircc snáma*] I take this as being made up of the Mid. Ir. prep. *ra* + vb. n. <*seirccid* 'dries up' + *snáma* 'tides/floods' but I have no corroborative examples.

70.30. *Chaín*] An instance of Mid. Ir. aspiration of the obj.; cf. §70.45, and see *OIP*, p. 146 n. 107.

70.34. *Fúcair*] The sense seems to require a 1 p. sg. here, but the form is very odd; *L* has *Fuacair*, which is no different. The *DIL*, s. v., fúacair cite this as an early form of the 2 p. sg. impv., but I fail to see how that matches the sense of what follows. Note that *P* emended to *Ro fuacair*, obviously intending a pret./perf. form of the vb. In fact, however, the *Lc* form: *Fuaicarthar* may be closer to the mark, as it accounts for the awkward *ar* as well.

70.49. *Olla, Oliua, Oliuana*] Cf. §§25, 28, and 31; these women are, of course, nowhere mentioned in the bible.

70.50. *Copha sétig Noé*] Note that this name does not occur in the prose text at §18, where we might expect to find it. The name is, however, well attested in Irish sources, from the 8th c. *Liber de numeris* (Percoua) to *Lebor Gabála* (Cobba), ed. Best, Bergin & O'Brien, Vol. 1 (1954) p. 2.

70.52. *Oliua indlaga*] Note that this material occurs early also in Anglo-Saxon tradition; e.g., Georg Baesecke, *Der Vocabularius Sti. Galli in der angelsächsischen Mission* (Halle 1933), who gives the following passage from

St. Gall MS. 913, p. 173 ff.: 'Regina Faberba nomine uxor Noe; nomen Suht uxor Sem, filii Noe; Narra uxor Cham; Susse nomen filiae Hiob; Olla et Oliua.. *(lacuna)* nomen latroni, qui cum Domino crucifixi sunt, Jonathas et Carmatres,' etc.

70.64. *hi teirt kalaind Mai*] See the notes to §20.

70.68. *cid bad dattu*] My translation of this is uncertain.

70.74. The following four stanzas are translated and discussed by James Carney, *Studies in Irish literature and history* (Dublin 1955/1979) pp. 103–10; cf. Charles Donahue 'Grendel and the Clanna Cain' *Journal of Celtic Studies* I (1950) pp. 167–75. Carney has noted that the monstrous species described in this poem, but which did not figure in the narrative of §§33 and 34, all derive from *Etym.*

70.90–3. Cf. §28.

70.92. *fo bruth na n-esgal*] This is difficult; I take *bruth* = *brúd* 'crushing' with *eas* 'waterfall' + *gal*, but this is very tentative.

70.97. *ónt sruth*] The Nile (to the Gulf of Aden).

70.98–9. Cf. §28.5–6.

70.102–5. Cf. §28.4; the word *athslaiti* is otherwise unattested. The form seems to have been concocted to provide a rhyme with *Affraice*, and may comprise *ath* + *slaite* (gen. sg.) 'the many staved'?

70.104. *sruth Nuchuil*] The Niger river; cf. Airbertach mac Cosse's 'universal geography', ed. Olden, pp. 240–1:

Sruth tic dar Affraic aníar
a sléib Athlaint ónd acían;
is Dara a ainm ica bun
mad tair is é a ainm Nuchul.

70.106–9. *Secht mórthuatha Cannáin*] These are not mentioned specifically in the prose account, §30.

70.116–17. Cf. §28.7–8.

70.118–20. Cf. §24.4. The geographical details are not cited in the prose account, though a text like mac Cosse's could have provided them.

70.124. *i tír na Laignech*] This at least gives a location for the poem.

70.126–9. Cf. §26.1–2; the source of the second couplet is §27.2–5.

70.130–4. The details are from §27.

70.138.41. Cf. §27.

70.142–5. Cf. §24.16 and §25; note that these verses follow the error of §25 in allotting eight sons to Japheth, including the phantom *Masseca.*

70.150–65. A pharaphrase of §25.1–15.

70.155. *ro-hailte fri ardríge*] A reference to the 'World Kingship' of the Medes and Persians.

70.166–205. A paraphrase of §25.16–25.

70.169. *ó Íbad rígrad Rómán*] This seems to imply that Alanius (Elonius) was regarded as ancestor of the Romans; cf. *Lebor Bretnach*, ed. van Hamel, pp. 6–7 §5, and lines 180–1 of the poem.

70.173–7. A reference to the sons of Míl.

70.181. *Rómán*] Note the nom. pl. with velar ending; see James Carney (ed) *The poems of Blathmac son of Cú Brettan*, Irish Texts Soc. Vol. 47 (Dublin 1964) p. 155 (note on *énán)*.

70.190. *mór ṅgelhua*] I take this word to mean 'grandson', i.e. a member of a *gelfine*, the kinship group represented by the agnatic descendants of a common grandfather.

70.191. *oénmac Negua*] Not the 'only son' of Negua, but the 'peerless son', for §25.22 names three sons for Negua: Uandalus, Saxus, and Bogardus; cf. Cecile O'Rahilly 'Varia' 4, *Celtica* 12 (1977) pp. 185–96, at pp. 193–5.

70.192. *no-chathed caslus calaid*] I take the second word to be a compound of *cas* + *lus*, but the whole line is obscure.

70.202–5. I have taken *mór do gliccus ro-chertaig* as referring proleptically to *Brittus*.

70.206–9. Cf. §25.5–7.

70.214. *Comlín*] The evidence of the other MSS suggests this emendation is required.

70.216. *ní faigbet*] Apparently from *fo-gaib* but the meaning of the second couplet is not clear to me.

70.218–3. Cf. §26.2 and §31.

70.220. *ó sruth Gaind*] Note that the name is not given in the prose; it does not occur either in mac Cosse's poem. Is the river Indus intended? *(sruth Gaind*, however, clearly means the Ganges).

70.232. *acra*] Is this from *accur* 'desire, wish' (vb. n. ⟨*ad-car*), or can we take it as an early attestation of the word *acra* 'acre'? Cf. *DIL* s. v.

70.233. *senathair na Callacda*] Cf. §31.7: *Arfaxad, is uad atát Caldei.*

70.237. *ó nád buidi*] The usual imagery in Irish has the scaldcrows being 'grateful' to a warrior for providing carrion; in this case then the use of *ó nád* is unusual. Cf. John MacNeill 'Three poems in Middle-Irish, relating to the battle of Mucrama' *PRIA* 3 C (1894) p. 534: *Messi ⁊ Macc Con dín bat budig brain.*

70.242–5. A paraphrase of §32.5–10.

70.243. *ros-horddaig Ísu an̄glech*] I do not know what this refers to.

70.252. *airdairc*] There is a slight erasure in *R* between the *a* of this word and the other letters, and it may be intended to read *irdairc* (: *inraic*); *L* has *o Ur erdairc* for line 253.

70.260. *ní hin̄glind, i n̄gait*] I am not sure what this means.

70.274–93. A paraphrase of §32.

70.292. *in cach thír*] The emendation is suggested by the readings of the other MSS.

70.294–7. Cf. §28.7–8.

70.298–305. Cf. §24.4–6 and 16–20.

70.305. *a dó, sain, sechtmogat*] Cf. §24.5–6 and notes thereto.

70.306–9. The doctrine of the 72 languages, corresponding to the 72 tribes descended of Noah; cf. §24.5–6 and notes.

70.312. *sídmag*] Either 'plain abounding in fairy-mounds' or 'plain of peace'; see Tomás Ó Cathasaigh 'The semantics of "síd" ' *Éigse* 17 (1977–8) pp. 137–55.

70.314–17. Cf. §§6, 7, and 24.

70.325. *cen aéb duilgiusa*] *R* has *con*, which hardly seems appropriate.

70.327. *hUa hUathgail a hUsenglind*] The monastery of Killeshin, Co. Laois.

INDEX OF PERSONAL AND TRIBAL NAMES

In the lists that follow the names are cited in the form in which they appear in the Irish text. In order to facilitate their identification I have indicated the paternal, filial, or matrimonial affiliation, as the case may be, by the use of the following abbreviations: m. = *mac* 'son'; i. = *ingen* 'daughter'; b. = *ben* 'wife'. References throughout are to the section and line numbers of the Irish text.